INSIDE
SEVEN DAYS

INSIDE
SEVEN DAYS

The show that shook the nation

BY

ERIC KOCH

Introduction by Peter Desbarats

Prentice-Hall/Newcastle

Produced by
Newcastle Publishing Limited
The Mill
Greenwood, Ont. L0H 1H0

Published by
Prentice-Hall Canada Inc.
1870 Birchmount Road
Scarborough, Ontario M1P 2J7

Design: Word & Image
Typesetting: Attic Typesetting Inc.
Editorial: Brenna Brown, Nora Underwood
Printing: Gagne Printing Ltd.

Publication of this book was made possible, in part, by a grant from the Gannett Foundation, which supports journalistic research in Canada and the United States, and with the support of the Graduate School of Journalism, University of Western Ontario.

Canadian Cataloguing in Publication Data
Koch, Eric, 1919–
  Inside Seven days

ISBN 0-13-467416-2

1. This hour has seven days (Television program) — History. 2. Television and politics — Canada — History. 3. Canadian Broadcasting Corporation — History. I. Title.

PN1992.77.T48K62   1986   791.45"72   C86-094268-6

I have yet to see any problem, however complicated, which, when you look at it the right way, did not become more complicated.

Paul Anderson, quoted in *The Ghost in the Machine* by Arthur Koestler.

Leiterman: In the control room

CONTENTS

INTRODUCTION

For two decades, a generation of Canadian television journalists has worked in the shadow of *This Hour Has Seven Days*. It was, as everyone then realized, as everyone now would acknowledge, the most spectacularly influential series of television programs that Canadian journalism had ever created or ever would create, up to this day.

It was the first Canadian public affairs television show to sweep the ratings. In this era of multi-station television in our major cities, cable, satellite and VCRs, it is difficult to imagine the impact that *Seven Days* had on all of us from its brave debut in October, 1964, until it faded into history after its 50th program on the evening of May 8, 1966.

Everyone watched it; everyone talked about it. On Monday mornings, in elevators, taxis, buses, commuter trains, coffee shops, offices and factories throughout English-speaking Canada, people turned to one another and said, "Did you see what they did on *Seven Days* last night?" They said it in admiration, amazement, amusement, outrage, fury—with every human emotion except boredom.

For two television seasons, *Seven Days* enthralled the country. It had something to do with the novelty of television itself. Canadian television was only 12 years old when *Seven Days* went on the air. Only a few imaginative journalists, Patrick Watson and Douglas Leiterman among them, intuitively sensed the role that television eventually would play as the most powerful news medium of our time.

Every Sunday, Watson, Leiterman, Laurier LaPierre and other members of the *Seven Days* team explored the limits of television in terms of journalistic practice and public acceptability. No one knew, at the outset, how far they could go. It was an era of pioneering and experimentation in Canadian television journalism that never would and never could be repeated.

Its success had something to do with the antiestablishment bias of the Sixties, an era more congenial to the American spirit than the Canadian. *Seven Days* coincided almost exactly with a brief moment when Canadians, in Quebec and elsewhere, challenged many of their institutions and dreamed of new departures.

It also had something to do with the journalistic virtues and bureaucratic vices of the Canadian Broadcasting Corporation, and the powerful role of public broadcasting in Canada, a North American anomaly.

Above all, its popularity and influence was due to a cast of characters that included the first Canadian journalists to become truly national figures, the most powerful broadcasting executives in the country, politicians, cabinet ministers and eventually the Prime Minister himself. For the saga of *Seven Days*, in its second and last season, spilled out from the screen to engulf the nation.

For the first and probably the last time, Canadians were involved passionately in a debate about the survival of a television program, and about questions that had to do with fundamentals of television journalism: What was "good" television journalism all about? Was it possible to have a "free press" in this new electronic medium?

These questions are as relevant today as they were when the future of *Seven Days* was a matter of national concern. We are still in the infancy of television journalism. Despite the already rigid conventions of this new medium, we have only begun to explore its potential. The story of *Seven Days* is a timely reminder of the hopes and excitement that attended its birth.

By coincidence, this history is published in the 50th anniversary year of the Canadian Broadcasting Corporation, at a time when the concept of public television is under scrutiny and attack in Canada, in the United Kingdom and western Europe, and in many developing nations influenced by their example. If the story of *Seven Days* throws the weaknesses of public broadcasting into sharp relief, it also reminds us that only within the CBC at that time did journalists have the freedom to challenge authority publicly.

It has taken 20 years for those involved in the story to begin to look at it objectively. In retrospect, the question that obsessed all of us—Who killed *Seven Days*?—seems less important than the larger questions that the whole affair posed about the ethics of television journalism and the relationship between television journalism and political authority.

Only Eric Koch could have presented them with such flair and insight. He has the instincts and training of a novelist, a historian's eye for relevant detail, and a zest for political intrigue that betrays his own history as a successful career producer within the CBC.

It is a story that had to be told. Anyone who has ever wondered what really happens behind the screens of television journalism will find this account as absorbing and as relevant as we all found *This Hour has Seven Days*.

Peter Desbarats
Dean
Graduate School of Journalism
University of Western Ontario

Laurier LaPierre, Dinah Christie, Patrick Watson: On set

PREFACE

Almost all the *Seven Days* alumni whom I could contact—on both sides of the barricades—generously allowed me to interview them at length. Their names are listed at the end of the book.

Among others whose patience I strained with countless questions were:

Don Bennett, Robert Blackwood, Harry J. Boyle, G.F. Brickenden, Bill Cunningham, Guy Coderre, Walter L. Gordon, Gordon Fairweather, Doug Fisher, Ron Fraser, Robert Fulford, Gordon Hinch, Stuart Keate, William Kilbourn, Barry MacDonald, Don J. Macdonald, Sheila Mackenzie, Peggy Nairn Liptrott, William Neville, Richard Nielsen, Richard O'Hagan, E.B. Osler, Frank W. Peers, Gerard Pelletier, Gordon Sheppard, Lister Sinclair, Ernest Steele, David Tasker, Marc Thibault, Bernard Trotter, Vincent Tovell.

To all of them I express my gratitude. I made ample use of their contributions throughout the book—without specific attributions. The footnotes usually refer to written or printed documents.

My thanks are due to the CBC for opening its archives to me and to Helen Carscallen, whose M.A. thesis, written when *This Hour has Seven Days* was still on the air, remains an important document. I also found *The Public Eye* by F.W. Peers, University of Toronto Press 1979, of immeasurable help.

Quotations from the Report of the *Standing Committee on Broadcasting, Films and the Arts* of 1966—an indispensable source—are listed in the footnotes merely as *Committee*.

My profound thanks are due to my editor Ramsay Derry, to the explorations program of the Canada Council, without whose generous help this book could not have been written, and to Peter Desbarats, Dean of the Graduate School of Journalism at the University of Western Ontario, who obtained a much appreciated grant from the Gannett Foundation to which I am deeply grateful.

My own memories of the events described are considerably flawed and I have tried to rely on them as little as possible. During the first season of *Seven Days* I was Supervising Producer

(Public Affairs), responsible—together with many others—for the administration of public affairs programs but not for their editorial content. Of course *Seven Days* absorbed much of my time. In the summer of 1965 I faced a serious dilemma. I was greatly impressed by the idealism, courage and vitality of the producers. But I had been a member of the Department of Public Affairs since 1953 and in many ways felt closer to the old guard than to the young turks. Moreover, I was in no position to deflect all those involved from what I was sure was a collision course with head office, nor was I temperamentally suited for such a task. I realized that the collision I anticipated would seriously damage the Corporation and I was acutely uncomfortable about being so helpless. Therefore, I took the easy way out and asked for a transfer to try my hand as a working television producer on *Take Thirty*. I am afraid I cannot claim that my real purpose was to survive the coming explosion in order to be able to write this book. Like other bureaucrats, I regarded survival as a good *per se*.

During the second season I watched *Seven Days*—both the program and the battle—from the outside.

PART ONE
BEGINNINGS

John Drainie

CHAPTER 1

FREEDOM, LTD.

He who moulds public sentiment goes deeper than he who enacts statutes or pronounces decisions.

Abraham Lincoln, 1858.

This book is about the rise and fall of *This Hour Has Seven Days*, the fast-moving, theatrical and innovative public affairs program presented by the Canadian Broadcasting Corporation on television for two seasons, 1964–65 and 1965–66, every Sunday night from ten to eleven.

It was invented by two experienced producers, Douglas Leiterman and Patrick Watson. Their personalities, their talent and their drive shaped the program. Together with Alphonse Ouimet, president of the CBC, they are the central figures in the story.

In the spring of 1966 the dramatic clash between the producers and Ouimet led to the greatest explosion in the history of Canadian broadcasting. It raised fundamental questions about the function of public broadcasting in a free society.

What follows is an anatomy of the crisis.

If it is true that there has been a love-hate relationship between English Canadians and the CBC from the beginning, then the time of the hottest love was when *This Hour Has Seven Days* dominated the airwaves, and the moment of the deadliest hate when it was killed, or when it killed itself.

The unfolding battle over *Seven Days* was the liveliest political battle over a cultural issue (other than language) in English Canadian history. By the time the smoke cleared, there had been banner headlines in all major Canadian newspapers, numberless stories and editorials, open defiance of CBC authority by the producers who claimed that it was they who were carrying out the true mandate of the Corporation and that management was betraying it, a strike threat by CBC producers, the formation of *Save Seven Days* committees across the country, a cloak-and-dagger meeting between a cabinet minister and one of the insubordinate producers, several requests for emergency debates by the Leader of the Opposition John Diefenbaker, intervention by Prime Minister Lester Pearson, demands in parliament for the abolition of the CBC as the only clear-cut way of getting rid of its problems, mediation efforts and parliamentary hearings covering more than a thousand pages of Hansard.

While the program was on the air the CBC was in its heyday of power and influence.

It has not been the same since.

The first battle over program content in broadcasting in Canada flared up in 1928. The issue was religion, not politics, morals or taste. At that time, several radio stations were operated by churches and religious groups, four of them by the "International Bible Students Association", that is, Jehovah's Witnesses. The federal government had been receiving petitions and complaints that these stations carried programs "under the name of Bible talks" that were "unpatriotic and abusive of all other churches". No administrative machinery had yet been constructed to adjudicate fairness and balance of program content. Therefore, the federal government simply decided to revoke the licences of the offending stations. There was an uproar in parliament and the Conservative government under R.B. Bennett began to wonder whether it should adopt a "policy of national broadcasting along the lines adopted...by the British government". The result was the appointment of a royal commission which, in 1932, led to the creation of the Canadian Radio Broadcasting Commission and later, in 1936, when the Liberals under Mackenzie King were in power, to the founding of the Canadian Broadcasting Corporation.[1]

The invigorating Canadian climate did not permit an exact cloning of the British Broadcasting Corporation's austerely paternalistic monopoly. But many of its attributes were successfully transplanted. (When the BBC had difficulties resolving problems of religious doctrine it printed its own hymn book.) The CBC shared the BBC's sense of social purpose and moral uplift and felt the same need to inform and entertain its audience without overstimulating it by trying to stretch standards of political or moral taboos. Unlike printing presses, airwaves were scarce and the CBC firmly believed that the public had to be protected from abuses of all kinds. In the years immediately following the creation of the CBC, during the war and the immediate postwar period—before the arrival of television—no earth-shaking controversies raised fundamental questions about the basic assumptions of the Canadian system. However, there was continuing debate, as there was in the United States, where a very different system evolved, about the social responsibility of the broadcaster.

Television arrived in the United States at the same time as the nuclear age and the Cold War and many dilemmas about freedom of expression in an open society suddenly became acute. At first the networks were uncertain how to handle television news. The natural medium for news reporting and analysis seemed to be radio. For television the only traditions to build on were theatre newsreels like *The March of Time* which had had its origin in a CBS radio series produced in conjunction with *Time* magazine. *The March of Time* had been shown in moviehouses from 1935 to 1951 and consisted of a string of topical short items which fell between spot news and mini-documentaries and dealt with significant issues of the day. In the early days of television the technology for quick, flexible film reportage had not yet been invented. Each camera crew required several hundred pounds of equipment, cameras, tripods, batteries and lights. But the new medium was a visual one and demanded visual news reporting.

> The notion that a picture was worth a thousand words meant, in practice, that footage of Atlantic City beauty winners, shot at some expense, was considered more valuable than a thousand words from Eric Sevareid on the mounting tensions in Southeast Asia. Analysis, a staple of radio news in its finest days and the basis for the fame of Swing, Murrow, Kaltenborn, Shirer and others, was being pushed aside as non-visual.[2]

There was a solution for this dilemma: the development of the television personality. Of these the greatest was Edward R. Murrow, who had made his reputation as a superb radio reporter for CBS News during the London blitz. After the war, he developed the documentary radio series *Hear It Now*, working closely with Fred Friendly, a young writer from Providence, Rhode Island. In 1951—a year before Canadian television went on the air—this series was transformed into *See It Now*, designed as a successor to *The March of Time* which was dying. The program slowly evolved into weekly half-hour think-pieces, each one introduced as "a document for television based on the week's news". Many of Murrow's programs, produced by CBS News and sponsored by Alcoa—the Aluminum Company of America—were far more controversial than *The March of Time* had ever been. Murrow was introduced as "the distinguished reporter and news analyst Edward R. Murrow". Such a combination of functions would have been unthinkable in the BBC and CBC where, in order to keep the news untainted by opinion, a careful distinction was drawn between reporting, handled by the news department, and news analysis, which was the responsibility of the department of public affairs, originally called talks department.

Murrow's and Friendly's decision occasionally to take a strong editorial line on controversial issues exercised a strong influence on the producers of *Seven Days* a decade later.

The cause *See It Now* served was the cause of American liberalism. This was new on U.S. television and took great courage at the time when the program was making its greatest impact. These were the years when Senator Joseph McCarthy was conducting a witch-hunt in his committee against "Communists" in public life, using as his weapons innuendo, smear, character assassination and guilt by association. To be accused by him often meant instant dismissal and blacklisting. Every institution in the country was terrified of him, including CBS.

But two years after *See It Now* went on the air, Murrow and Friendly decided to expose the senator.

They proceeded with the greatest care. Throughout 1953, their staff gathered all available McCarthy footage. When they were ready to go ahead they informed CBS management that they were about to do a program about McCarthy and asked for advertising support. CBS declined. Murrow and Friendly paid out of their own pocket for quarter-page advertisements in *The New York Times* and *Washington Post*.

The date was March 4th 1954. The program made television history. It contributed decisively to the senator's eventual downfall.

To demonstrate McCarthy's technique, Murrow showed film clips from the senate hearings. One of these, at the end of the program, was McCarthy's cross-examination of Reid Harris, for many years a civil servant in the State Department. In 1932, twenty-two years earlier, in a lawsuit against Columbia University, Harris had been represented by an attorney from the Civil Liberties Union. McCarthy asked Harris whether he knew that the organization had been listed as a front organization for the Communist Party. The very fact of asking that question in his inquisitorial committee room was intended to convict Harris of high treason.

This was Murrow's conclusion:

> Twice he (McCarthy) said that the American Civil Liberties Union was listed as a subversive front. The Attorney-General's

list does not and has never listed the ACLU as subversive, nor does the FBI or any other federal government agency, and the American Civil Liberties Union holds in its files letters of commendation from President Truman, President Eisenhower and General MacArthur. The actions of the junior senator from Wisconsin have caused alarm and dismay among our allies abroad and given considerable comfort to our enemies, and whose fault is that? Not really his. He didn't create the situation of fear; he merely exploited it, and rather successfully. Cassius was right: "The fault, dear Brutus, is not in our stars but in ourselves... Good night, and good luck."[3]

Nearly a month later, Senator McCarthy replied at CBS's expense, on the same spot on the network as *See It Now.*

Now, ordinarily I would not take time out from the important work at hand to answer Murrow. However, in this case I feel justified in doing so because Murrow is a symbol, the leader and the cleverest of the jackal pack which is always found at the throat of anyone who dares to expose individual Communists and traitors.[4]

Ed Murrow's attack on McCarthy demonstrated the effectiveness of television in bringing to the surface of American political life the revulsion felt by many for the senator's rabble-rousing and self-serving demagogy. This was a new kind of television—a fearless, eloquent and skilled "reporter" with the charisma of a movie star slaying a dragon who had succeeded for many months in terrifying large sections of normally responsible people in the political arena, in the media and in the universities. A morality play, performed with high passion and deadly seriousness, had been acted out in the living rooms of America.

In Canada, until the arrival of *Seven Days,* no television journalists with theatrical star qualities had ever aspired to the role of dragon-slayer. Canada was spared a McCarthy, but even in the years preceding *Seven Days* there had been no shortage of social evils which public-spirited, though unspectacular, broadcasters were determined to expose. They often did so while conscientiously trying to observe the existing guidelines governing controversial broadcasters, but always risking the charge of sensationalism. Among these social evils were the antiquated divorce laws, a subject for lively debate in parliament in the spring of 1960. On May 19th the CBC's *Close-Up* made its contribution. The executive producer was the enterprising and imaginative Ross McLean who had an enormous influence on the producers of *Seven Days.* The program caused the greatest row of the first decade of Canadian television. It entered history as "The Case of the Shady Lady".

Close-Up staged an interview with an anonymous young lady, discreetly presented in silhouette, who claimed to be a professional corespondent. One hundred and twenty times, she said, she had manufactured evidence of adultery, for a hundred dollars per occasion. Immediately following the program, the Attorney General of Ontario ordered an investigation and the director of public prosecutions declared "If this sort of thing is going on, we've got to stop it." Charlotte Whitton, the combative former mayor of Ottawa, called the interview "decadent and revolting". Two months later, the *Toronto Telegram* stunned the country with the revelation that the young woman was an employee of a detective agency who had concocted the story for a fee of $150.00 and hoaxed the CBC. She herself had never been a corespondent, she said. But many divorces were granted on the strength of the sort of rigged evidence of which she had spoken on the program. The embarrassed CBC took little comfort in the fact that the hoax had exposed, in more senses than one, the hypocrisy of our times. While the producers had no defence against the charge of having been duped, they could console themselves with the knowledge that they had been duped for a good cause. As for top management in Ottawa, the episode strengthened their distrust of what they regarded as irresponsible sensation-mongering among the production staff in Toronto.

In the early sixties, investigative television journalism began to flourish in Canada, the United States and England. The example of the kind of courage Ed Murrow displayed when he exposed McCarthy inspired many young journalists, and broadcasting institutions on both sides of the Atlantic found it increasingly difficult to devise appropriate rules to guide controversial broadcasting. New magazine programs sprang up, the most important of which was the BBC's *Tonight*. In matters of news presentation, the official announcer who read prepared bulletins gathered from wire services was making way for reporters with individual styles and reputations.

The CBC was a broadcasting organization, but once television arrived on the scene it soon became evident that it had to enter the area of film production. The National Film Act of 1939 had established the National Film Board as the only public agency to make films in Canada, and for many years the CBC had to conduct delicate negotiations in order to legitimize its film production. That is why, until 1965, in spite of prolific film-making for thirteen years, no credit on the screen was allowed to indicate that any program was a CBC TV film production. Management constantly reminded its senior people that they "were not in the film business".

However, a handful of far-sighted people in the CBC, confident that jurisdictional problems would sooner or later be resolved, made some wise decisions at an early stage. Before the first television program went on the air in 1952, a CBC working group had to decide whether the corporation was to use 16 or 35 mm film. The U.S. networks and the Europeans, including the BBC, considered 16 mm 'substandard'. Yet the CBC decided in its favour, partly because in a country the size of Canada the cost of shipping 35 mm film would have been prohibitive. It was this decision which quickly made the CBC a world leader in three vital areas: it established high standards for private film processing laboratories from coast to coast; it developed entirely new methods of evaluating film quality for television; and it adapted telecine systems for 16 mm film. These pioneering efforts proved to be highly beneficial. It was irrelevant that for a time CBC standards were ahead of those used abroad, since the question of marketing Canadian programs outside the country did not arise until the rest of the world had caught up with Canadian innovations.

The introduction of light and mobile cameras at this time made it possible at last to shake off the "tripod syndrome" enforced by the heavy and bulky 35 mm sound equipment. This had a liberating effect on the coverage of television news, with political consequences of immeasurable importance. It enabled the networks to cover the civil rights marches in the South, and the Kennedy assassination in November 1963, in a direct and vivid manner inconceivable before. It may have been television which kept the country together, in Fred Friendly's opinion, after the traumatic shock of the Kennedy assassination.[5] It was also the time when American and French film-makers were experimenting with *cinéma vérité* and candid camera techniques were being designed to catch people and situations *au naturel*.

In matters of editorial content, too, the early sixties was a time of new breakthroughs. In Canada, as elsewhere, producers constantly stretched the limits of public acceptability, and these limits were very different in different parts of the country. When in February 1962 *Quest*, the CBC's Sunday night series of avant garde programs, presented *Crawling Arnold*, a play by the cartoonist Jules Feiffer, E.W. Blunden, Conservative M.P. for Medicine Hat, Alberta, quoted letters from his constituents calling it "depraved...disgusting...immoral...garbage...and a rank violation of the sanctity of the Canadian home and family", and asked that steps be taken "to institute some control over the apparently degenerate minds which often appear to have completely taken over CBC programming".[6] John Diefenbaker called *The Open Grave*, a contemporary allegory of the Resurrection shown on Easter Sunday 1964, "a flagrant, scandalous and sacrilegious insult to the majority of Canadians" *before* he had seen it, merely on the basis of press reports.[7]

The built-in tension between broadcasters and politicians invariably becomes most noticeable in the coverage of political news. In his private life the politician may wish to be left alone, undisturbed by the glare of publicity. But he cannot perform his public activities without the attention of the media, especially television.

> The politician needs...the appearance of dignity, the right to time his actions and statements and the right to change his mind; he wants to address his public when it is in his own interests to do so. The broadcaster claims the rights of traditional journalism and employs additional tools; he demands the right of timing and scheduling, the right of constant publicity, together with the pretension that he represents the 'public' (which they both claim); the broadcaster wants the politician to appear when it is to the latter's disadvantage as well as when it is to his advantage.[8]

In Canada, the natural tensions between politicians and broadcasters became exacerbated after John Diefenbaker's surprise victory in 1957 which followed a long era of Liberal governments headed by Mackenzie King and Louis St. Laurent.

Diefenbaker, as a Westerner from the Bible Belt, had little sympathy for sophisticated city-slickers in Toronto and Montreal. The CBC had a difficult time during the six years he was prime minister. In 1963 the Liberal Lester B. Pearson took over, and, though he was more urbane, relations between his government and the CBC were also marked by frequent skirmishes. During both governments the socialist CCF, which in 1961 became the New Democratic Party, was a consistent and reliable supporter of the CBC and conducted a vigorous opposition whenever the government in power was in conflict with the Corporation.

In the spring of 1964 the CBC commissioned a film to present "an intimate, behind-the-scenes look at the prime minister's day". It was to be called *Mr. Pearson*. The director was Richard Ballentine who, together with Gordon Sheppard, had recently made a film portrait of Hugh Hefner, the originator of the new magazine *Playboy*, for which he earned five international awards. Ballentine chose as his cameraman Donn Pennebaker, a master of *cinéma vérité*. They shot film of the prime minister at the U.N. and in his office in the East Block, watching the World Series during the lunch break while the Minister of Labour Allan MacEachen tried to discuss the longshoremen strike with him. They shot film of Pearson conducting a cabinet meeting, receiving Haile Selassie, the emperor of Ethiopia; they shot the prime minister on the way home to 24 Sussex Drive and at home with with Mrs. Pearson. There were uninhibited remarks about his predecessor in office, unguarded comments by Allan MacEachen and minor indiscretions by Mrs. Pearson. The prime minister uttered one "Lord" and one "God". There was also a partisan political remark by James Coutts, the prime minister's appointments secretary.

All these uninhibited, unguarded and indiscreet remarks were removed during the editing at the request of Pearson's public relations advisers who were worried about blemishes on the prime minister's image, though one "hell", one "damn" and one "God" survived. The special arrangements between the producers and the Prime Minister's Office which had permitted such "corrections" during the editing process were subsequently changed by mutual consent to conform to the CBC's traditional practice of not allowing politicians and their advisers to exercise any influence on the way programs were produced.

When the president of the CBC, Alphonse Ouimet, saw the film he was appalled—not by the swearing, nor by any political aspects of the film, but by the quality of the production. *Cinéma vérité* struck him as completely amateurish. He decided the film was not to be shown and a statement was issued to the effect that "it was deemed unacceptable for showing on the basis of broadcast standards".

There was an outcry in parliament. The opposition was convinced that Pearson, or Pearson's people, had put pressure on the CBC not to show an unfavourable portrait of the prime minister. On June 19th John Diefenbaker thundered "There has not been a more serious matter before parliament than this!"

Pearson replied.

Well, the Leader of the Opposition has suggested that one way of clearing up this particular allegation would be to have a showing of this film for members of parliament. I hope that can be arranged and that this can be done without interfering with the CBC, who have custody of the film. I will take the right honourable gentleman's request to the CBC and join in that request that the film be made available to members...I hope I shall not be accused of interfering with the affairs of the CBC if I get in touch with the president of the Corporation and express my view that this film should be shown publicly.[9]

That afternoon Pearson called Ouimet.

PEARSON: *It's Lester Pearson speaking.*
OUIMET: *How do you do, sir.*
PEARSON: *You probably know what happened in the House this morning.*
OUIMET: *Yes, I do.*
PEARSON: *Then you know that the Leader of the Opposition Mr. John Diefenbaker has asked me to use my good offices to try to get you to release this film.*
OUIMET: *I know you were asked and that you would do your best. Are you calling me as the prime minister of Canada, sir?*
PEARSON: *Oh, no.*
OUIMET: *Are you calling me as Head of the Liberal Party?*
PEARSON: *Oh, no.*
OUIMET: *Then you must be calling me in a personal capacity.*
PEARSON: *Yes.*
OUIMET: *We will consider your views in that light. Thank you very much.*[10]

Alphonse Ouimet stood firm. Without being influenced by any political considerations, he had made up his mind that the film was not up to CBC standards. It was not shown on the CBC until April 1969, after Ouimet had resigned. Joan Irwin commented on it in her column in the *Montreal Star* on April 21st:

Technical excellence will not be among the film's achievements. Who cares? It's not every day that the public is allowed to get that close to its prime minister and I doubt that any member of the audience would object to the blurry, out-of-focus shots, the too-fast zooms, or the muffled conversations.

The excitement over the 'banning' of *Mr. Pearson* gave Canadians a whiff of things to come. Three-and-a-half months later *Seven Days* went on the air, breaking convention in very much the same way. Once again, it was the style—the eclectic mix of new ways of presenting information, conveying experiences and 'getting close' to the subject matter—which shocked the older generation. They thought it was the content of the program which was upsetting them. But it was the form.

CHAPTER 2

THE SHOW

The first program of *This Hour Has Seven Days* went on the air from ten to eleven on Sunday evening, October 4th 1964.

It set the style for the fifty programs to come. This is what appeared on the screen:

HUSHED WOODWINDS AND DRUMS. SUSPENSE MUSIC.

A GREY-HAIRED LADY WITH HORN-RIMMED GLASSES APPEARS ON THE TELEVISION SCREEN.

THE CAMERA ZOOMS IN ON A THICK BOOK.

ANNOUNCER WARREN DAVIS, voice-over:

> *Seven days ago this report was delivered to the White House. It confirmed that the shots that killed President Kennedy were fired by Lee Harvey Oswald.*

THE CAMERA RETURNS TO THE GREY-HAIRED LADY.

> *This woman is Lee Harvey Oswald's mother. She says the report is ridiculous. She has come to our studio in Toronto tonight to defend her statement and her son. Her story is one of seven awaiting you in the next sixty minutes.*

MUFFLED DRUMS.

THE CAMERA ZOOMS IN ON LAURIER LAPIERRE, SITTING AT A TABLE NEXT TO JOHN DRAINIE.

> *Ladies and gentleman*, This Hour Has Seven Days.

FANFARES: THE *SEVEN DAYS* THEME.

JOHN DRAINIE:

> *Since last July the police of two countries have been searching in vain for Harold Chamberlain Banks who jumped twenty-five thousand dollars bail in Montreal to avoid facing an assault charge. Hal Banks was the undisputed tsar of Canada's sixteen thousand merchant seamen until he was fired from the Seafarers International Union last year by government action. On Thursday this week, while the Justice Department, the FBI and the RCMP claimed no knowledge of his whereabouts, Hal Banks was discovered sitting on the deck of his yacht in Brooklyn smoking a cigarette.*

WE SEE HIM.

The man who found Banks was Toronto Star *reporter Robert Reguly.*

ROBERT REGULY:

This is what happened. The SIU was leaking out stories that Banks was either in Puerto Rico or San Francisco. So I decided to look for him in New York. I hired a tough character to protect me as I went nosing around the waterfront. On a pier in Brooklyn we saw a white Cadillac with Quebec licence plates. It was lunchtime and nobody was around, except a man sitting on the deck of a sixty-foot Chris Craft cruiser. I recognized him as Hal Banks. I went up to him and said "Mr. Banks?" and he said "Yes, what do you want?" I said I wanted an interview and he told me to beat it. I went to a nearby gas station and phoned in my story. Then I went to a drugstore and bought a Brownie camera and went back to the dock. This time Banks saw me coming. There were seven SIU guards waiting. I grabbed two quick shots with the Brownie and they came racing at me. I ran. But one of them managed to clout me on the side of the head. But I kept on going. My driver luckily saw what was happening and he wheeled around on Flatbush Avenue, cut off the goons and I jumped in.

JOHN DRAINIE:

Tomorrow in Ottawa an attempt will be launched to defeat the government on the issue of Hal Banks. The opposition wants to know the answers to these questions: Why was Banks left free on bail? Why was he charged with the conspiracy offence for which he could not be extradited from the United States? Why could the RCMP not locate him when Bob Reguly found him in two hours? Will he be brought back to Canada now to face the music? The opposition attack will fall on the shoulders of Minister of Justice Guy Favreau. He is in our Seven Days *studio in Ottawa to answer the questions of Warner Troyer and Laurier LaPierre.*

We switch to Ottawa. Guy Favreau, a middle-aged lawyer with a black moustache, appears on camera. He is not entirely comfortable expressing himself in English but he does his best to answer the questions. The tone of the interview is respectful but the questioners—especially Warner Troyer—are mildly persistent. It is evident that the interview has been edited. They discuss the legal problems involved in granting bail to Hal Banks.

After the interview, a film sequence is shown.

WARREN DAVIS, voice-over:

Our Seven Days *cameras found Banks on the yacht in Brooklyn this morning. Our reporter Larry Zolf and cameraman Mike Lenny spotted the boat from the air. Then, they approached by motor launch. They were warned off by thugs who threw rocks when they came too close. On the dockside they mounted a vigil. Goons warn Zolf if he passes the 'no trespassing' sign they will break every bone in his body. But at ten thirty-five this morning the familiar white Cadillac pulled up and Hal Banks himself climbed out. He ignored our cameras, walked jauntily down the pier, and mounted the gangway to the deck. Here he awaits tonight word of the next moves which are bound to be made to take him into custody.*

FANFARES: THE *SEVEN DAYS* THEME.

Harpo Marx died this week at the age of seventy. John Drainie pays tribute to the silent Marx brother and presents a clip from an interview Joyce Davidson conducted with him on the CBC program *Seven-O-One* in December 1960. Harpo, wearing a moth-eaten wig, baggy pants and an outsize raincoat, mutely pretends through eloquent gestures that he has walked all the way to Toronto from Hollywood. Clowning throughout the interview, he makes a pass at Joyce Davidson, climbing all over her. Then, in another film clip, Harpo hammers his way through Rachmaninoff's famous C sharp minor prelude at the keyboard until the piano collapses. A short telephone interview with the aging actress Margaret Dumont follows, while stills of her appear on the screen. She has acted with the Marx brothers in many films and speaks of Harpo with affection and admiration, stressing his consummate musicianship.

MUSIC: A SOLEMN MILITARY MARCH.

JOHN DRAINIE:

Since this is the first edition of Seven Days *we would like to display some of the fare you can expect from us in the months ahead.*

CAROLE SIMPSON:

And to begin with, we would like to show you the following excerpts from the manifesto so boldly conceived by the executive producers of this show just a short nine months ago . . .

Cartoons of gloomy birds in various humourous poses appear on the screen while Warren Davis reads the manifesto with mock pomposity:

This Hour Has Seven Days—*the show ranging over the complete spectrum of responsible journalism, of such natural interest, such vitality and urgency, that it will recapture public excitement in public affairs television and become mandatory viewing for a large segment of the population.* This Hour Has Seven Days *will present vigorously produced public affairs material. Each item must have something to say. Tone will be energy, maturity, intelligence. The program will be provocative, thoughtful—the all-seeing eye. It will view the human spirit with dignity.* Seven Days *will range Canada and the world. Reporter-cameramen teams will look not only at the news but the reasons behind it, pouncing on*

*significant events wherever they occur. With perceptive
comments on urgent national concern we will provide greater
depth.* This Hour Has Seven Days—*probing dishonesty and
hypocrisy, drawing attention to public wrongs and encouraging remedial action, presenting tough encounters with prominent guests hot in the news and prepared to be grilled.* This
Hour Has Seven Days *will accommodate the experimental
and the artistic. Cameras in strange places will provide new
insights.* This Hour Has Seven Days *will set a pace with live
reports and interviews on top of the news, treating the world
as our own backyard.*

TRUMPETS.

A cartoon appears of a gloomy bird, bent down under the weight of a
huge globe on his shoulders.

VOICE: *Good grief—we're carrying all that on this show!*

A filmed interview with the mother of a murdered civil rights worker
in the South follows, a prelude to next week's film documentary by
Beryl Fox, *Summer in Mississippi.*

Next: a visual report on the investigation of the crash near Ste. Thérèse, Quebec, of an Air Canada jet on December 23rd 1963, in which a
hundred and eighteen people were killed.

This leads to a short skit by the *Second City* satirists who will, according to Carole Simpson, "regularly siphon a little of their private recipe
for acid out of their native Chicago and into our *Seven Days* studios.
Tonight they bring you this important message":

WOMAN: *I'm tired of these modern novels.*
MAN: *Have you tried William Shakespeare?*
WOMAN: *Who?*
MAN: *William Shakespeare. He gets way down deep inside life,
         where ordinary writers fail to penetrate.*
WOMAN: *Sounds good.*
MAN: *He is good, and good for you. Here's a passage from modern
         novelist A: "I don't feel well. I'd kill myself but I'm afraid."
         Now listen to William Shakespeare: "To be or not to be,
         that is the question."*
WOMAN: *That's much better.*
MAN AND WOMAN: *Get William Shakespeare today for a richer, fuller
         life, available at booksellers everywhere.* [1]

FANFARES: *SEVEN DAYS* THEME.

LAURIER LAPIERRE:

John Fitzgerald Kennedy was pronounced dead at one p.m on
November 22nd last year. Fifty-one minutes later, Lee Harvey
Oswald was arrested at a Texas theatre in Dallas...

JOHN DRAINIE:

Oswald was questioned for approximately twelve hours

between two thirty p.m. on November 22nd and eleven a.m. on November 24th. Throughout this interrogation he denied that he had anything to do with the assassination of President Kennedy... Lee Harvey Oswald did not stand trial. Shortly after eleven that Sunday morning, with half a hundred newsmen, three television crews and seventy police on hand, he in turn was fatally wounded as publicly as any man in history.

MRS. OSWALD APPEARS ON SCREEN.

ROBERT HOYT: *Mrs. Oswald, were you watching?*

MRS. OSWALD: *No, I wasn't.*

ROBERT HOYT: *Where were you when your son was killed?*

MRS. OSWALD: *I was with my daughter-in-law Marina at the Executive Inn. Just about fifteen minutes before the terrible tragedy, I said to Marina "Honey, let's turn the television off." I turned it off myself. I didn't see the actual killing.*

ROBERT HOYT: *You saw the films then later?*

MRS. OSWALD: *I saw it for the first time this past Sunday.*

ROBERT HOYT: *What did you think as you saw that picture of Ruby approaching toward your son with a gun in his hand?*

MRS. OSWALD: *Well, I was prepared for it. Because for the last ten months I have investigated just every lead and everything there was. The reporters had told me repeatedly that they had never seen such an astonished look on any man's face as my son's. And then suddenly I heard him say: "The President? Who said anything about the President?" This is important, to hear him say this.*

ROBERT HOYT: *No matter what kind of preparation you had, could anything prepare you for seeing a scene like that? Certainly you must have felt something.*

MRS. OSWALD: *Yes. Of course I did. I immediately went to the screen. I went as close to the screen as I possibly could because I wanted to catch every word that my son said. I had asked the officials to show me this picture because this would have helped me in my immediate investigation. But I was denied that privilege. So this was the very first time...*

ROBERT HOYT: *You are certain, Mrs. Oswald, that your son could not have killed the President...*

MRS. OSWALD: *Well, my investigation shows nothing other than that Lee was a patsy and this was a frame-up. I don't say that I'm right but...*

ROBERT HOYT: *Who's framing him, Mrs. Oswald?*

MRS. OSWALD: *I wish I had the time to go into the complete story. You must understand that there's many many aspects to this case. Who framed Lee Harvey Oswald?... My investigation shows that our trouble is in our State*

> Department, that there are a few men in our State
> Department who wanted President Kennedy out of the
> way. I'm a very unpopular person.

ROBERT HOYT: Do you really believe this, Mrs. Oswald?

MRS. OSWALD: It isn't that I believe this. It is because I think I have
circumstantial evidence to back me up.

ROBERT HOYT: What evidence do you have?

MRS. OSWALD: Well, I have a document that is explanatory. I went
before the Commission with my documents, with one
in particular they were supposed to inform me about
and they didn't. It's just really too much to understand
the impact of all of this...

ROBERT HOYT: Mrs. Oswald, do you accept or feel any guilt at all for
what has happened to your son?

MRS. OSWALD: No, and this is the deplorable part of the report on the
assassination, that Lee was a misfit and that I didn't
give him the emotional lead that he needed.

After the conclusion of this interview, a short visual reconstruction of
the assassination follows. It focuses specifically on the flight path of
the bullets. After that, an attack of the Warren Commission Report by
lawyer Mark Lane, the chairman of the Citizens' Committee of Inquiry, who is grilled hard by Warner Troyer and Laurier LaPierre. Next
comes a short appearance, taped the previous summer, of Lord Denning, "an unpredictable British Appeal Court justice whose colleagues
are said to regard him with affectionate anxiety. It was he who last
year probed into the celebrated affection of John Profumo for a girl
named Christine Keeler." Lord Denning reminisces about a suicide
case in which he was involved before the British parliament had decided that neither suicide nor attempted suicide was a crime.

The last feature in the show is a graphic film sequence about the
Beatles' recent performance in Toronto, with Larry Zolf interviewing
shrieking teenagers and their older fans, including approving grand-
mothers.

This is John Drainie's introduction:

> This past month the British Board of Trade rejoiced in public
> over the contribution that four young performers from Liver-
> pool had made to the British economy. Of the millions they
> earned abroad for Britain this year, $198,000 came from their
> September songs in Canada where they spent a fruitful three
> days. The day they hit Toronto was Labour Day for most of
> us. For some others it was the Day of Worship.

The program concludes with a reference to the Queen's impending
arrival in Canada. John Drainie:

> Twelve hours from now a U.S. airliner takes off from London
> to bring another famous British visitor to our shores. We will
> be with her and reporting back in seven days. Good night.

That first show contained most of the ingredients which guaranteed success and were to cause trouble later: subjects close to the bone, an edited interview with a politician, irreverence, irony, satire. In the spring of 1966, when the program was not renewed for a third season, the camera work and production techniques were more sophisticated and the performers more at home in the studio. But the concept had remained the same.

Soon the producers deliberately began to sprinkle it with more unorthodox borderline entertainments than had been permissible before in a public affairs program. These were specifically designed to attract attention and to shock.

The subject matter was traditional.

The mix was new.

The effect was immediate.

•••

On September 25th 1964, eight days before the launching of the show, the CBC staged a press conference, connecting Toronto with Ottawa and Montreal on closed circuit. Jeremy Brown, the entertainment editor of the *Toronto Telegram*, was there.

> It must have been the Corporation's most expensive publicity gimmick to date. There was a showing of a satirical film clip about Diefenbaker. With ruthless single-mindedness the producer of that item had culled hundreds of feet of film of Dief at his oratorical best and visual worst, and lumped all the shots together, without the oratory but with the music. Another satirical segment lampooned the hot line between London and Moscow and even played with the British homosexual theme.

Brown concluded that if this press conference was an indication, *Seven Days* will be "the smash of the season—out of Parliament as well as in."

The press was not unanimous in its praise of the first program. While conceding that no program should be judged by its first appearance, Frank Moritsugu of the *Toronto Star* thought it was too much like the *Ed Sullivan Show*. He enjoyed the last item, "a dazzling film coverage of the Beatles' visit to Toronto". But he was concerned.

> Will most viewers be willing to stick to the end of *Seven Days* to sit through its fizzes? The interviews with lawyer Mark Lane and Mrs. Marguerite Oswald (both flown here yesterday for the show) were rushed and inconclusive, and with the Favreau interview made three which wound up as abruptly as a Sullivan turn usually does.

•••

During the preceding 1963–1964 season the Sunday night spot at ten following *Bonanza* had been occupied by the public affairs program *Horizon*, which had an average audience of 650,000 viewers. Four weeks after *Seven Days* went on the air—by mid-November 1964—its average audience was 1.6 million, by December 2 million, by March 1965 2.1 million. By January 1966 it was 2.2 million, by March 2.9 million, and the program's final appearance on May 8th 1966 had an audience of slightly under 3.3 million. This was almost half the total audience across Canada for all English television broadcast at that hour on Sunday evenings. It was the biggest audience of any *Canadian* program aside from *Hockey Night in Canada*. However, *Bonanza* and *Ed Sullivan* each consistently attracted more viewers than did *Seven Days*.

The show had more university-educated viewers than any other CBC network program except *Hockey Night in Canada*. At the same time, more than half of its viewers never completed high school. It was one of the very few fast-moving magazine show anywhere on television up to that point which was specifically designed to appeal to all sections of society.

It did not matter whether you were a PhD in philosophy, a cabinet minister, a waitress or a garbageman, the program was designed for you. Every Sunday night, it contained something for every taste—tough interviews on domestic issues, ombudsmen items often based on complaints sent in by viewers, international stories, obituaries of high-brow cult figures like T.S. Eliot and Edith Sitwell, human-interest features, stories celebrating the positive aspects of society, "show-biz" items, humourous pieces, all presented by the hosts in a manner that spoke directly to viewers and engaged them as entertainingly as possible in the common cause of exposing human folly, hypocrisy, injustice and exploitation.

This common cause could be served only, the producers believed, if the program adhered to the middle of the road in its overall character. The Beatles film in the first program was a good example. There was a scene at the airport as the Beatles took off, when shrieking Beatlemaniacs practically tore down the fence. It was intercut with a laconic observation by one of the Liverpudlians who said "They appreciate what we're doing", in very much the same amused and detached tone as host John Drainie's wry introduction. Both he and the reporter-interviewer Larry Zolf made a special effort to convey the impression that *Seven Days* was on the side of the puzzled and helpless parents rather than on that of their hysterical pubescent children who were shown on the screen as temporarily insane.

Seven Days was middle of the road. But the program also had an implied message which had become clear very quickly. It presented itself as one of the few public institutions on the people's side and suggested subliminally that there was no need any longer to look up to the guardians of authority with respect. It consistently championed the little man in his encounters with large bureaucracies, including large commercial bureaucracies. *Seven Days* introduced consumerism to prime-time television in North America. Soon after the first show, it began to present ombudsman items, exposing negligence and wrongdoing in high places. The consumer advocate Ralph Nader, whose book attacking the car industry, *Unsafe at any Speed*, came out in 1965, appeared on *Seven Days* before any American network had given him airtime. For the first time since the radio days of the forties—since *Citizens Forum* and *Farm Forum*—the CBC was putting on a program in which the public took a proprietary interest. Though the word "feedback" had not yet become common usage, the producers and performers forged a bond with their audience which made it possible for them to respond quickly to the audience's reactions and to solicit—and to take seriously —the audience's wishes.

Seven Days was the people's show. It was exciting, revealing, cocky, fearless, accusatory, emotional, titillating. Watching it was like going on a sleigh ride.

You got on and it would not let you off until the hour was over.

CHAPTER 3

GENESIS

Change was in the air. After the prosperity and complacency of the fifties, serious questions were being asked about fundamental matters. Previously, dissent from middle-class materialism had taken the form of leftwing radicalism. But in the sixties protest was beginning to take another form: a new lifestyle was emerging among the young, showing up in their music, dress and long hair. In 1960 the U.S. Food and Drug Administration had approved the use of the Pill, thereby unleashing the sexual revolution. Thanks to the postwar baby boom, by 1961 the Canadian university population was fifty percent higher than it had been in 1956. Seventeen new universities were built in seven years. There was talk of participatory democracy, not only in the universities, but throughout society. People were beginning to believe that through direct action they could more effectively influence events.

However, in Canada the winds of change blew much more gently than they did in England and in the United States. But there was considerable internal growth which strained the fabric of Confederation.

> Few thought simple readjustments would ease the strain...
> The grey threads now seemed merely dull, not stolidly respectable, and in any case that respectability which had marked Canada's earlier style was no longer a value Canadians or others cherished. Throughout the country we cleaned out our closets, but we were uncertain whether we would refill them with the new fashions we saw.[1]

In England in the late fifties, working-class writers and dramatists like John Osborne had already been looking back in anger at centuries of suppression, while no comparable cultural trend had emerged in Canada. In the United States, the middle sixties were marked by increasing racial tension, by violence in the inner cities and by increasing involvement in Vietnam. In 1964 the Free Speech Movement was launched at Berkeley, followed by student rioting on almost every campus.

In Canada, too, the political scene was becoming more lively, but for different reasons. Diefenbaker's election victories in 1957 and 1958 had demonstrated that it was at last possible to change governments after the long period of Liberal rule. There were elections 1962 and 1963 when Diefenbaker's administration collapsed in disarray and Lester Pearson formed a minority government. The next few years were characterized by bitter acrimony between Pearson and Diefenbaker. There were a number of political scandals such as the Gerda Munsinger affair which reached back to the years when Diefenbaker was in power. It was an era when young people had increasing doubts about the morality of politics. It was a perfect period for a popular television program dedicated to exposing the seamy aspects of public life.

In Quebec important things were happening. Even before the death of Maurice Duplessis in 1959 it had become evident that rapid industrialization was causing far-reaching social changes which dramatically accelerated under the Liberal government of Jean Lesage. In English Canada these events were regarded very much in the same light as the civil rights marches in the South. Well-meaning people looked at the Quiet Revolution with tolerance and patience. After all, change in the backward province was long overdue. In fact, numerous observers in Ontario and in other parts of English Canada, frustrated by the dreariness of their own political life, had envious admiration for rising Quebec nationalism. But many underestimated the implications.

> The English-Canadian media showed a generosity towards the Quiet Revolution that rested upon too superficial an appreciation of the nature of the social, economic, and political changes occurring in Quebec. The first stirrings of separatism...troubled English Canadians: the bombs in Montreal mailboxes outraged them. Too often, all dissent was lumped into a general mass called separatism.[2]

Throughout the Pearson years there was a feeling of malaise and uncertainty in Canada, as though the old clothes no longer fitted while no new ones had as yet been designed. Events unfolded slowly until the climactic explosion of the October Crisis of 1970. But this more than four years after the end of *Seven Days* and three years after the great federal feast of the Centennial Year and Expo 67. By then the sixties had come to an end.

••••

The men at the top of the CBC were men of the radio generation. With the arrival of television, they not only had to make judgments on moral and aesthetic issues raised by new styles of

CBC productions but they also had to deal with young people who were developing a mystique of their own.

Only a few radio producers like Ross McLean had found the transition from the old to the new medium stimulating, but McLean's youth, his prodigious talent as a producer and his reputation as an *enfant terrible—vide* his role in "The Case of the Shady Lady" and in a few other adventures and misadventures on which the authorities had frowned heavily —precluded him from being considered managerial timber. Older men like Andrew Allen, the greatest of all CBC radio drama producers in the forties and fifties, had found the tradition painfully difficult. The prevailing myth was that the one indispensable qualification for television production was raw youth. The gap between the generations was defined by the differences in styles, skills and experience. Allen invariably appeared in the control room to direct his plays impeccably attired, addressed his actors by their surnames and insisted on formality and distance. One could not imagine him in the uniform of the television producers—the turtleneck sweaters, the slacks or jeans, talking in a jargon of their own. A radio producer could learn the technical requirements of his craft in a week or so. His effectiveness depended on his artistic and intellectual gifts, not on his technical skills. Nor were vast batteries of technicians and assistants required to put his programs on the air. All this was different in television. The command of cameras, lighting, sound, design and graphics required an entirely different approach. No wonder the young producers who had learned their craft on the battlefield—doing programs *live* in the studio—looked down on their bosses as elderly armchair generals who had never faced the enemy in eyeball-to-eyeball encounters on the firing line.

What marvelous fun those pioneer producers had in the fifties and early sixties, and what self-confidence! They were exhilarated by the joys of the control room. They relished their hairbreadth escapes from disaster. Everything was new and they were the centre of the world. They took little interest in the CBC as such. They were far too busy and too absorbed in their daily adventures to worry about corporate politics.

They were not deeply impressed by CBC rules and regulations. There was an old-established rule, for example, that permitted producers only to speak to the press through proper CBC channels. This rule did not make much sense to the producers and the more enterprising of them consistently ignored it. They chose to follow only those rules which suited them. The Toronto bureaucracy, much aware of growing producer power, bent backwards to avoid disputations about minor infringements. This was in some measure due to the liberalism of Keith Morrow, the benevolent director of the Ontario Region. A former farm broadcaster from the Maritimes, he invariably exercised his authority with easy good humour. It was Morrow and Doug Nixon, the director of programs who had a natural flair for innovations, who created the climate for courageous and original programming.

Late in 1958 or early in 1959 Douglas Leiterman and Patrick Watson had lunch with Ross McLean, the producer of *Close-Up* and the *wunderkind* of CBC public affairs television, in whose units they were working. Much admired for his flair for the new medium, his prowess as a director in the studio, his critical gifts and his eye for talent, McLean was breaking new ground. He had a popular touch and commissioned as much investigative journalism as his resources allowed. *Close-Up* was produced within the bounds of traditional CBC public affairs programming but management considered him an *enfant terrible* and he was frequently in hot water.

When McLean had lunch with his two colleagues the ratings had just come out. How come, Leiterman and Watson asked him, that whatever they did, whether their shows were brilliant or not quite so brilliant, *Close-Up* got around fourteen percent of the audience? The competing stations might put on sitcoms, Hollywood films, game shows or dreary educational programs, it made no difference. *Close-Up* got fourteen percent. That was the hardcore public affairs audience. Wasn't that depressing?

Surely it was possible, Leiterman wondered, to make reality every bit as fascinating and compelling as fiction. And, he added, with typical high-mindedness, weren't they irresponsible if they didn't at least try?

Some time later, in the fall of 1960, Watson went to Ottawa to produce a network series of his own, *Inquiry*. This was his initiation into the political life of the nation's capital. During the next three years he conducted, as he put it, a "non-stop telephone conversation" with Leiterman. They criticized each other's programs relentlessly. While doing so, the idea grew in their minds that, somehow, they must get together and produce a public affairs program of their own that would appeal not only to the traditional hardcore public affairs audience but also to truckdrivers and cleaning ladies. University professors didn't need it anyway, they said. Didn't truckdrivers and cleaning ladies pay taxes?

Ross McLean: Mentor

Leiterman formulated his ideas in more political terms than Watson. Eight private stations had been licenced in 1960 to compete with the CBC in larger cities. The following year they were linked by the CTV network. However, there were as yet few public affairs shows on the private network and many communities had no Canadian television service at all other than the CBC's. Leiterman repeated again and again that the CBC had a responsibility towards them which it was not discharging.

Watson talked more about the nature of the medium. Television was a mass medium, he said. It cut across social barriers by its very nature. At its best—a baseball game, a hockey game—it appealed to everybody. To him, the image was one of a balloon enlarging so that it encased everybody. If they produced good theatre, everybody would watch automatically. They soon agreed that if they were given the chance to produce a network program jointly they would do something which traditional public affairs television, including *Close-Up*, had never done. They would make the conquest of a mass audience their highest priority. If an item did not force the eye of the viewer on the screen it would not go on the air. Nobody in CBC public affairs had ever said such a thing. Other producers may have made all kinds of programming and technical innovations. But nobody in the department had ever deliberately set out to attract char-women and truckdrivers.

They met at their cottages at Go Home Lake in Muskoka and hammered out a submission to the network. In January 1963 they proposed the production of a one-hour show for Sunday nights at ten in the solemn language of which they themselves made mild fun in the first program of the series. It would become 'mandatory viewing for a large segment of the nation'; every item would have something to say; it would be provocative, thoughtful, the all-seeing eye, and so on.

One of the major influences on them was the BBC's *That Was The Week That Was*, popularly known as TW3. They hardly dared to hope that their projected program would be a similar success. Designed for a substantial minority audience, it had made its debut in November 1962. The first program had an audience of three million. Within four weeks that figure had grown to five-and-a-half million and by the end of the eleventh week the audience was a record twelve million.

Against all expectations, TW3 became a mass audience hit, the biggest hit in the history of European television. John Crosby of the *New York Herald Tribune* called it "the best TV show in the world... A BBC spokesman happily told me that in one program, the third in the series, 'I counted at least five skits that were legally actionable'."

On Saturday evenings the streets of Britain were empty while the nation had its eyes glued to the telly. The wittiest writers, critics and poets wrote for it—John Braine, Kenneth Tynan, Carol Brahms, Keith Waterhouse and Willis Hall, as well as obscure newspapermen for whom TW3 was the major outlet for their talents. It made performers David Frost, William Rushton and Bill Oddie household words.

TW3 was produced by BBC Current Affairs, not by the variety or light entertainment departments. Not all of its content was satirical but most of it was. Bernard Levin's pungent editorials were often serious and moving, for example the piece he contributed after the death of the former Labour Party leader Hugh Gaitskill. The show following the assassination of President Kennedy was read into the record of the United States Senate on the motion of Senator Hubert Humphrey.

••••

On May 17th 1964 Watson was in Shanghai on CBC assignment, shooting the first major documentary on China for North American television.

> Yesterday was superb (he wrote to Leiterman). Fine street and harbour stuff and an ecstatic hour in a pig slaughter house that handles a thousand pigs an hour. Good propaganda posters and people stuff and lots and lots of sweet, fat gorgeous close-up sound... For goodness sake send news of the MAG. I'm still zero on title and host.

MAG, of course, was the code name for what was to be *This Hour Has Seven Days*.

Two days before Watson had dispatched his letter, Leiterman had written to him.

> Well, I've been putting in a month of the kind of thing that made you ready to quit TV; I'm immensely jealous of you guys out shooting; and when you get back by gawd I can't wait to dump the administration on you for a while! Ugh. It's been like a SIU hiring hall around here... Actually there have been some interesting people... My proposal on six *Document* subjects enclosed... Re space, our needs are up to twenty-five offices or cubicles which must be enclosed and if possible soundproofed for good work. That includes editing rooms. Since we'll have a film unit under our roof but need easy access to studio and VTR facilities I'm pressing for Jarvis Street area, which seems promising... Hurry home.

When Watson was back and he and Leiterman had their brainstorming sessions at Go Home Lake, all their problems, title, hosts, space, facilities and, above all, choosing the right team, were gradually resolved in time for the show to start on October 4th 1964. Once a month there was to be a *Document* film, one hour in length, to which Leiterman owed his reputation in television. This would give them a chance to deal with a specific subject in depth. Leiterman had suggested six topics to Watson in his letter to Shanghai. Up to then these documentaries had been scheduled irregularly. One of the purposes of the new magazine show was to give the hour-long visual think-pieces, regularly scheduled and promoted, a large audience at last.

For both of them it was a magic spring and summer.

●●●●

Leiterman was thirty-seven when *Seven Days* began, Patrick Watson two years younger. Both were too old to be on the side of the rebellious youngsters. Neither was leftwing.

Leiterman was a loner, private, remote, ascetic—no alcohol, tea or coffee. He commanded respect, admiration and inspired a little fear. Brought up in Vancouver, he was a congenital outsider.

His Jewish paternal grandfather had swum naked across the Dnieper River around 1860 to escape military service in the Czarist army. But, like his American-born mother, Leiterman was a Christian Scientist. Christian Science is an optimistic, activist religion. It gave him his passionate belief that the world could be a better place and that, at a time when society was groping for new certainties, he could help people understand the world around them. His religion also taught him that, with persistence, he could control his destiny.

By the time he had joined *Close-Up* in 1958 he had been a newspaperman for eleven years.

> As a police reporter, business reporter, and general assignment writer I came to see all the suffering and misery which was not part of my own life. And I came to believe that much of it could be avoided, and that society could take steps in our country to lead its members to happier and more worthwhile lives... Out of it all, almost imperceptibly, I began to develop a sense of the power of the press and a modest sense of mission. Wrongdoing could be exposed. The captains of industry and politics often had clay feet.[3]

Between 1947 and 1958 he was reporter, editorial writer, foreign correspondent and Ottawa correspondent for the Southam News Service. The year before he went to Ottawa he spent at Harvard on a Nieman Fellowship, studying economics, government and Soviet affairs, and attending intensive sessions with such luminaries of the American political scene as Adlai Stevenson, McGeorge Bundy, Karl Friedrich and Zbigniew Brzezinski.

Leiterman was at Harvard in the early fifties, at the time when Senator Joe McCarthy was at the height of his terrifying influence. Leiterman became aware of the immense power of television as he watched Ed Murrow's historic *See it Now* which exposed McCarthy as a brutal, irrational witch-hunter and demagogue and thereby, almost overnight, changed the climate of opinion towards him. Up to that moment he had not given it any serious thought. He saw the program in the very university which had good reason to fear the onslaught of McCarthy and which had suffered many casualties. The university had not been effectively defended by the faculty or by the press until Murrow had taken his public stand.

After Harvard, he returned to Canada and resumed his career as a newspaperman. Then he joined the CBC and spent some time on McLean's *Close-Up* team. After that, he became one of Canada's great documentary film makers. He directed biographical portraits of Louis St. Laurent, Mackenzie King, John Diefenbaker, Richard Nixon and Anthony Eden, in addition to making films on topics as diverse as *The American Presidency*, *Forty Million Shoes—A Report on Brazil*, *U.N. in Peril*, *Report from the Wasteland* (a film on the state of television), and *The Image Makers* (a film on public relations). For his documentary about the American south—*One More River*—he received the first Wilderness Award, the annual prize for the best CBC documentary. The films were scheduled irregularly under the title *Document*.

Leiterman's style was confident, lucid, conscientious, earnest and restrained. In the case of both the Diefenbaker film and *One More River* viewers found their personal prejudices—pro and con Diefenbaker, pro and con American blacks—confirmed. Nothing was further from his mind than to become a film pamphleteer for a cause. He had no cause other than to present to the public as revealing a view of reality as he could. Moreover, with characteristic thoroughness he had quickly become master of his craft, eager to exploit every new technical innovation. He became fascinated with all aspects of the equipment. As to the methods of obtaining the pictures he needed, like all enterprising film makers he used every trick in the trade. If he had to conceal a camera in the baptismal tank of Victoria's First Baptist Church to film John Diefenbaker while he read the lesson, he did so, and was amused when the choir girls fed the cameraman chewing gum as he lay on the floor, swathed in red velvet.

In 1964 Douglas Leiterman wrote a piece for *The Globe and Mail* about *cinéma vérité* and the new methods of gathering pictorial information. It appeared just after the argument over *Mr. Pearson* had made headlines.

> The creepy-peepy cameras put a new premium on the old-fashioned virtues of judgment and responsibility. Privacy will be much invaded and conversations more often overheard.
>
> Viewers will gradually accept the new conventions and more candid appraisals of leaders and led will be sought and accepted. Perhaps, as we all mature, scenes of prime ministers preferring baseball games to business will not be alarming.[4]

The new program *Seven Days* helped decisively to make this prediction come true.

••••

Patrick Watson complemented Leiterman. He was relaxed, sociable, versatile and congenial.

Unlike Leiterman, Watson came from mainstream Canada. He had had a golden childhood in a large Toronto family, filled with talk, music, reading, laughter, friendship and games. Early in life he performed magic tricks at neighbourhood parties and at thirteen he won the part of Jake in the radio series *The Kootenay Kid*. Unlike Leiterman, who had always wanted to be a newspaperman, Watson could not make up his mind. He was good at too many things. Excellent in mathematics, he wanted to be an aeronautical engineer. But then, in his last year at high school, he became infatuated with Shakespeare. At the University of Toronto he took no particular interest in politics. In his second year he switched from sociology and philosophy to English. After receiving his M.A. he joined the Toronto publishing house of Gage, which was planning to do a textbook on English grammar for primary language instruction. Gage sponsored him to do further graduate work towards a PhD in linguistics at the University of Michigan.

In 1955, at the age of twenty-five, Watson had his first television experience as freelance host for several weeks of *Junior Magazine*, produced by the CBC's Children's Department. He was still working on his PhD. He did not own a television set and had approached the new medium with the snobbish disdain of a bright young academic. But he was immediately entranced by the medium, and especially by the prospect of becoming a television producer. Therefore, it was not difficult to talk him out of going on with his PhD work. He took a production training course and not much later, after a stint as the producer of *Mr. Fixit*, he found himself in Ross McLean's unit in public affairs.

The transition from academic life to television was made easier by Watson's acquaintance with Marshall McLuhan's work. They had never met at the university, but once they did meet they became good friends. McLuhan confirmed Watson's realization that the impressions created by images on the television screen had a stronger effect on the viewer than information conveyed verbally or in print.

In 1959 *Close-Up* had carried an interview with Bertrand Russell, conducted by Elaine Grand and filmed by Allan King in London. Russell was old and frail, and there was a touching element of sexual tension between him and his young and pretty interviewer. In his precise, high-pitched voice he reminisced about his Victorian childhood, his discovery of mathematics and physics. He talked about his opposition to nuclear weapons, about religion, and about his "private, passionate relationships".

Watson tested his friends. It was a memorable interview, they said, because of the impeccable logic of the old man's mind and his steel-trap intelligence. But no one could precisely remember what he said. It was evident that it was not information in the traditional sense which Russell had conveyed but watching him had been a significant experience. One had the feeling of having been "in the presence of greatness".

It was theatre.

••••

Leiterman was too hard-headed a newspaperman to have much use for McLuhan. His ambition was to give ordinary people in every walk of life enough information in the traditional sense on which to base judgments. Such information should:

> ...transcend their historic ignorance and prejudices and invigorate the body politic with intelligent response to major national issues. The process would...lead to some modern equivalent of the Greek city-state, with discussions in every home and hamlet of the important matters of the day as brought to them by the new medium...[5]

Seven Days was to combine Watson-McLuhan's global village with Leiterman's Greek city-state.

••••

Inventing the right title for the show proved to be an intriguing task. As Leiterman and Watson sat on their rocks at Go Home Bay they scribbled down dozens of names. None seemed appropriate. One weekend Peter McFarlane came up. He was a genial variety producer with a lively mind and great skill as a studio director. McFarlane announced categorically that the only possible name for the new program was *This Hour Has Seven Days*. Leiterman and Watson laughed. It struck them as absurdly extravagant. It would never stick.

Then there was the problem of choosing the right hosts. Watson would have liked to have been one of them, but there was a rule in the CBC which prevented producers from hosting their own shows and at that stage it was more important for Watson to be one of the producers.

Among those auditioned was James Sinclair, the father of the former Margaret Trudeau, who seemed to Leiterman to have the required charm and authority. Sinclair had been a member of the St. Laurent government from 1952 to 1957. In 1964 he was head of the Fisheries Association of British Columbia. Leiterman knew and admired him from his days in Vancouver. Other candidates were Peter Gzowski, Percy Rodriguez, Robert Fulford and the young Peter Jennings. Another Vancouver man with whom they negotiated was Bernard Braden, who had made a great splash for himself on the BBC as the star of *On the Braden Beat*. He had the necessary common touch, the attractively flippant insouciance as an interviewer which they liked very much, a style similar to that which Larry Zolf later developed in his man-in-the-street pieces. In the end they couldn't afford Braden.

Eventually they chose as one of the two hosts John Drainie, Canada's most eminent radio actor. He appealed to Leiterman and Watson because of his quintessentially Canadian Honest-John image and flawless professionalism. Drainie had recently become widely known for his portrayal of Stephen Leacock. The role of host in a public affairs television program was new to him and he was a little unsure at first whether he would be adequate. While the material was, of course, written for him, it was understood that he would never deliver lines with which he could not associate himself personally.

Tragically, he was able to act as host for only one season. In the spring of 1965 he became ill with cancer and on October 30th 1966 he died.

Watson proposed as the second host the man who had performed for him for a year on *Inquiry*, after A. Davidson Dunton, the former chairman of the CBC, had left in 1963 to become co-chairman of the Royal Commission for Bilingualism and Biculturalism.

At that time, when he was looking for a replacement for Dunton, Watson had made appointments with two Montreal professors on the same day, a professor of law at the University of Montreal and the director of French Canadian studies at McGill. The law professor was Pierre Elliott Trudeau, whom Watson had met once or twice. The McGill historian was Laurier LaPierre, whom he had never encountered.

Watson's friend and colleague Cameron Graham had auditioned LaPierre for his new program *Twenty Million Questions* and found him interesting. But he had a pronounced accent. Cameron was launching a new program. To do so with an accented host was perhaps a little dicey. *Inquiry* was an established program. Watson was prepared to take a risk.

Watson went to see Trudeau first and asked him whether he might like to succeed Davidson Dunton as host of *Inquiry*. The professor was interested in Watson's proposition, no doubt aware of the magical way René Lévesque had become a household word in Quebec as a television personality.

"Perhaps it is time I got into the mêlée," he mused. But how did it work? How free was he to say what he wanted to say? Oh, very free, Watson replied. Almost completely free. There was only one limitation: it was the producer, not the host, who had the final authority, as an officer of the Corporation, to determine the political balance of the program. That was his responsibility.

Trudeau regretfully declined. He needed more freedom than the CBC was prepared to give him as host of a public affairs program. After all, Watson had not offered him the job of commentator. That would have been the role he cherished for himself.

LaPierre would not have minded at all if Watson had confessed that Trudeau had been his first choice. He admired Trudeau enormously and Trudeau had often been the LaPierres' guest for dinner in their apartment in Westmount. Their views on Quebec's place in Canada were similar. Both were anxious to open windows and let the fresh air blow in. In August 1965 LaPierre was to write a piece for the *Canadian Forum* in which he argued that unless English Canadians accepted French Canadians as equals, there might be an "eventual dismemberment of Confederation as French Canadians...concentrate all their energies within the confines of their province which they will ultimately transform into an independent state".

Before inviting LaPierre to be the co-host with John Drainie on

Seven Days Watson once again approached Trudeau. He tracked him down in Barcelona and popped the question on the telephone. Trudeau once again declined a regular role but agreed to act as freelance interviewer. He had one memorable assignment: an interview with René Lévesque, done jointly with Larry Zolf, presented on December 6th 1964.

At first Leiterman was a little lukewarm about LaPierre for the same reason that Cameron Graham had been unenthusiastic a year earlier: it seemed risky to start a new program with someone with a French accent. But Watson was sure LaPierre was the right man and he prevailed. Neither of them ever regretted it.

Born in 1929, just as the Depression began, one of LaPierre's earliest memories was the arrival of the bailiffs at their home at Lac Megantic in the Eastern townships. They were about to take everything away, even the beds. There were two brothers and two sisters: two other sisters had died. His father, whose education had finished with grade three, had lost his ice cream business. Later he became a lumberjack—*un draveur*—but because he drank he could not hold a job. It was LaPierre's mother, a maid and a cook, who kept the family together and even managed to send the children to board in a convent at Disraeli, near Thetford Mines, for twenty-five dollars a month each. LaPierre was an ordinary student who was not recognized as particularly gifted. He stayed until he had finished grade six. The nuns took the view that unless the boys learned English they would never amount to anything. LaPierre therefore went to St. Patrick's Academy in Sherbrooke. He was thirteen and had never been in Montreal, ninety miles away. In his last year he took a commercial course. At seventeen he found a job as clerk at the Dominion Rand Company in Sherbrooke and worked for it and for other companies for two years. He was bored to tears, utterly dispirited.

LaPierre had been to mass every day since he was a little boy. He now decided to become a priest—not a mundane parish priest in Sherbrooke, but a missionary priest in a religious order. He was not particularly anxious to spread the faith but determined to get away. But what religious order to apply to? He had a good friend at the time, a priest. LaPierre put the names of three religious orders into a hat. The priest put the hat into a chalice and both of them went to church together and knelt down at the high altar. The priest prayed to the Holy Ghost: *Veni Creator Spiritus*. LaPierre picked the winner out of the chalice: the Congregation of St. Paul in Baltimore.

He stayed in Baltimore and at a Novitiate in New Jersey for

four-and-a-half happy years. The world opened up for him: he discovered that he had a mind. He had not read a book until he was eighteen. Now he read hundreds. He learned to care about people, to make friends. The Sulpicians who ran the congregation were excellent teachers. He took Latin, Greek and German.

Above all, he learned to be an orator. This was part of his training as a missionary. Experts from the theatre gave elocution classes. He discovered his extraordinary powers of expression. The only place the students could go to outside the seminary on Saturdays and Sundays was the public library. There he found a superb record collection. For hours he listened to Laurence Olivier playing Henry the Fifth. An Oxford-trained priest told him that, in order to perfect his English, he should read Dickens aloud to him for an hour a day. This he proceeded to do. He was constantly reminded to project his voice so that he could be heard even by those who sat in the last pew. It was no surprise therefore that the accent which became his trademark was distinctive and different from that of other French Canadians speaking English.

His French, too, was a little unusual. While in the States he never spoke his native language. When he returned to Quebec again many years later he could still speak *joual* as well as anyone but he practically had to learn 'proper' French from scratch.

Though LaPierre's faith remained unshaken he changed direction after finishing his religious studies in the States. He decided to pursue an academic career as an historian of French Canada. Since he lacked a degree from a collège classique he could not be admitted to the University of Montreal. Therefore he went to St. Michael's College at the University of Toronto.

Now another world opened up for him—the world of the secular academy. Suddenly the antiquated structure of Quebec society was revealed to him as abominable. He developed a profound anticlericalism though he continued to admire many priests personally. While at the University of Toronto he concentrated on his work and was not deflected by political activism or extra-curricular diversions. He also got married—to Jo Armstrong, a direct descendant of Edward Blake, the premier of Ontario who became a dominant figure in the federal Liberal Party and had been a brilliant opponent of Sir John A. Macdonald. Recently an article recalled LaPierre's wedding:

> Half the guests spoke no English and the other half no French. Goodwill prevailed but communication was impossible until one of the guests burst into song and broke the impasse.[6]

In 1959, after only three years, he received his PhD. LaPierre's first teaching job was at the University of Western Ontario. After that he went to McGill. He remained at McGill when he first became the host of *Inquiry* and a year later the co-host of *Seven Days*, commuting from Montreal every weekend.

••••

The beautiful girl who together with Laurier LaPierre and John Drainie was to form the third part of the on-air trio at the beginning of the first season was Carole Simpson, a·revue performer from England. The model was Millicent Martin of the BBC's satirical program *That Was The Week That Was*, the singer who, to quote John Crosby of the *The New York Herald Tribune*, introduced each program by "singing the week's news in witty wicked rhymes that Sir Arthur Gilbert wouldn't have minded writing".

After three months, at Christmas 1964, Simpson had to leave Toronto for California for personal reasons, to be succeeded by the luminous twenty-one-year-old, guitar-strumming Dinah Christie. Both her parents, Robert and Margo Christie, were prominent Canadian actors, and in her teens she had been a "call-boy" at Stratford, calling actors when they were due to appear on the stage. Later, she performed as a folk-singer in various musical revues, including some at Old Angelo's in Toronto.

Seven Days went on the air before the women's movement was launched. Today, no talented performer would accept, without protest, the sexy cover-girl roles assigned to Simpson and Christie, who were clearly of secondary importance. But they did, without hesitation. Simpson vanished from the Canadian scene. For Christie, however, *Seven Days* meant the beginning of a distinguished career as a major popular singer and actress.

CHAPTER 4

THE CORPORATION

When *Seven Days* was launched in October 1964 the Corporation was on the defensive, facing a host of enemies. Rarely since its foundation in 1936 had its role been challenged with comparable intensity. One of the reasons why the CBC's top management welcomed the *Seven Days* concept was that they shared Leiterman's and Watson's ambition to attract a mass audience to a public affairs program. If successful, it would once again demonstrate the CBC's social purpose, imagination and vitality. These were traditional CBC qualities and it seemed important to remind the country that the CBC was better than ever and was making a determined effort not to be elitist—a term, by the way, which was not yet in common usage. There had been severe criticism in parliament—especially from representatives from the West—of a number of avant-garde programs which were considered self-indulgent, immoral or simply incomprehensible.

Besides, viewers were beginning to watch more American than Canadian programs. This was the situation in 1965:

> Considering all stations together, CBC, private Canadian and U.S. stations where available, the viewing of Canadian-produced programs was only 30 percent of the total evening viewing. In our seven major cities the average CBC-owned station devoted 57 percent of its evening schedule to Canadian-produced programs and drew 53 percent of its audience with these programs. The average Canadian 'second station' devoted about 34 percent of its evening schedule to Canadian-produced programs and these draw 28 percent of its total evening audience.[1]

It was not only the increase of American viewing which worried CBC management. There was also the frequent criticism of its efficiency. In 1963 the Glassco Commission took the position that the Corporation was in need of extensive reorganization and that it had failed to develop positive goals. In May 1964, another committee of inquiry was appointed to investigate the broadcasting scene and make recommendations for the future. Once again, it was to be headed by Robert Fowler, who had been the chairman of a royal commission from 1955–1957.

●●●●

Until television arrived on the scene, the CBC was financed through an annual licence fee of $2.50 a year for each radio set. This insulated the Corporation from the political process and no parliamentary appropriations were required. (The BBC in England is still financed this way.) But this system had proved impracticable once television arrived and from then on the CBC received its money primarily from the public purse, and secondarily from commercial revenues. The new method of financing changed the Corporation's relationship with the politicians noticeably, especially those occupying the government benches.

Until 1958, parliament had delegated to the CBC all regulatory powers in broadcasting. The Corporation had the power to grant and revoke the licences of all private stations and was responsible for setting and maintaining program standards. At the same time it provided the national service. Private stations served local and regional needs. Many of them helped to distribute CBC programs across the country.

Adversaries of public broadcasting had criticized the system from the beginning. But public opinion generally accepted it as a sensible way to achieve a cultural consensus and a workable combination of public and private interests designed to prevent the domination of Canadian networks by the Americans.

Critics of the system had sharpened their attack after the arrival of television. Not only did television make larger demands on the public purse than radio, thereby imposing a greater obligation by parliament to demand accountability from the Corporation, but it also offered private broadcasters greater opportunities for making money than radio had ever done. The private broadcasters saw themselves increasingly as competitors of the CBC and balked at the idea of being regulated by it.

John Diefenbaker, while campaigning in the federal election of 1957, promised that, should the Progressive Conservative Party win under his leadership, he would deal with this situation. He kept his promise.

Diefenbaker had a large measure of support. The political climate was no longer friendly towards the CBC. Every M.P. outside the big cities had a long list of grievances about inadequate coverage and program service. The CBC's impressive achievements in building the most extensive television networks in the world sharpened the appetite of those who felt, often with some justification, that they were not getting a fair share and were not treated by CBC management with the attention they deserved.

On achieving power in a landslide victory in the 1958 election, Diefenbaker's government quickly passed a new Broadcasting Act which took the regulatory power away from the CBC board and placed it in the hands of a new board, the Board of Broadcast Governors, the BBG. In the following years it granted licences to private television stations in the major cities to compete with the CBC. Up to that time private stations had only been established in smaller cities which did not have a CBC station. The second stations in the major centres soon formed a new network, the CTV. In the years between 1956 to 1965 the number of private television stations increased from twenty-nine to fifty-nine, CBC stations only from nine to sixteen.[2] It soon became clear that the dominance of the public sector in broadcasting which had been a cardinal principle of Canadian broadcasting since the thirties was seriously endangered.[3]

At the end of the fifties, the prospects of serious competition and the tensions with the Diefenbaker government made CBC management increasingly sensitive. This was hardly the time for major conflicts with its employees.

••••

Trouble came first in Montreal. In Quebec dramatic social changes were imminent. The Quiet Revolution was about to challenge established authority. From December 1958 until March 1959 the television producers of the CBC's French network, now usually called Radio Canada, were out on strike. They wanted to form a union. This demand had been denied to them, on the grounds that producers, since they had authority to spend money on the talent they employed, were part of management.

There was a marked difference between attitudes towards unions in English and in French Canada. In English Canada unions were considered legitimate primarily among working people in industry, less so among professional people, and certainly not among creative people in the arts. In French Canada the attitude was fundamentally different. Not only did many of the most prominent intellectuals, journalists and creative people—among them Pierre Trudeau and Gérard Pelletier—support organized labour but they also saw nothing wrong with syndicalism for professionals.

In the last years of Duplessis' government there had been growing labour militancy throughout Quebec. The conflict, which broke out shortly before the end of his regime (he died on September 7th 1959) soon became acutely ideological and led to increasingly bitter confrontations. It radically politicized many of those involved, among them the French network's most popular commentator, René Lévesque. The struggle turned large sections of the Quebec intelligentsia, its artistic and academic communities, against CBC management. It also created painful French-English tensions within the Corporation and demonstrated CBC head office's ineptitude in dealing with its creative elements.

Some seventy producers were soon joined by three thousand members of the technical, journalistic and clerical unions, some in violation of their contracts.

> The fact was that in the decade's long list of strikes this was the first one involving wage-earners who led a comfortable life. The producers were certainly not, as Mr. Duplessis put it, plutocrats cushioned by enormous incomes... But their average yearly salary of $7,500 (which they were then earning) placed them among the privileged.[4]

The strikers spent long hours on the picket-lines in sub-zero weather and even longer hours in study sessions. There was violence. Non-strikers were beaten up, cars damaged, houses splattered with paint, families intimidated. There was a march to Ottawa. Pierre Trudeau had recently broken a bone in his foot in a skiing accident in the Laurentians, but, according to witnesses, this did not prevent him from taking a taxi to the picket line on several occasions to lend his support.

On March 2 twenty-one strikers were arrested on Dorchester Street, in front of the Radio Canada Building. René Lévesque was among them. He had not previously been active in the struggle against Duplessis. Throughout the fifties he was primarily interested in international affairs and his program *Point de Mire* on the French network had made him one of the most popular television personalities. The strike converted him to Quebec nationalism and launched him on his political career.

On March 7 he spoke to the press in English with bitter irony:

> Some of us, and maybe many, come out of this with a tired and unworthy feeling that if such a strike had happened in English Canada, it would... have lasted no more than half an hour. To this day, ours has lasted sixty-six days. Of such signal advantages is the privilege of being French made up in this country. And even at the risk of being termed "horrid nationalists", we feel that at least once before the conflict is over we have to make plain our deep appreciation of such an enviable place in the great bilingual, bicultural and fraternal Canadian sun.[5]

It was true that English Canada had showed little interest in the dispute. CBC producers in Toronto conspicuously failed to rally to the support of their French colleagues. They regarded the idea of a union for creative people with distaste.

Nor did the federal government want to get involved. Jean Marchand, the general secretary of the CCCL, had requested the intervention of the Minister of Labour, Michael Starr, since the conflict affected "the whole population of Quebec", but to no avail. The government took the position that management should deal with this dispute on its own. It only made a half-hearted offer to mediate the dispute through a deputy minister of labour.

On March 7th the CBC yielded on the main point. The producers were allowed to form a union. But affiliation with the CCCL was denied to them. That, in management's view, would have been an intolerable infringement of the producers' political independence because it would have created an institutional connection between them and a large segment of society sharing a specific point of view.

It would take many years for the scars left by the Montreal producers' strike to heal.

••••

Trouble in Montreal was followed by trouble in Toronto in June 1959. There, the public affairs department, which six years later was to launch *Seven Days*, dramatically played out its traditional role as the conscience of the Corporation before the admiring eyes of the nation.

Every weekday morning after the eight o'clock news there was a short program called *Preview Commentary* in which carefully balanced members of the press gallery in Ottawa voiced their views on the previous day's happenings in parliament. It had been on the air for two years. But now there was a new government in power, John Diefenbaker's. Some of the views expressed failed to please him. Undoubtedly he made his displeasure known to George Nowlan, the minister through whom the CBC reported to parliament, and a consistent supporter of the Corporation. It is hard to imagine that Nowlan failed to pass the prime minister's displeasure on to the executive vice-president of the CBC, his old friend Ernest Bushnell. He may have done so over drinks, coupling his complaints to lamentations about his own uneasy relations with the prime minister, together with horror stories about the moves afoot to punish the increasingly expensive and, from the government's point of view, *embarrassing*

Corporation. In fact, he may have observed wryly that his job was on the line unless something was done about *Preview Commentary*. Moreover, it seems probable that Mrs. Ruby Meabry, his devoted executive assistant and one of those impressive and independent-minded Ottawa ladies who enjoyed having a drink with the boys, took it upon herself to phone Bushnell to give him a graphic account of the terrible position in which the minister would find himself unless *Preview Commentary* was taken off the air.

The General Supervisor of Talks and Public Affairs in Toronto at the time was Frank W. Peers, an austere but very human official with academic inclinations, originally from the West, who enjoyed universal respect. On Monday June 10 he was summoned to head office in Ottawa to be told that, starting the following Monday, a factual report, based on the dispatches of The Canadian Press and United Press about parliamentary developments, would take the place of *Preview Commentary*. The excuse given was that a careful assessment of parliamentary debates, government policies and opposition criticism demanded more than five minutes and a longer interval from the events under review.

There was no precedence for such a peremptory order from head office. No important program decision had ever been made in Ottawa without consultation with responsible departmental officials. Peers and his colleagues had no choice but to conclude that the order had been given as a result of political influence. Yielding to pressures of this kind was the one unforgivable sin, the gravest conceivable offence against the mandate of the Corporation. Explanations were sought but not given. The board of directors upheld head office's decision.

Peers and his two immediate deputies, Bernard Trotter and Hugh Gillies, resigned in order to be free to make their case public. Their resignation was followed by that of thirty-five program organizers (in effect executive producers) and producers across the country. Patrick Watson was one of them. These were formal resignations. It was not a walk-out. Although all those who resigned hoped they would be reinstated when the dust settled, no one could be sure. There were headlines and editorials everywhere. It was a major crisis. The press overwhelmingly supported Peers and his colleagues. The battle-lines were clearly drawn. Peers and his high-principled followers were the good guys. Management was the bad guy.

Under the headline *CBC Rebels Stood Up Like Men*, the

Reverend J. Franklin Chidsey wrote in the *Toronto Star* on June 25th:

> In the life of every man at one time or another, perhaps many times, there comes a dark night of the spirit, a decisive hour in which he must come to terms with himself and his world, his ideals and his acts. This week that hour came for Frank Peers of the CBC.

On June 30th Bushnell appeared before the parliamentary committee and emphatically denied that an order or directive had ever been given to him by anybody. The committee did not press him. He was asked whether it was true that he had ever said "heads would roll" unless *Preview Commentary* was taken off the air. He neither confirmed nor denied it. He said he was convinced that "with this tragic series of unfortunate circumstances that we have had in the last six months, that if we did not pull up our socks, certainly somebody's head would roll—and quite properly." He said he had various general conversations with Mr. Nowlan, who had expressed the view that there were some things in the Corporation "which were not properly administered".[6]

Four weeks later George Nowlan appeared before the committee. Doug Fisher of the CCF asked him whether he had any idea how his name came to be included among those whose heads would roll. Nowlan said he had no idea but was wondering whether that was a threat or a promise. He was sick and tired of the criticism coming in from all over the country. There was nothing he would rather do than get rid of the responsibility of reporting to parliament for the CBC.[7]

Having upheld Bushnell on June 22nd, the board, yielding to the universal clamor, reversed itself on June 24th. *Preview Commentary* was restored and none of the resignations were accepted.

Bushnell left the CBC early in December 1959. In the following year he received the licence for CJOH-TV in Ottawa. In October 1960 Frank Peers—"Mr. Integrity", as Nathan Cohen called him in the *Toronto Star* of June 24 1959—was promoted to the position of Director of Information Programming at head office in Ottawa.

••••

Both the *Preview Commentary* crisis and the Montreal strike had a deeply demoralizing effect on CBC management, considerably weakening its authority both inside the organization and outside. The *Preview Commentary* crisis, the last great battle of the radio era, strengthened the moral position of the public

J. Alphonse Ouimet: president of the Canadian Broadcasting Corporation

affairs department vis-à-vis senior management. It had successfully fought for a principle central to the Corporation's integrity. This principle top management appeared to be prepared to jeopardize, at least for a few days, in the interests of good relations with the government. The public affairs department's morally impeccable role during that dispute strengthened its self-confidence and increased its prestige. These were to be important elements in the battle over *Seven Days*.

The Montreal producers' strike was the first confrontation of the sixties. The memory of the deep wounds it had inflicted was to haunt Alphonse Ouimet, president of the CBC, for years to come, particularly during the bitter confrontation with the Toronto producers in the spring of 1966.

••••

In 1919, when Ouimet was eleven, his father, who had a wholesale gentlemen's furnishing business on St. Paul Street in Old Montreal, wanted to reward him for his good marks at school. He suggested buying him a bicycle. But the boy preferred a crystal radio set which cost about the same. Instead of sleeping, the boy listened to his set night after night, spellbound. He performed all kinds of experiments with it. He also began to read about the theoretical possibilities of television.

A few years later, when he was a student at the Collège Ste. Marie in Montreal, he became a skeptic. This may have had something to do with the way the philosophy classes were conducted. Instead of presenting the ideas of Leibnitz, Hume, Kant, Hegel, John Stuart Mill and Karl Marx at face value, the Jesuits would present their ideas in such a way as to imply that, even if it had to be admitted that they were great minds, it was a matter of regret that they were unenlightened souls who had failed to recognize the Truth. Ouimet resented this bias. To him objective detachment and Cartesian rationalism were all-important. He could use the tools of scholastic philosophy as well as anybody, and, using St. Thomas' methods, prove anything. But that was not at all what he wanted to do. He had firmly made up his mind to develop his scientific and technical gifts.

The École Polytechnique of the University of Montreal only offered a course in civil engineering. He could not afford to go to the Massachusetts Institute of Technology in Boston. He therefore decided to study electrical engineering at McGill, even though his English was not as good as his Latin.

The Ouimets were a well-known Outremont family, with a reserved pew at the church. Alphonse's great-grandfather had been a church architect and his grandfather a judge.

"You will hardly believe this," the priest declared in church the Sunday after he heard about Alphonse's decision to go to McGill. "The oldest son of one of our most distinguished families is going to risk losing his faith and his tongue at a foreign university". McGill was about a mile from the Ouimet house in Outremont.

The university hardly recognized the existence of French Canadians. But Ouimet headed his class within two months, in spite of his halting English. When he graduated in 1932, in the depth of the Depression, he was one of three out of a class of nineteen who found a job. He was hired as junior research engineer at Canadian Television Limited. After a year the company went bankrupt but re-emerged as Canadian Electronics Limited. Together with two associates he designed and built a sixty-line mechanical television system using a rotating lens disc to project the picture on a small screen. After that he knew television could be made to work. In 1934 he joined the Canadian Radio Broadcasting Commission, which in 1936 became the CBC. He rose quickly in the hierarchy. By 1948 he was Chief Engineer and Coordinator of Television. By 1953 he was general manager. He was forty-five.

As chief engineer he had masterminded CBC television, as general manager he directed its explosive growth. In five years the staff quadrupled from fifteen hundred to six thousand and the Corporation's budget increased from twelve to forty nine million. The whole organizational structure was recast, new departments were created and existing services expanded. Industrial relations suddenly became a major factor. New production centres were built.

Ouimet hesitated before he accepted the presidency. He had spent all his life on the technical side, he told Gérard Pelletier one day at lunch. Pelletier was then working for a labour organization and appeared regularly on the French network. Now, Ouimet went on, he had to add "the cultural and political dimension". Was it wise to accept?

Pelletier encouraged him. "You are far more intelligent than Frigon," he told him. Augustin Frigon, also an engineer, had been general manager from 1944 to 1951. "He had a sterilizing influence on the Corporation. You are more open and have more imagination. But you must be aware of the problem. You should surround yourself with a brains trust on whose advice you can count."

In mid-November 1958, Ouimet was appointed president of the CBC. For the Christmas holidays he went to Florida for a few days' rest. Hardly had he arrived when he was summoned back to deal with his first crisis, the Montreal producers' strike. It was an excruciating experience. The producers' main—but by no means their only—target: the Director of Television. They considered him a high-handed, insensitive autocrat.

His name: André Ouimet, Alphonse's younger brother.

Like Alphonse, André was a forceful character. He had played a dominant role in building the French network during its years of phenomenal growth. But he lacked his brother's tact. The two brothers hardly knew each other. By the time André was thirteen, Alphonse was twenty-four and married.

André's career path had not been as straight as Alphonse's. He dropped out of McGill and, without Alphonse knowing anything about it, joined the CBC as a sound man. He worked his way up the ladder. Alphonse scrupulously avoided participating in any decision involving his brother's promotions.

Human relations were not André's forte. The sixties were about to begin. Had there not been growing tensions within the society as a whole, the producers' quarrel with him could have been dealt with through normal channels. That Alphonse was not at all close to him did not matter at all. In the perception of the producers André would not have been their boss had it not been for his being the president's younger brother.

Three weeks after returning from Florida, in the middle of the negotiations, Alphonse Ouimet had a heart attack. For the following six months Ernest Bushnell was acting president.

●●●●

Throughout his years as president, Ouimet had trouble "adding the cultural and political dimension". He had made the transition from engineering to administration with ease. To him the two were closely related activities. Devising organizational charts was like composing blueprints for the construction of a machine or an electronic circuit. He had an unusual facility for grasping complicated intellectual and technical problems and would only reluctantly concede that any question was unanswerable. He found people more interesting on a chart than off.

Alphonse Ouimet was genial, courtly and talkative but he was also proud and stubborn. From the Jesuits he had learned a strong sense of hierarchy, and from his engineering professors a structural approach to organizations. Suitable people could always be found, he thought, to fill most of the empty boxes on the charts.

He did not go out of his way to hire qualified men from outside if he thought he could find them inside.

Programming was only one of many CBC functions. He would not allow himself to show any bias in favour of the "the creative people" in the organization, even though the production and distribution of programs was the CBC's *raison d'être*. To him engineers, technicians, salesmen, studio supervisors, station managers were just as entitled to attention as programmers. Ouimet could not accept that the writers, artists and musicians who make programs have chosen their profession, not to be good corporate citizens, but in order to express themselves and indulge their vanities and that without such desires they were not likely to be any good. He had some feeling for the visual arts but was not particularly interested in literature and music and felt more at home with technocrats than with poets.

Towards intellectuals—especially intellectuals in the public affairs departments in Toronto and Montreal—Ouimet was ambivalent. He was always a little impatient with the assumption that one department more than any other was responsible for upholding the ancient traditions of balance, fairness and impartiality, of remaining aloof from the government in power, and of being incorruptible. On ethical matters generally, he was irritated by what he considered the presumption of certain CBC people who regarded themselves as the guardians of the Corporation's institutional morality.

> Speaking generally, I have seen no evidence for a number of years that the high priests of the CBC's intelligentsia have much to teach their less pretentious colleagues in the field of ethical behaviour. If anything, it is generally the other way round.[8]

But there was little question that political and moral crisis-management was the daily bread and butter of the "intellectuals" in the public affairs departments of both the French and English networks and that they had developed special skills in dealing with inflammable issues.

Still, like many of those who had risen in the Corporation in the days of radio, Ouimet had a strong feeling for the social purpose of the Corporation. Once television had arrived and the CBC became increasingly dependent on commercial revenue, the social purpose inevitably became blurred, creating grave dilemmas for the man at the top. In 1957 the Fowler Commission had recommended that the CBC pursue more vigorous commercial policies, apparently without fully understanding that this inevitably implied a new orientation for the CBC.[9] An increased reliance on commercial sponsorship meant a more determined attempt to appeal to mass audiences. This in turn was bound to encourage the acquisition of more American entertainment programs, which always tended to be more popular than their Canadian counterparts. This would naturally alienate many old friends of the CBC, the academics, the artists and performers, the adult educators, the unions, the churches, the nationalists.

The Corporation seemed to be faced with one crisis after another.

On the day Mother Margaret d'Youville, the founder of the Grey Nuns, was beatified in Rome, the French network presented a play about her. Convents rented television sets. Young nuns were allowed to stay up late to watch. What did they see? Daringly racy scenes from the beatified mother's early married life. The switchboard lit up. Quebec M.P.'s demanded that the parliamentary committee be given the names of all those responsible for approving the script and the production. No doubt there was gleeful amusement in the *café des artistes* near the Radio Canada Building. The executive vice-president Ernest Bushnell had to admit that there had been "a breakdown in the chain of command", not exactly surprising after the destabilizing strike.

Then there was trouble in Ontario. Premier Leslie Frost was outraged by the CBC's allegedly biased and distorted election coverage in favour of the Liberals and the CCF. The hot water in which Bushnell found himself was brought to boiling point when Joyce Davidson, the beautiful interviewer whom Ross McLean had made famous on *Tabloid*, said on NBC's *Dave Garroway Show* in New York that most Canadians were indifferent to the impending visit of the Queen. The scene shifted back to Montreal. Algerian rebel leaders had been interviewed on film giving their unflattering views about the French. This naturally elicited a violent protest from the French ambassador who contended that Canada was giving aid and comfort to France's enemies.

When Ouimet heard about the *Preview Commentary* affair, and perhaps about the most famous of all Bushnellisms, namely that "heads would roll" unless *Preview Commentary* was taken off the air, he was again in bed, this time recuperating from a gallbladder operation. Therefore he was not directly involved. But he pleaded with Bushnell to tell the board exactly what had happened. If there had been political pressure, the board should deal with it. He insisted that the Corporation had never yielded to political pressure. It would be disastrous if it ever did. Ouimet had an engineer's congenital aversion to politicians and he was deeply imbued with the conviction, shared by his predecessors, that the CBC could function only if it kept even a friendly government at arms' length, let alone an unfriendly one.

Ouimet has always expressed admiration for Frank Peers' handling of the affair. He thought Peers and his colleagues had good reason for suspecting improper political influence. He had to "take off his hat" for the manner in which they conducted themselves. They had resigned before speaking out.

●●●●

Relations between Diefenbaker and the CBC were tense. He thought the CBC was a handmaiden of the Liberal Party. At one point Ouimet thought the time had come for some personal diplomacy. He called Reeves Haggan, who was then Area Supervisor for public affairs in Ottawa.

"Reeves," Ouimet said, "do you think you could introduce me to the prime minister some time when he is at CBOT? I've never met him, you know."

"Of course. I would be glad to."

"How do you think a meeting like that would go?"

"I'm afraid he won't say very much to you," Haggan answered cautiously. "Prime ministers only concern themselves with people they have to concern themselves with. They rarely have the time and energy just to be pleasant."

Ouimet was in the lobby when Diefenbaker arrived.

"Sir," Haggan said. "I would like to present to you Mr. Alphonse Ouimet, president of the CBC."

Diefenbaker shook Ouimet's hand, made a grunting sound, and left him standing there.

On a later occasion Ouimet was in the studio when, during one of Diefenbaker's political telecasts, the *Teleprompter* broke down, leaving him stranded in mid-sentence.

Diefenbaker held the president of the CBC personally responsible.

For over five years Diefenbaker's government kept Ouimet's salary at $20,000, the same salary he had received as general manager.

For the CBC the political atmosphere situation did not improve very much after the Liberals came to power under Lester Pearson in 1963. To them CBC management also appeared weak and inefficient and unable to prevent a continuous rash of complaints to parliament. One inquisition followed another. Ouimet was, as he reported later, "only a half-time president", the other half time he had to devote to answering questions. Life would have been infinitely easier for him had there been a separate chairman of the board to look after "the political and cultural dimension", but, according to the new Broadcasting Act, the president also chaired the board.

Before the advent of television, nobody had been much concerned with the lack of central control in the CBC. Program leadership was exercised in Montreal and Toronto, not in Ottawa. There had always been tension between Toronto and Montreal and between program people and administrators, but the management style had been personal and gentlemanly. But now television had made the CBC big, expensive and complicated and the old familial arrangements did not seem tenable any more. Ouimet felt he had to demonstrate that management knew how to manage, that it was responsible and accountable. The only way to proceed, he thought, was to centralize. Of course head office did not produce programs but it could at least formulate firm program policies.

But who would do this? Would the French accept program leadership from the English? And the English from the French? How could the resistance of "the intellectuals" in either group to being run by Ottawa bureaucrats be overcome? Ouimet had no illusion that this was merely a structural problem. The right leader had to be found.

He was never found. Certainly not among "intellectuals". They can't manage anything, Ouimet thought. He could give a dozen examples of distinguished program people on both the French and English side who failed to lead spotless personal lives, drank too much and couldn't even manage their own budgets. One or two of them might have been all right but they were too leftwing. Very few of them, in any case, could work in both French and English.

Besides, what distinguished program person was prepared to leave his natural habitat and move to Ottawa in order to work in that large new head office building on Bronson Avenue? It seemed indistinguishable from any other government building in the capital's suburbs, deliberately removed from the centre of Ottawa as a symbol of the CBC's distance from the seat of power. There was nothing in the building's design and appearance to indicate that this was the nerve centre of a secular church, a national newspaper, a collective university, theatre and concert-hall, Hollywood-North, and the policy-making body of a sales organization for network time to private sponsors. Its architecture suggested prudence, blandness and efficiency, rather than vitality, excitement and devotion to Truth and Beauty. Whatever it was, it wasn't Athens of the North. The executive suites on the sixth floor were particularly awesome in their hushed cheerlessness. The converted girls school on Jarvis Street in Toronto and the old Ford Hotel on Dorchester in Montreal, near some of the best restaurants in town, were Greek temples, London Bloomsburys and Latin Quarters, in comparison with Ouimet's remote and insipid new edifice in Ottawa.

What "intellectual" would want to work there?

By far the most impressive personality in the building was Alphonse Ouimet himself, the beleaguered president who bridged the French and the English cultures and the sciences and humanities and was not completely at home with any of them.

His new headquarters was inaugurated on June 26th 1964, three months before *Seven Days* began to rock the nation.

Leiterman and Hoyt: In front of the camera

CHAPTER 5

INSIDE THE PRESSURE COOKER

In May 1964 Leiterman had outlined in his letter to Watson, then in Shanghai, that he had asked the CBC to supply them with a certain number of offices, film facilities, and so on. The CBC met most of his requirements. Production quarters were at the corner of Maitland and Jarvis Streets, half a block from the studios and CBC Toronto headquarters, the former Havergal College.

From the beginning the *Seven Days* spirit was distinct from that of the CBC as a whole. This was underlined by the unit's location: no other program shared the premises. The team had loyalty to Leiterman and Watson and not to the CBC, which merely provided the money, the staff support and the airtime. The group was largely oblivious to the exigencies of the mother organization which had given the program birth and nursed it and which now had high hopes of benefitting from its success. Even the unit's immediate boss, Reeves Haggan, rarely came to the Maitland Street offices. Leiterman and Watson conferred with him, if necessary, in his office down the street. Film editing was done in the building unless it was farmed out because the facilities were overbooked. The production management of *Seven Days* devised its own accounting procedures because the normal CBC system appeared to them too cumbersome, too unreliable and too slow. Also, once trouble started with upper management, they were afraid that they were vulnerable to attacks on the grounds of careless and extravagant waste unless they scrupulously controlled their own expenditures.

The program had the support of the higher echelons of the CBC and was endowed with a generous but not excessive budget of $31,850 for each show, of which $14,700 were available for direct costs, such as cash expenditures, including salaries for members of the team who were on contract. The rest covered internal CBC services and staff salaries. Out of this budget many, but not all, of the monthly films *Document* were to be financed. It was the largest budget ever given to a one-hour public affairs program. The figures make sense only in relation to other shows.

Seven Days:
Total Budget: $31,850
Direct Costs: $14,700

The Public Eye, a half-hour public affairs program:
Total Budget: $18,000
Direct Costs: $ 6,000

Telescope, a half-hour film program:
Total Budget: $13,660
Direct Costs: $ 8,200

The Nature of Things, a half-hour science program:
Total Budget: $9,000
Direct Costs: $5,000

Take Thirty, a daily half-hour afternoon public affairs program:
Total Budget: $2,310
Direct Costs: $ 860

CBC Drama *The Ideal Husband* by Oscar Wilde (Jan 5th, 1966):
Total Budget: $56,850
Direct Costs: $16,500

Drama *Show of the Week*:
Total Budget: $30,128
Direct Costs: $ 9,058

Festival Rigoletto (February 3rd 1965):
Total Budget: $192,800
Direct Costs: $ 97,200

In the first season Leiterman and Watson alternated as producer and director. Each had his own team with which he put every second show on the air. In the second season Robert Hoyt and Ken Lefolii followed a similar pattern, with the difference that they acted as producers while David Ruskin directed. Separate units were put together for the hour-long *Document* every month or six weeks, to be directed by Allan King, Daryl Duke and Ross McLean. Laurier LaPierre, still a full-time professor at McGill, only flew in on the weekends.

••••

Watson had decided from the beginning to let the pictures speak. He did not need McLuhan's "probes" to convince him that television derived its power not from its ability to convey ideas and information but from its extraordinary facility for making an impact on the senses. Watson was influenced by McLuhan but, thanks to his theatrical and analytical insights, he had come to that conclusion himself. He was thinking in terms of pictures, not words. His eyes had been opened long ago by his friends' reaction to Elaine Grand's interview with Bertrand Russell.

In his years as creator of documentaries, Leiterman too had mastered the craft of image-making. But his approach was more journalistic than Watson's. He had begun his career as a newspaper reporter in Vancouver.

> I early learned the old saw about a picture and ten thousand words, and I began a long apprenticeship in reportage which claimed me for the old values of objectivity and integrity in news. I learned what it was like to rouse folk from their beds and tell them that their son (daughter) had just been killed, listen to their grief, and steel myself to write a story based on what they told me *in extremis*. In those days we were also taught that grief-stricken families would really wish to have a photograph of their loved one published in the paper, but were in no condition to make a sensible judgment on the matter, and we therefore might on occasion pocket a photograph from a mantlepiece, returning it after brief exposure in the photo-engraving shop of the paper. I was astonished to find that the practice was not quite as disgusting as I had imagined, since on two or three occasions when I was required to perform it I would return the photograph and invariably found that the family approved of its publication. (Had they not approved, I very much doubt that the city editors for whom I worked would have failed to publish anyway.) . . .
>
> I suppose I believed then and I believe now in the perfectibility of man made in the image of the Creator.
>
> But I was aware how much needed to be done before man would inherit the earth.
>
> Yes, these were apocalyptic problems, but surely they were not beyond the ability of civilized, thinking man to solve—*if he was informed*.
>
> That's what television could do, lure the common man, if you could reach him, tear him away from the hockey game, capture reality with your cameras, display it before his very eyes, then the common sense of the common man could be enlisted for meaningful change.[1]

Leiterman's journalistic idealism had some problematical aspects. He always took the position that it was proper to commission any story, however questionable in ethical terms it may seem at first. The decision whether to put it on the air or not was to be made later. But on one or two occasions he commissioned stories which some members of his staff considered of dubious ethics from the very beginning. This is an example:

On March 4th 1966 there was a plane crash of a D.C.8 belonging to Canadian Pacific Airlines at the Tokyo airport. Seventy-one persons, including twenty Canadians, were trapped in the wreckage. Only seven survived.

On November 29th 1963 another D.C.8, belonging to Trans-Canada Airlines, had crashed at Ste. Thérèse in Quebec. That disaster was the subject of a *Document* presented on November 7th 1965. Air safety was very much on *Seven Days'* mind and there was widespread suspicion that federal authorities were not sufficiently scrupulous in investigating disasters.

Among those on board the C.P.A. plane was the husband of Peggy Nairn Liptrott, a CBC public affairs producer whom some members of the *Seven Days* team knew.

Mrs. Liptrott had heard about the crash on the news in the early morning. She feared that her husband was probably on that flight. This was confirmed at about ten thirty in the morning. In the early afternoon, while she was frantically waiting for information whether or not he was one of the few survivors—he was not—a *Seven Days* researcher called her twice to try and make arrangements to film a statement from her "about aircraft safety". This was to be done in the presence of her daughter who was three and her little boy who was a year and a half. Later she learned that what *Seven Days* had had in mind was to film the scene of her being told of her husband's death. She also found out that the crew had taken a vote and decided not to carry out the orders. The filming never took place.

••••

Rarely had producers outside the CBC drama department shown as much interest in technique as Leiterman and Watson. They had already established friendly relations with the Technical Department during their years on *Close-Up* and had maintained them ever since. They both understood that in order to create powerful pictures they must treat cameramen and studio technicians with whom they worked as equals. This, most other producers had not bothered to do. Many of the technical people shared Leiterman's and Watson's interest in innovation and experimentation and rewarded them with enthusiastic cooperation and supported them in the coming battles far beyond the call of duty.

The same applied to film and tape editors. Only recently had it become technically possible to edit tape close to the program release time and *Seven Days* made excellent use of this invaluable facility. It had been part of the two producers' original concept that "if an item did not force the eyes of the viewers on the screen it would not get on the air." Once they were in

Left to right: Jean Burnett, Doug Leiterman, Ken Lefolii

production, the rule was that no item would be longer than six minutes, except when there were very special reasons. Many of the interviews they presented were shot on film or tape at many times that length. When cutting them down, they naturally chose the lively rather than the lifeless sections. Leiterman and Watson were convinced that on television truth is revealed when men and women are shown under pressure and not when they are calmly reflecting about the issues raised. On many occasions they were severely criticized for unfair editing. In their defence they insisted that television should have the same right to edit as print journalists. Leiterman often quoted Fred Friendly who had called the film equipment the *See It Now* teams used "the one-ton pencil". Newspaper editors don't hesitate to cut out what they think are irrelevant or boring passages. Why should television journalists be held to putting on the air faithfully all the material they film or tape?

Every Monday morning—the morning after the show—the whole team would assemble in the board room. Every one was asked to give marks between one and five for each individual item (five was tops), plus the reasons.

Not everyone agreed that this exercise in participatory democracy was an effective device in building a team spirit. A few resented the awarding of brownie points for having gone three days without sleep, for having squeezed in five or six interviews in a day of flying trips to New York, Boston, Dallas or Los Angeles.

They all knew, of course, that participatory democracy only went skin-deep. It was the staff's job to gather the material. But final editorial judgments, including judgments on delicate ethical matters, were made by Leiterman and Watson during the process of putting the show together. Often members of the team had to wait for months for the usually inaccessible Leiterman and Watson to make up their minds whether to put the material they had gathered on the air or not, or in what shortened form.

It was not only the opinion of the staff which was on the agenda at these Monday morning meetings, nor the responses of the newspaper columnists. These were avidly read the moment the papers came out. Occasionally the reactions of the Maitland Street charladies were solicited.

Due weight was also given to Leiterman's fourteen-year old daughter:

Daddy:

Birth control more interesting this week but too long. Some attempts at humour failed. If you are going to have so many shots of the studio they should be better shots (closer up, more definite). Show was entertaining, but you should have spent less time on unworthy subjects.

Love

Lachlan.

P.S. I'm writing this because I never see you.

Sometimes Larry Zolf was asked what his mother thought, back home in North Winnipeg.

She had only one criterion. If her son was on the show she loved it.

••••

After the program had gone off the air, one member of the team, using his memory rather than the scientific method, jotted down some figures on a piece of paper. Out of some forty people whom Leiterman and Watson assembled, he found, between nineteen and twenty-three were married when *Seven Days* started. Only three of them were still married to their original spouse at the end of two years' continuous service and two of these three marriages disintegrated later.

Seven Days was not a hotbed of immorality but an emotional pressure cooker. The pace was incredible, the psychological tension enormous, the excitement unbelievable, the loyalties fierce. The reason so many marriages broke up was simply that the domestic lives of *Seven Days* people could not conceivably have the same emotional intensity as their professional lives. Besides, they hardly ever saw their spouses. In a pressure cooker you are, by definition, close to your neighbour and, naturally, one thing leads to another.

Without Watson's humanizing diplomacy, few members of the team would have been able to endure the fanatical drive and inexhaustible energy of Leiterman, the man of iron. His imperturbability gave him immense strength and authority. If ever an aggressive-compulsive fighting spirit was concealed behind an air of utter calmness and total self-control, it was Leiterman's. Most of his people had enormous admiration for him. No one ever heard him raise his velvety, muted voice. Even towards the end of the second season, when it was evident that Watson was exhausted and no longer able to keep pace, the two never had any disagreements in public.

It was impossible to say no to Leiterman. He would wake up his people in the middle of the night, during the few hours of sleep he granted them, and they would jump out of bed and do whatever was requested from them. There was little grumbling. People worked too hard. Those hoping to take a few moments off to catch their breath were wise to stay out of the way. If he ever spotted a producer or story editor in the corridor, or on the parking lot, or in the elevator, who did not seem to be in a hurry to go somewhere to shoot or edit film, scout out a story or catch a cab to the airport, he would ask in his soft voice "What's your load?" and if there was no immediately satisfying answer, he would instruct him or her to fly forthwith to Mexico City to interview a convict on death row or to Berlin to catch a Russian spy. He always had hundreds of story ideas up his sleeve.

There were three signs stuck to his wall:

THE REAL MEASURE FOR MAN'S LOVE FOR HIS PROFESSION IS HIS WILLINGNESS TO TOLERATE DRUDGERY.

THERE ARE NO INDISCREET QUESTIONS ONLY INDISCREET ANSWERS.

NEVER UNDERESTIMATE THE INTELLIGENCE OF YOUR AUDIENCE AND NEVER OVERESTIMATE THEIR INFORMATION.

Not everybody could stand the pace. Leiterman was too absorbed in his work to have much time for other people's feelings.
In any case, he knew that there were scores of applicants lining
up outside his door only too anxious to work for the show for
twenty-four hours, if necessary.

Here is a letter of resignation from a script assistant:

> I am writing this because I don't really feel I can communicate
> with you as well as I should.
>
> I spoke to Patrick last night and I'm afraid I became some-
> what hysterical. And this is really the reason I am leaving.
> After a year of daily and weekly crises and working to deadlines
> and frustrations, etc. etc. I find that my sense of proportion and
> standards and ideas are not level-headed ones and this worries
> me and what I would normally ignore would become a huge
> drama and this is wrong. The delights and pleasures somehow
> get lost, which, I feel, is sad. Even my drinking has increased
> somewhat—mainly because when one has a free moment you
> have to cram so much into it. I don't mind hard work, but
> because of the enormous amounts of hours I find I have
> nothing else in my life except *Seven Days*. Thus, except for
> hard work, not much inspiration from me is forthcoming.

In the summer of 1965 Leiterman directed a crew filming a
scene for a documentary about a motorcycle gang. Its working
title was "Youth and Morality". They were filming two boys and
two girls on the downside of a hill. A car came down the hill,
straight in the direction of one of the girls. She didn't see it
coming. Leiterman threw himself in front of the car. The car ran
over both his legs and broke them. While he was pinned under
the car, the radiator burst, gushing boiling water on him. One of
the boys lifted up the car and pulled him out. Leiterman was
taken to the hospital.

Christian Scientists have a special attitude towards pain and
death and are convinced, as Leiterman was, that their religion
had special significance for the healing process. While not being
at all doctrinaire about the medical profession, he tended to take
a "show me" attitude towards it.

No one dared to express solicitude about his accident, just as
when there was a death in his family no one dared to offer
sympathy.

(The denial of death had some concrete applications in journalism. On April 12th 1945 President Roosevelt died. The headline
in the *Christian Science Monitor* on April 13th read TRUMAN
PLEDGES U.S. TO ROOSEVELT POLICY; CAPTURE OF VI-
ENNA ANNOUNCED BY STALIN.)

Patrick Watson: "He eroticized the environment"

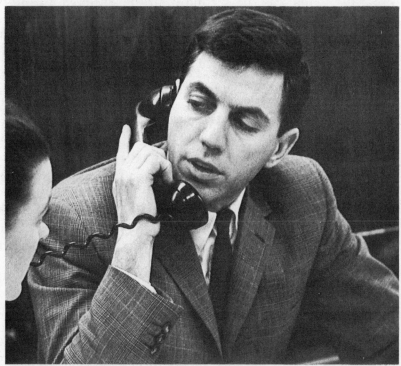
Doug Leiterman: "Get me Mao Tse Tung"

Unlike Leiterman, Watson was usually relaxed. His sense of theatre and gift with words tempered Leiterman's fierce determination. He used his charm to whip the troops into shape. For a smile of approval from him no effort would be spared. His charisma, to quote one of his many female admirers, "eroticized the environment".

Watson's loss of a leg was the result of a very different kind of accident from Leiterman's. The difference was characteristic. Each was a hero in his own way. Watson's accident, typically, was the direct result of his addiction to avant-garde thinkers. Buckminster Fuller was the inventor of the geodesic dome. Watson was fascinated. In 1960, he tried to construct one on top of his cottage at Go Home Lake in Muskoka, with his own hands. He was alone and fell off the roof, breaking his leg. There were almost unendurable delays and gangrene set in. In the end, the leg had to amputated.

A bad leg was a trademark of the team. For various reasons, John Drainie, Warner Troyer and Warren Davis also limped. So did Leiterman who had had polio as a child. In the summer of 1965 he had the dreadful accident while filming "Youth and Morality". This was the second injury he suffered during that year: in the previous winter, childhood polio notwithstanding, he had a skiing accident and broke his bad leg. It so happened that on the same day another member of the team, Sam Levene, also broke his leg.

While in the hospital after his skiing accident, Leiterman turned his room into an office. Outwitting his doctors and nurses, he ordered a moviola installed so he could look at film footage. On Sunday he was transported to Studio One on Jarvis Street and spent the day rehearsing and directing his show from the stretcher. Since he could not go the bathroom, the women in the studio had to leave during critical moments.

With unlimited devotion and enthusiasm it was relatively easy to overcome merely physical obstacles. It was not evident at first that other qualities were required to win the battle with CBC management.

PART TWO
WARFARE

Reeves Haggan: Head of public affairs

Throughout its first season *Seven Days* was criticized for "being overloaded with frivolous or sensational material" and for having "neglected sober and responsible coverage of current affairs". Therefore, Leiterman asked his researchers to conduct a study. This was their finding:[1]

International Affairs (not U.S.)	14.5% of airtime
U.S. Affairs	7.5%
National Affairs	12.6%
Social Problems	26.6%
Business, Industry and Labour	4.3%
Satire and Entertainment	15.3%
Sports	1.4%
Science and Medicine	9.3%
Religion	4.3%
Arts	1.4%
Education	1.4%
Seven Days "Navel-Gazing"	1.3%

Such statistical surveys were necessarily arbitrary. For example, which items were counted as "entertainment" and which as "arts"? Besides, it was the tone of the program and not the subject matter which had given cause to the criticism, though in internal exchanges this was never stated explicitly. Compiling figures was merely a strategic exercise designed to score debating points.

In its two seasons *Seven Days* presented fifty magazine programs containing four hundred and sixty items, plus nine one-hour films in the series *Document*. No more than a dozen stories caused major confrontations with management, including one or two which never went on the air.

However, certain subject areas, such as the coverage of the war in Vietnam, "sleazy" items and satire were recurring themes in the warfare between CBC Toronto and head office in Ottawa. In the matter of style and general approach, management frequently accused *Seven Days* of lack of objectivity, unprofessional interviewing techniques and unfair editing which, in the Corporation's view, constituted breaches of established journalistic policy. It was on this ground of policy that the unfolding battle was fought out until, in the spring of 1966, matters of principle were overshadowed by a power fight between legitimate corporate authority and a rebel group which, with considerable public support, claimed to represent the true mandate of the CBC.

This is a summary of the episodes which caused the most controversy:

GUY FAVREAU

The original interview with the Minister of Justice, Guy Favreau, about the Hal Banks case covered seventeen minutes of film. Once it was edited, it had been reduced to six minutes.

Two days after it was shown, Favreau's executive assistant complained to management about unfair editing. Reeves Haggan who as general supervisor of public affairs was in charge of *Seven Days* was asked to give his opinion. (A description of Haggan and of other CBC officials mentioned in this section will be found in Chapter 6.) This was his reply:

> I do not consider that people in public life can expect everything they say to be transmitted as they said it. In my opinion, all the points made by Mr. Favreau in the recording were in the broadcast. This would seem to be very much in his favour.
>
> It may very well be that an occasion will arise when the weighting given to the points made in a recording by an interviewee may differ radically from the weighting given to them by the producer of the show. That I think is something that people in public life must expect and endure...
>
> I should also make it clear that both Mr. Favreau and his principal officials have told us that they don't question our right to edit, nor do they suggest that this right has been abused. Their feeling expressed to us is that, on this occasion, we could have done better.[2]

THE QUEEN

Trouble arising out of the second show was more serious.

Throughout September 1964 the CBC had made elaborate preparations for the mammoth coverage of the forthcoming royal tour. First, the Queen was to attend ceremonies in Charlottetown to mark the centennial of the pre-Confederation conference. Then, at Premier Jean Lesage's invitation, she was to visit Quebec.

The Queen was due to arrive there on Sunday, October 11th,

the day of the second *Seven Days* show. There was violence in the air. Eleven months earlier President Kennedy had been assassinated in Dallas. Lesage had received threats on his life if he actually allowed the Queen to come. Also, there had been a threat to kidnap his eight-year-old son Raymond.[1]

A week or two earlier, Larry Zolf had been in Quebec, filming man-in-the-street interviews with local citizens. He asked them about their views on the monarchy. He sounded out two Irish nuns as they emerged from a convent, a few students and a Jewish couple. They all took the position that this was not the time for the Queen to visit Quebec.

The British satirical review *Establishment* happened to be in Toronto that week to give a performance at the Eaton Auditorium. They had in their repertoire a skit which portrayed Her Majesty as a cockney housewife in curlers, mop in hand, delivering the annual Christmas message. *Seven Days* made arrangements with the company to film the skit, for presentation on October 11th.

When Reeves Haggan heard about this plan, he thought the idea inappropriate and instructed *Seven Days* not to go through with it. But luck was not on his side.

Ted Briggs, the CBC's executive vice-president who as an announcer had himself covered many royal tours, was in Quebec. For old times' sake, his friends in the CBC Outside Broadcast Department had invited him, just to give him pleasure. After all, no royal tour was complete without him. He was to perform no official duties there. In the plane to Quebec Briggs happened to sit next to a CBC cameraman. He asked him what he was going to film. The cameraman replied that he was going to film the people who were against the Queen.

As soon as Briggs arrived in Quebec he issued a managerial order that outside the news there was to be no reference whatsoever on any CBC program to any activities and demonstrations critical of Her Majesty's visit. This meant, among many other things, that Larry Zolf's man-in-the-street filmed interviews could not go on the air.

Haggan screened the film. The network people screened it. Keith Morrow, the regional director, screened it. They all agreed there was nothing wrong with it. They asked Briggs to look at it himself. Briggs refused. He vetoed any further discussion on the subject.

"That," according to Haggan, "was a drop of poison that tends to stay in the bloodstream."

The morning after October 11th, Canada's front pages were filled with stories about the Quebec demonstrations, with vivid pictures of hundred of young separatists clubbed by the police and the Queen being booed. *Globe and Mail* reporters witnessed thirty-two arrests, two at gunpoint.[2] But most CBC viewers were deprived of this reportage. There was a football game and the National News did not go on the air until two a.m. in the morning. The live Outside Broadcast coverage, carefully following Briggs' orders, did not show a single demonstration or placard. The script had been pre-written and large segments of the "reportage" had been filmed ahead of time. The program created the impression of just another happy royal occasion.

But not *Seven Days*. While carefully avoiding any flagrant infringement of the executive veto, it mocked the event in a short *cinéma vérité* sequence showing candid shots of the aging Governor-General Vincent Massey and Prime Minister Lester Pearson as they emerged from their respective limousines, clearly unaware of the camera, and members of the Guard of Honour yawning and scratching their noses. Then there was a solemn clip from a meeting of the Ladies Orange Benevolent Association, United Lodge 379, in Niagara Falls. They adopted a resolution, "with deep concern", to have silent prayers said every morning at eleven for the safety of Her Majesty, "while visiting our land".

This was Laurier LaPierre's concluding commentary:

> Tonight the ladies of the Orange Lodge will have a grateful sense of relief that Queen Elizabeth came through the bizarre adventure in Quebec City unharmed. The government and the RCMP will be congratulating themselves that my compatriots in that city, with a few noisy exceptions, behaved. But, ladies and gentlemen, is that enough? Is it good enough to say "We got away with it?" It seems certain that my compatriots this week in the midst of admiring Her Majesty's courage and in the midst of feeling relieved, wondered very deeply whether the Crown can still realistically be a symbol of Canadian unity and whether their government had been wise in acceding to the wishes of the Quebec government that she be invited in the first place.

There was one further reference to the Queen in the program. In a skit about birth control pills which followed an interview with Dr. John Rock, one of the originators of oral contraceptives, there was a reference to pink birth control pills with pictures of Her Majesty on each side, to differentiate them from normal pills.

GEORGE LINCOLN ROCKWELL

The American Nazi leader, a former navy pilot, was placed high up on the hot seat. He was wearing a uniform with a swastika armband and the camera showed the phalanx of armed storm troopers who had come into the studio with him. He was smoking a corncob pipe. The backdrop was a large swastika flag.

The interview covered a wide range. The questioners were Douglas Leiterman, Robert Hoyt and the director Beryl Fox.

Rockwell said he believed in free enterprise and was opposed to the corporate state. He was basically a racist, he declared, who wanted to preserve a white Christian nation for the white Christian people who built it. To negroes he would offer a chance to go back to their own nation in Africa. He thought most negroes would be more comfortable travelling back to Africa in cattle cars—or in cattle ships—than in Greyhound buses.

"I think," he said, "they would prefer to go the way they live."

> As for the Jews, the constitution provides for that... Death is the penalty for treason and I believe that. That's the only way to deal with a traitor. I think they should be placed before American juries in American courts of law, federal courts, and if they're convicted by law of treason I think they should be executed... I think Hitler dealt with the Jews in Germany in the same way he dealt with all traitors, the same way we will. I think he has been lied about more than any other human being in history except Jesus Christ.... I think Hitler was a gift from Providence... I think he was so far above everything I'll be able to accomplish that it's almost sacrilegious for me to speak of myself in the same way as Hitler.

CBC middle management in Toronto had prescreened the program and approved it. It had been announced on the air the previous Sunday and duly publicized. Consequently, thirty Jewish organizations representing twenty thousand people immediately appealed to the Corporation not to go through with the plan, though no one outside the CBC had seen the interview. When CBC Toronto, conditioned to resist pressure groups, went ahead anyway twenty-five pickets were organized to walk along Jarvis Street and Mutual Street on Sunday, before and during the program. The signs read CBC COOPERATES WITH NAZIS and THERE IS NO PLACE FOR NAZIS IN DEMOCRACY.

Some leading members of the Jewish community contacted

middle management to ask how it could be sure that some residue of Rockwell's message might not subliminally be retained even in the minds of those who would never admit to being anti-Semitic and who would in fact deny it vigorously. They pleaded with the CBC to reconsider its decision. After some hesitation, Toronto management stood firm.

The morning after the interview had gone on the air, Diefenbaker rose in the House and said he saw no reason why the "so-called leader of the United States Nazi party... should receive the attention of the CBC across Canada, nor why Nazism should be glorified in this way."[1]

The press was divided. Under the headline *Sensation-seeking on CBC*, George Bain wrote in his column in the *Globe and Mail*:

> The complaint that any viewer might legitimately make about the Rockwell interview was that, since he represents no problem of the real world—not in the United States, far less here—then holding him up for examination constitutes a total waste of time and money.[2]

The *Toronto Star* had carried a favourable editorial, but in his column Ron Haggart asked "What's so bold about filming a Nazi?"

> Is this brave, bold, penetrating journalism? Is this probing into the soul of America... or is it just blather, blather which could be filmed as easily, and with as much meaning, at 999 Queen Street West in Toronto.[3]

That was a reference to the institution which housed the mentally sick. However, Bob Blackburn in the *Toronto Telegram* (which had run a critical editorial), Frank Penn in the *Ottawa Citizen* and Dusty Vineberg in the *Montreal Star* wrote favourable pieces. Vineberg's was headlined *Rockwell Hard To Play Straight*:

> It was all so extreme that it was funny, containing the same elements of sadism and inhumanity as a sick joke.[4]

On August 26th 1967, Rockwell was shot to death in a parking lot in Arlington, Virginia, from the roof of a coin-operated laundry, by a fourth-ranking member of the party who had been expelled the previous April.

••••

Judy LaMarsh was secretary of state at the time of the *Seven Days* crisis in 1966. Ten years later, in January 1976, she was the host of the daily CBC radio program *Morningside* and devoted the week of January 12th to nostalgic interviews with Leiterman,

Watson, LaPierre and Zolf to observe the anniversary of the program's demise. The subject of sensationalism and controversy arose. She asked Leiterman whether he consciously chose sensationalism as a device to present public issues. He said, in a sense, yes.

"Well then," LaMarsh observed, "you must have been in trouble with management almost from the beginning."

> Sure, yes, (Leiterman replied). The basic thing is we were not afraid of controversy. In fact, it was vital. It was essential to the kind of thing we wanted to do. Because the essential nature of controversy is that we're dealing with material that's very high in the public consciousness, or should be. By its nature it will bring out conflicts and stir up all the pressure groups of every kind of cherished favourite interest or favourite prejudice. It will stir up the politicians and the government and particularly the CBC brass, which over the years has had an enviable reputation of having their heads buried in the sand...so they won't hear the controversy and won't see it and won't smell it and won't be disturbed by it. For as soon as controversy reaches the upper levels of the CBC, as you very well know, it goes directly by some sort of osmosis into parliament and into politics, and the CBC is quite properly very much afraid of being exposed to public pressure.

As an example of the *Seven Days* policy of presenting a controversial issue in a consciously sensationalist manner, Judy LaMarsh proceeded to play back—to Leiterman's surprise—an excerpt from the Rockwell interview. This was her introduction:

> It's the kind of thing we don't do in this show. I didn't like it then. I don't like it now. I consider it an incitement to violence and to all kinds of rotten sorts of things.

After having played back this excerpt LaMarsh said that there can't be anybody within the sound of her voice who didn't feel that what Rockwell had said was such filth that it had made a statement itself. Was that why Leiterman had put it on?

> I think (Leiterman replied) I would say it a little differently. You see, I don't believe that we should pretend the world is different from the way it is. I think that if we're going to help change the world and improve it we'll have to recognize what kind of world it is and I don't think we should pretend that there are not people like George Lincoln Rockwell around.

As to the danger that some marginal people already "off their rocker" might be swayed by Rockwell, Leiterman said that you may have to balance the damage against the good you do for the vast population who may learn something they need to know.

"In my view the balance is all in favour of letting them see what it's like and make up their own minds."[5]

The following day was the last day of Judy's commemorative series on *Morningside*.

WATSON: The most interesting thing of all was said when you talked to Douglas yesterday and you played an excerpt from the Rockwell interview, you said, "This is the kind of thing I would never put on my program because it's disgusting and revolting. However, to illustrate the point, I'm going to do it but I want you to know, dear audience, that I think it's revolting and disgusting..." If you do that kind of thing you must not be surprised if you're accused of hypocrisy.

LAMARSH: I should be accused of something even worse...I didn't have a chance to listen to that tape first and I took someone else's word for it. When I listened to it I could hear that Douglas Leiterman and Robert Hoyt were not sympathetic, and their coolness when they let that rotten, foul man talk like that, that was itself important. I changed my mind.[6]

Three weeks after the Rockwell interview had gone on the air, The *Globe and Mail* carried an article by Watson.

When television really starts to work on the community why does the word sensationalism leap to the lips so readily?

Television is essentially a sensation instrument, a device for communicating, or inducing, sense impressions. It works on the senses. Marshall McLuhan says it's tactile. And whether or not you accept the McLuhan metaphor, it is true, for example, that the sharp confrontation of a political figure, the challenge hurled by the inquisitors at the man in the hot seat, produces a feeling for the nature of the man. A sensation. It does other things, too. And this kind of sensationalism (and I confess to a certain amount of flim-flammery here) is communicating at a level that can get to all the people at one time.[7]

REV. RUSSELL D. HORSBURGH

Chatham, Ont., was an ecclesiastical Peyton Place, a conservative community torn by conflicts between the generations and by racial strife. On November 13th, Rev. Russell D. Horsburgh, the minister at Park Street United

Church in Chatham, had been found guilty of contributing to juvenile delinquency by encouraging sexual relations between young people on church premises. He was a graduate of McMaster and Queens Universities and had been a respected minister for twenty-three years in various places. It had been a lengthy trial which received a great deal of attention. There were six large volumes of transcripts.

While the Rockwell case had caused an uproar among the public and hardly a ripple within the Corporation, the film feature about Rev. Russell D. Horsburgh, carried on November 15th in the sixth program, became a major internal issue.

Produced under Watson's guidance, the film could not go on the air while the case was *sub judice*. A difficult legal question arose: could it go on the air after the verdict had been reached but before the sentencing? Lawyers were consulted who advised that, after certain sequences were deleted, the item was not in contempt of court.

However, while these deliberations went on, Ottawa gave confidential instructions to Doug Nixon, the program director, that the Horsburgh case was not to be touched. Presumably, these instructions were prompted by moral, not legal, considerations.

After hectic last-minute meetings and screenings till late into the night, Doug Nixon agreed with Reeves Haggan and Peter Campbell that Ottawa's instructions were unreasonable. Campbell, a former senior official from External Affairs, carried on the diplomatic discussions between Nixon, Haggan and the producers as though he was still practising his old trade. The story went on the air.

Ouimet held his regular Monday morning meeting at head office the day afterwards. This is an extract from the minutes:

> The question was raised whether the Corporation should continue with the program of the sensitivity of *Seven Days*, keeping in mind its considerable measure of success as well as the total corporate situation.
>
> Management must be concerned with any new venture in programming to make sure that it stays within our policies and standards of production. In this instance the program is a type of journalism which the Corporation has never attempted before and Management has given a great deal of time to detail, item by item, week by week. It was felt that, after all the discussions on specific points, on philosophy, on the need for strict supervision at the network level, it should no longer be necessary for detailed senior Management supervision. It was also felt that the program needed more time to improve. There

is a place for provocative, controversial, aggressive, sometimes sensational or satirical, journalism on television. Such a program could bring credit to the Corporation without running too many risks and without creating too much difficulty. We must keep in mind when trying to bring things of interest in current affairs to the public's attention that we have audiences with diverse interests.

There must be complete confidence in whoever is in charge of a program of this type, in his ability to make sound policy judgments and to use common sense in choosing items for treatment in the program. At the same time it is important that there be strong leadership from Management in exercising the kind of editorial responsibility that is required.

It was suggested that, after very careful study, Management should make a clear statement of broad editorial policy to cover the various types of current affairs journalism. The statement should not only qualify the editorial policy to be followed, but should also qualify the rules to be followed on this particular program. The limits of individual authority must be emphasized. There should be room for flexibility as long as there is no licence.[1]

●●●●

The film feature included interviews with young people in the Chatham streets. "Hanging is too good for Horsburgh", a young man said. "Life in jail," another recommended. "Let him suffer." But some remarked that the minister had done a lot to straighten them out.

Horsburgh himself told the interviewer that he had tried to establish contact with young people. He had hoped to gain their confidence and thought that he had achieved a great deal when a young person came to him and said "I'm having a problem with sex. I'm carrying on in an immoral way."

He was asked why he thought it had all blown up in his face.

We have a group of young people in our church who had never seen the inside of the church until recently. These young people have a chip on their shoulder. They think they have been maltreated, and many of them were, in their own homes. They don't think they've had a fair deal in society and they turned against society. Sometimes they turned against the very hand that reached out to help them.

On February 13th 1966 *Seven Days* carried a follow-up story. Horsburgh had been in prison for a hundred and seventeen days and was home on bail, pending an appeal to the Supreme Court. In his second interview he told *Seven Days* that he had made the best of his imprisonment. He was writing a book *From Pulpit to*

Prison and wouldn't have missed the experience for anything.

In the same program Watson interviewed the Rev. Ronald Smeaton, a friend of Horsburgh's, who had written a book about the case.[2] There is a reference in the book to the accusation that Horsburgh was a homosexual. Watson asked him about that. Smeaton replied that he definitely did not consider Horsburgh a homosexual and that Horsburgh had gone to a psychiatrist on his own volition and been given a clean sheet. Then Watson suddenly asked Smeaton whether it had ever been suggested to him that there was a homosexual component, real or imagined, in his relationship with Mr. Horsburgh.

No, said Smeaton, he didn't think so. Then he added: "The real person you should be asking about that is my wife."

Shaun Herron, himself a former United Church minister, made this comment in the *Winnipeg Free Press*:

> Smeaton's reply is much admired around the CBC... But if it was an admirable reply, it is possible to wonder how an interview about Horsburgh with a man who had done no more than defend his friend, legitimately got round to the intimate physical relations between Smeaton and his wife—before some three million people... (It was) an impertinent, irrelevant and intrusive question which was introduced not because Watson thought it likely, but because the sudden confrontation would make good "impact television"... This was an unforgivable abuse of the privilege of interviewing an author: it was an abuse of a decent man...it was an abuse of the vehicle itself and it was an assertion that the professional use of the vehicle comes before every other consideration.[3]

In 1967 the Supreme Court allowed Horsburgh's appeal. A new trial was ordered. He was exonerated. In January 1971 the United Church reinstated him without qualifications and in October he died.

DIEFENBAKER AND LÉVESQUE

Seven Days invented its own terminology for the probing interview of a prominent politician: the "hot seat". For each of these interviews, Warner Troyer and Laurier LaPierre mapped out their strategy in detail beforehand. They tried to anticipate the answers, always hoping for illuminating theatre. When John Diefenbaker was their guest, he delivered precisely what they had hoped for—the raised finger and the shaking jowls in high indignation. LaPierre pressed him hard, giving the old performer a golden opportunity to accuse him in his best courtroom manner of being a cynical tool of the Liberal Party.

There were so many complaints about LaPierre's provocative interviewing technique that head office issued a statement expressing its regrets. It was approved by R.C. Fraser, Vice-President and Assistant to the President.

> A number of people have objected to the manner in which Mr. Diefenbaker was questioned and we regret that the attitude of the interviewers should have been objected to by anyone. So far, this program has had its good interviews and some bad ones. I would agree that some of these have been marred by the quality and manner of the questioning. The Corporation is aware of this and has endeavoured to make *This Hour* a program which measures up to CBC standards.[1]

The next hot-seat interview, on December 6th, elicited no such communiqué from head office. It upset the press more than management. The guest was René Lévesque and this time the interviewers were Larry Zolf and Pierre E. Trudeau. Lévesque was still a member of Jean Lesage's Liberal government of Quebec and Trudeau professor of law at the University of Montreal.

Watson explained later that *Seven Days* had intended to dramatize the French-English situation. They had chosen Zolf, the "impatient western Canadian who doesn't really understand why the hell we should put up with this kind of nonsense from Quebec", and Trudeau, who was to slip the knife from quite a different direction, "in a very French, humourous, wry way".[2]

As it turned out, the audience saw a great deal of Zolf and very little of Trudeau. What it saw was, as Watson had intended, excellent theatre.

ZOLF: In all fairness, how do you expect English Canadians to distinguish between separatists and extremists when separatism is the end of Canada? When Quebec comes out of Confederation, the rest of the country folds up.

LÉVESQUE: I can't answer your question. That's an English-Canadian problem, not mine. It will eventually unravel itself in the collective English Canadian mind.

ZOLF: You sit there, as you have in the past three or four minutes, and you try and tell me that you don't care what English Canada thinks?

LÉVESQUE: I didn't say I didn't care. I said I couldn't answer your question about how the heck, if the problem exists the way you say—you know more about it than I do—an English Canadian mind which confuses separatism and extremism is going to get out of the confusion... I didn't say I wasn't concerned. How can you be anything but concerned if you're interested in Quebec's needs, priorities and interests?

This was followed by a sharp exchange on the conditions under which violence was justified. Lévesque said Fidel Castro's revolutionaries had every right to resort to violence. If Canada turned into a police state, the same would apply here. This was not disputed. Trudeau then told Lévesque that separatism was considered by many in this country as a force of disorder. Lévesque agreed, but added that a measure of disorder was compatible with a democratic system.

TRUDEAU: I completely agree with that. But what I'm afraid of is the backlash against disorder. We live in a social and political context where forces of authority have traditionally behaved in a very authoritarian way. Some of the things that are happening now...do seem to indicate that there will be a backlash of the forces of order against the forces of disorder. How would you assess that danger?

LÉVESQUE: I don't think there is any real danger of that.

Robert Fulford commented on the interview in his column in the *Star*:

I winced with embarrassment when Larry Zolf either demonstrated or pretended a level of stupidity which was, as far as my memory goes, unique in CBC history.

There sat René Lévesque, who is, whatever you think of his views, the brightest of all the important politicians in Canada.

And there sat Pierre Elliott Trudeau, the lawyer and writer, who is one of the civilized men of Canada.

And there, within the same frame, representing Toronto, and me, and the English-language TV network—and even perhaps representing you, dear reader— was this boor, Larry Zolf, either failing entirely to understand Lévesque or (worse) pretending to misunderstand him.

To Lévesque and Trudeau, and to the French Canadians who watched the program, this must have proven what they've suspected all along: English-speaking Canadians are both thick-headed and frivolous, and there is nothing that can be done about it.[3]

RICHARD ELY

Just before Christmas 1964 Briggs received a letter of complaint from District Judge Avila Labelle, of the magistrate's court in Hull. His decision in the case of Richard Ely had been subject of the most recent *Seven Days* program. Judge Labelle enclosed a hand-written, undated note sent to him by a viewer:

Labelle—

Shame on you. You whiskey-smelling skunk. How in hell were you ever appointed to the Bench.

God has promised to forgive the repentant. They have to atone for their sins but they are forgiven. Your sentence was terrible. If you wanted to set an example you could have used somebody else. Not a poor unfortunate mixed up young man who never had a chance in life. *You* had every chance in life: a successful father etc. and look what you are: a blind fool, silly, drinking fool, lucky enough to get a political appointment as a judge.

Shame...

Happy Christmas if you have the heart to be happy after such a blunder. It must have been a morning after the night before.

Disgusted.

As it happened, it wasn't Judge Avila Labelle who had made a major blunder. It was *Seven Days* which had made by far the most serious factual blunder in its career and the producers weren't allowed to forget it. The following week they had to set the record straight and apologize. However, for the "poor unfortunate mixed up young man" the blunder had a decidedly beneficial result. On appeal, Ely's sentence was reduced from seven to three years, presumably—though this cannot be proven—as the direct result of the public indignation the program had aroused.

The facts, as stated on the program, were as follows: Richard Ely was twenty years old and lived in Hull. On a recent Friday night he had told his mother and sister that he had committed a robbery and wanted to surrender to the police. He had been thrown out of his home when he was fifteen and since then "his life had been irregular, but, as far as we know, not criminal". He wished to go to jail, he said, to learn a trade. He had spent $150 of the money he had stolen on text books on drafting. The family called a social worker who thought that, as a first offender, the boy would receive a sentence of between eighteen and twenty-four months for robbery and for possession of an offensive weapon. The next morning, on Saturday, on the recommendation of the social worker, he appeared before District Judge Avila Labelle in magistrate's court, without a lawyer and with no witnesses. It took the judge three minutes to convict him to seven years in St. Vincent de Paul penitentiary. John Drainie's commentary concluded: "In passing sentence, Judge Labelle said 'examples must be given. We thought you might be interested in this example'."

At the top of the show on December 27th *Seven Days* made this announcement:

> Last Sunday on the program we reported the case of Richard Ely of Hull, Quebec, who had pleaded guilty of robbing a hotel clerk of $497 while armed with a revolver and was sentenced to seven years' imprisonment by District Judge Avila Labelle. A review of the circumstances shows that in our report last Sunday we did not present all the relevant facts. Ely who had appeared as a first offender had surrendered to the police but this was not a short time after the crime. In fact the robbery was committed on November 9th and Ely surrendered on December 11th, nearly five weeks later. The *Seven Days* report did not indicate as it should have that Ely had used violence by beating the clerk of the Fontainebleu Motel, kicking him and hitting him with the butt of a revolver and threatening to shoot him and as a result of the attack the clerk was treated in hospital. The charge carries a maximum penalty of life imprisonment and whipping... The court was told that Ely had gone hunting for a week immediately after the robbery and then to Florida and the police was looking for him at the time he surrendered... We regret the facts presented by our previous program were not sufficiently complete to allow the viewer a full assessment of what took place in the courtroom, and before sentence was rendered.

Seven Days did not have a leg to stand on.

FRED FAWCETT

The next case was different. It raised the question how far CBC journalists may legitimately go in pursuing a story. In the Fred Fawcett case, William Hogg, Director of News and Public Affairs, thought they had gone too far. Of all their misdemeanors, their handling of this case was by far the most reprehensible and until the very end he did not forgive them.

Fred Fawcett owned a large cattle farm near Owen Sound, Ont. He was a large man, weighing more than two hundred and fifty pounds, and was well respected in the community. For twenty-five years he had tried to persuade the township of Euphrasia to provide an access road, a service rendered to all the other farmers in the community. When the township refused, he declined to pay taxes, taking the position that a Crown Grant title to his land rendered him immune to taxation. He had taken a correspondence course in law from an American university and considered himself an authority. He fully realized his argument was unusual. The township, on the other hand, didn't think his argument was merely unusual. It thought it was evidence of insanity.

On August 28th 1961 events occurred about which there was disputed evidence. The Crown contended that when two elderly tax assessors appeared on his land he shot a hole through the front tire of their car with a pistol. There was a great deal of contradictory evidence about the circumstances of this incident. Mr. Justice J. Spence in the Ontario High Court decided that, Fawcett's sworn testimony notwithstanding, Fawcett considered his farm "his own armed citadel" and that he had threatened to use his rifle against any person who came close.[1]

Two court proceedings in 1962 and 1963 dealt with the legality of his detention, not with his alleged criminal offences. The question was whether the confinement was constitutional under the provisions of the Mental Hospital Act. First, he had been remanded in a magistrate's court in Owen Sound for a mental examination. Later he was declared insane. He was held in various Ontario hospitals and was finally transferred to the Penetanguishine Hospital for the Criminally Insane where, by the time the program went on the air, he had been for almost four years.

It was Fawcett's sister Rita who had first gone to the *Toronto Star* and then to *Seven Days* to tell them that a gross miscarriage of justice had occurred. Sidney Katz of the *Toronto Star* spent many weeks researching the case though he was never given permission to enter the hospital's compound to see Fawcett.

The Crown's four psychiatrists had testified that Fawcett was insane. His neighbours unanimously agreed that he was as sane as they were. Katz's research led him to agree with the neighbours. His editor Ralph Allen supported him and the paper began a campaign to have Fawcett released.

Peter Pearson, having recently returned from studying film with Fellini in Rome, was one of the *Seven Days* researchers assigned to the case. He and his colleagues agreed with the *Toronto Star*. On March 18th 1965 Pearson called Dr. M.B. Dymond, the minister of health in the Ontario government, and asked for permission to interview Fawcett. Permission was refused. Patients were "not on exhibition but are sick people in hospital for treatment".

The same day the director Michael Hastings and a crew of two proceeded to Penetang with Rita Fawcett. In two suitcases, later described as "picnic baskets", they carried their equipment. Miss Fawcett identified them as "friends". The guards knew Rita Fawcett and escorted them through the gates straight to the reception room. Hastings interviewed Fawcett, filming near the window without lights. There was no interruption. For a few minutes an attendant looked in on the filming. After they had finished they took some silent shots of the grounds and called on Dr. B.A. Boyd, the superintendent, in his office, and asked whether he would agree to be interviewed. They did not tell him than an interview with Fawcett was already "in the can". Boyd agreed and answered questions about the nature of psychiatric evidence.

As soon as Haggan heard about the Fawcett interview he raised serious objections, and so did Bill Hogg to whom Leiterman also reported on the day of the filming. Leiterman did not tell either that Dr. Dymond had refused to give permission. Hogg made it categorically clear to Leiterman that unless proper permission *ex post facto* was obtained the film could not go on the air.

It was ready for screening on Sunday morning, the day of the show, March 21st. Haggan and Campbell were deeply impressed. They tried to persuade Hogg that it was in the public interest that the interview go on the air. Hogg replied that unless permission from the authorities was obtained he would oppose this. Hogg and Haggan jointly called Dr. Boyd in Penetang. They told him that by the time the crew called on him they had already filmed an interview with Fawcett. They apologized for the way this had been handled. Dr. Boyd said he would not object to the interview going on the air since both Fawcett and his sister had consented to it.

Leiterman then confessed to Haggan that Dr. Dymond, the minister of health, had vetoed a visit to the hospital before the crew had left for Penetang. Haggan was extremely annoyed and irritated. But by now he was so anxious for the interview to be shown that he himself called Dr. Dymond. Once again he obtained an agreement and Hogg softened his objections to the program going on the air. The minister later complained in a letter that he had been misled.[2]

Two weeks after the program, Premier John Robarts of Ontario called a press conference to announce the Fawcett case would be reviewed by a special medical board in July. But Fawcett did not have to wait that long. Dr. Boyd had discretion to use his medical judgment and decided on his own to order his release.

On May 28th Fawcett left Penetang. "I feel great," he told reporters. "I've never worried about my sanity. I never had any doubts about it."[3]

The next morning Leiterman had a long conversation with Hogg and expressed his regrets that it had never occurred to him to mention Dr. Dymond's veto to him or Haggan. He said he now recognized its relevance.

On Tuesday Hogg made his report to Ottawa.

> Leiterman feels that at times there are circumstances that justify opposing or indeed circumventing "constituted authority". As an example, he mentioned going through police lines or otherwise flouting state authority in Alabama. He would extend this view to the Fawcett case, and he was also inclined to argue that there is nothing wrong in going from one official to another to seek permission, without disclosing the results.
>
> I challenged both of these concepts and made it quite clear that if the circumvention of authorities was contemplated, the senior people responsible for the program must be informed well in advance, to have a chance to consider all the circumstances, and that I intended to exercise my responsibilities. After some discussion, Mr. Leiterman came around to my view, and there the matter was left.[4]

This was a misunderstanding: Leiterman never "came around" to Hogg's views on journalistic propriety. But he respected Hogg, and on his way out of the office he may well have said something conciliatory to placate the older man.

VIETNAM

Head Office was inclined to look at the world through rose-coloured spectacles. It found it unpalatable that *Seven Days* dwelled with such relish on injus-

Beryl Fox: Producer, Mills of the Gods

tice, cruelty, prejudice, greed and other manifestations of human frailty. But there was no CBC policy against doing so unless the producers broke the rules.

In the way they handled the Vietnam War they certainly did. They were not being objective about it at all. Of course they knew that their concepts of objectivity were different from management's. But they shrewdly avoided direct confrontations on the subject. They preferred to discuss it in terms of television versus radio. In radio, as in print, it was possible to give equal weight to opposing views by allocating the same airtime, or space, to both. In television, one striking image was more powerful than any number of words. It was the medium and not any new ideas about fairness, they said, that had rendered the old rules obsolete.

In 1964 and 1965 there was as yet no consensus in Canada about the war in Vietnam. The producers of *Seven Days* were among those who led the way in opposing it. They were in step with advanced opinion in the press, both in Canada and in the United States. Also, many people in the Canadian government, including Prime Minister Pearson, agreed with them. Still, no one could say they were being objective about it. During the parliamentary hearings in 1966 the matter came up repeatedly. Some of the M.P.s severely chastised them for making a consistent effort to "portray the Americans as warmongers and professional killers".[1]

On January 30th 1966 *Seven Days* presented a skit by Dave Broadfoot, following a straight interview conducted by Beryl Fox with American political scientist Bernard Fall, who had been in Vietnam when the French were expelled in 1954 and who had written several books about Vietnam, including *The Two Vietnams*.[2] (On February 21st 1967 he was killed in South Vietnam by a Vietcong mine.) Fall was acutely critical of U.S. policies in Southeast Asia. Head office had always been sensitive about the juxtaposition of straight material and satire. This occasion was particularly galling.

INTRODUCTION: *There are still a few men in America who want the United States to win at any price. On Thursday Mississippi Senator John Stennis, who is chairman of the Senate Defence Subcommittee, called for a tougher line. Said he: "I would never put our boys in mortal conflict against the hordes of Red Chinese coolies without using every weapon we have". Well, a fellow senator had this to say:*

BROADFOOT IMPERSONATING SOUTHERN SENATOR: *Mr. President, fellow senators. God gave this great country nuclear bombs and we must use them. We must not be intimidated by remarks from France or England or any other communist country. Some senators have asked for my feelings on nuclear war on a global scale. I say, yes, that's the only way to do it. Some say it could mean the eventual destruction of America. I say it's good for business. Some say they're going to be incinerated. I say, let them remember their ashes will be privately owned. We have the money to pursue this all-out war, Mr. President, if we could stop these silly projects, like taking pictures of the moon. Let us use our resources and our bombs to take freedom to North Vietnam, to Cambodia, to Laos, China, East Germany maybe, and—last but not least—Harlem. Let us look upon this as the war on poverty. And let us get on with it while the military dictator in South Vietnam is still friendly to us.*

CBC policy forbade satire on matters "involving intense personal feelings" by large sections of the audience. Following this presentation there was an exchange of memos between H.G. Walker, vice-president and general manager of network broadcasting (English), and the Toronto supervisors about the question of whether the war in Vietnam was a suitable subject for satire. Walker thought not.

> Canadians cannot help but be distressed at the loss of lives in the Vietnam War, and of course there is an awareness that but with a few more rounds of firing Canada itself could be directly involved. This being the case, I think it is quite improper to satirize war or the involvement of a nation in it. Certainly it runs counter to the intent of the policy to have a serious item on the Vietnam war, and in the same program satirize some aspect of it.[3]

Peter Campbell, the supervisor of current affairs specifically concerned with *Seven Days*, chose to differ. Before joining the CBC he had been a senior officer in the Department of External Affairs and had been Canadian Commissioner on the International Supervisory Commission which was watching over the truce in Laos in the late fifties. He therefore had first-hand knowledge of the war in Indochina. In fact, it was in Laos that he had first met Leiterman, who one day arrived in the capital Ventiane as a newspaperman accompanying Paul Martin, the Canadian minister of external affairs. Martin was on an inspection tour, anxious to see Canadian military personnel in Communist-held territory. The only way to proceed was in a small Beaver plane. Leiterman demanded to fly to the jungle with Martin. Campbell had to tell Leiterman that no arrangements could possibly be made at short notice to go with the minister, since the Communists rigidly controlled access to their territories and had to be notified well in advance. Leiterman replied that it was his right as a reporter to see what the minister saw. If this right was denied to him, he would have to publish— without being able to verify them personally—unfavourable reports he had heard about the sordid living conditions of Canadian soldiers stationed in Indochina which they would not like back home. The answer was still no, but no was not an answer Leiterman was prepared to accept. After he had attempted to board the Beaver in the vain hope of getting his way after all, he had to be escorted off the small airfield in Ventiane.

In their new CBC relationship, Campbell, a classical scholar, was able to be of greater assistance to Leiterman. This is what he replied to Walker's memo:

> I take it that the *Seven Days* item in question was a satire on the extreme views of Senator Stennis, not upon the war itself.
>
> Nevertheless, war has been long established in the traditions of Western civilization as a subject for satirical treatment. This is not surprising, since the object of satire is to make objection and there is much to be objected to in the matter of war. The great comic dramatist Aristophanes wrote a trilogy lampooning war (*The Knights*, *The Peace*, and *Lysistrata*), which are still successfully produced today, at a time when his country was engaged in a life-and-death struggle with its mortal enemy. Aristophanes was a patriot. But he thought the war immoral...
>
> As to the war in Vietnam, the cartoonists in North America and European newspapers have no hesitation in satirizing it when the occasion arises...
>
> There can be no doubt that the intense personal feelings of *some* Canadians are engaged in this war, those of the Student Union for Peace Action, for instance, and, probably, their counterparts on the extreme right. For most Canadians, however, the war must inevitably be somewhat remote, whether their intellectual or sentimental predilections predispose them towards or against the United States' military involvement in Indochina.[4]

On February 7th 1965 the bombing of North Vietnam began and soon afterwards the American evening news began to show pictures of the first American casualties. On February 14th *Seven Days* presented a feature on the war. First, there was a short interview with the aged Bertrand Russell who had just deposited an open letter of protest against the bombing at the U.S. embassy in London. In the interview Lord Russell accused the U.S. of engaging in a war of conquest. It wishes, he said, to subdue its satellite in Southeast Asia under a military despotism and was running a serious risk of war between the U.S. on one side and Russia and China on the other. The interview was followed by a short clip from a statement by McGeorge Bundy, the special presidential assistant on national security, who stated that the United States did not seek a wider war.

"If Mr. Bundy and his employer President Johnson don't want a wider war," John Drainie commented, "what are they doing bombing the north?"

Drainie then introduced Henry Cabot Lodge, the former American ambassador to Vietnam. He defended the bombing as "sagacious and courageous". He said that "if we're going to let all the rough and tough places go to the Communists and we're going to interest ourselves only in the nice quiet places which don't need our help, then we're soon going to find that the Communists have taken over the world." If the United States persisted and avoided being "petulant, impatient and easily discouraged", it could win the war.

This was Drainie's conclusion:

> A Soviet leader is supposed to have said: "What does the U.S. think it's doing? They know we're going to help North Vietnam. Do they want war?"
>
> Well, let's hope our neighbours know what they want.

The May 2 edition, the last but one of the first season, once again offended Bronson Avenue because of its lack of objectivity. A skit by Stan Daniels about a Pentagon general directly preceded an interview with McGeorge Bundy, filmed in Washington. The juxtaposition of straight material with satire invariably raised eyebrows at head office. Daniels played the general who was being questioned.

QUESTION: I see you're prepared for war with Monaco.
ANSWER: Oh yes, we won't take any chances. With the proper deployment of our nuclear forces we can kill any man, woman or child in Monaco 745 million times, and that includes tourists.
(BREAKS INTO SONG TO THE TUNE OF THE "BATTLE HYMN OF THE REPUBLIC")

At any moment's notice
Using this computer here
We can wipe out any nation on the globe
From Chile to Japan.

> It's the most complete and comprehensive
> Military plan
> That has ever been devised.

QUESTION: But it's only meant as a deterrent, general, isn't it?

ANSWER: *Oh, we'll never use it,*
Oh, we'll never use it,
Oh, we'll never use it,
That's not what it is for.

After the pretaped interview with McGeorge Bundy, Watson made a final comment.

> Although they find it sometimes hard to feel cheerful in the face of it, advice from Canada is listened to in Washington. Mr. Bundy told me so. If you feel Canada should exercise its influence in a major way on Vietnam, I suggest you write to the prime minister in Ottawa. He's already expressed some counsel to the president. He might be interested to hear your views. You don't need postage stamps.

The next day, head office instructed Hogg to make sure that *Seven Days* should never again engage in such direct crusading. The *Edmonton Journal* carried this editorial.

> Viewers were urged to write Prime Minister Pearson their opinion on U.S. policy in Vietnam so that he may relay them to Washington.
>
> What obviously was wanted was condemnation of that policy.
>
> Mr. Pearson would be better occupied in making an apology to Washington for this use of the Canadian taxpayer's money for an attack on a good neighbour, the leader of the free world, that was, in large part, as vicious and ignorant as it was childish and banal.
>
> Many regard the CBC as an arm of the Canadian government, If any of them saw *Seven Days* Sunday night, some of them may regard it more as an arm of the Chinese Communist Party.[5]

The two interviewers, Pat Watson and Tom Koch, had asked McGeorge Bundy questions about the U.S. role in Vietnam for forty-three minutes. Only eight minutes were shown. The State Department promptly issued a statement protesting what it considered unfair editing and, in an unprecedented move, made the full text available to U.S. consulates in Canada for public inspection. Some Canadian papers published the deleted portions.

Knowlton Nash was the CBC's Washington correspondent at the time. The incident had "damaged the CBC's operations in Washington," he wrote to Hogg. "In time the effects likely will be diluted, although the residue may remain for some time to come... I have been told privately that the CBC was now regarded as the most untrustworthy network with which the Department dealt."[6]

●●●●

Beryl Fox's hour-long Vietnam film *The Mills of the Gods*, shown on December 5th 1965 in the monthly series *Document*, made television history. It was the first of its kind anywhere in the world and it was unforgettable. Her guide was the author Bernard Fall.

The film began with scenes of disembarking and marching American soldiers, with the *Battle Hymn of the Republic* ironically on the sound track. There were images of rice paddies and helicopters, beautiful children, funerals in pouring rain and of destroyed and deserted villages, conveying the feeling that lurking in the jungle there was an invisible enemy so powerful that he was beyond the reach even of the most powerful military machine in the world.

The film was about Vietnam but not about the question of why the Americans were there. "I could not wrap my mind around that," she said. It was about "the honour of the little guy", about the victims of war which included American soldiers, their innocence and thoughtless brutality.

There was a sequence at the end of the film, shot by the cameraman Erik Durschmied from the co-pilot's seat, which Jack Gould called "without parallel in the annals of television". It showed a handsome, clean-cut bomber pilot exulting on the intercom on his mission's success as he flew over rice paddies and jungles along a curving river in an attempt to drive the Viet Cong into the open.

> There you go! Look at it burning! Just short of the treeline. Up we go! Real fine, real fine! That was an outstanding target! We can see the people running everywhere. Fantastic!... By Jove, that's really great fun. I really like doing that... I really like the Napalm because when we get there the VC are just addled because of the bit bombs, you see, it breaks their eardrums and makes them kind of senseless. Boy, we put a lot of ordnance on target. I would really like to see how effective it is.

Walker sent a personal note to Beryl Fox:

> I have already expressed to Toronto my reaction to the program but it is not unusual for these signals to die on the line down.
>
> I thought the film was tremendous. You richly deserve the international reputation you already have, and this film is yet another example of your fine creative work. Congratulations.[7]

The BBC showed the film, and so did the National Educational Network in the U.S. Jack Gould wrote in *The New York Times*:

> It is a work of art in its summation of the Vietnamese war. Miss Beryl Fox of Toronto is a producer of exceptional sensitivity and, with the camera, has caught with searing accuracy the overwhelming tragedy of war. Her program was not the shrill cry of the pacifist. It was a chilling poem of resignation to the inevitability of man's inhumanity to man.[8]

The most memorable praise came from the novelist Hugh MacLennan.

> This was the most beautiful, disturbing and moving work of art I have ever seen on television anywhere at any time. It had the indescribable beauty of absolute truth revealed in perfectly selected counterpoint. Its irony was subtler than Swift's. But unlike Swift or Orwell it was full of beauty, and that's why it was positive.

MacLennan's last sentence was the greatest tribute.

"It left one, curiously, with hope".[9]

THE ELECTION OF 1965

The new season in the fall of 1965 opened with the worst row in the history of *Seven Days*. The issue was whether, during the campaign, LaPierre was an acceptable interviewer of the party leaders when they appeared on the hot seat, as Leiterman contended, or whether he was too emotional and provocative. That was management's view.

At the outset Hogg and Haggan took the same view as management. Warner Troyer was a less flamboyant interrogator than LaPierre and, generally speaking, safer. Late in September LaPierre was ill, and Troyer stood in for him in a mock-up rehearsal in the studio while Haggan walked in. Haggan did not know the circumstances of the substitution and on September 27th reported to the Program Council in Ottawa—a top management committee—that Troyer was the interviewer. That was an honest mistake and a grave error.

When LaPierre recovered and heard rumours that he was *persona non grata* for the political interviews he made a fuss and threatened to resign. Leiterman firmly believed that not to use him would be misconstrued as "a reflection against the French

Canadian race".[1] Though "the bicultural feeling" he thought the show should have was an important point, it wasn't the only one he raised. The two hot-seat interviewers in the second season were to be Watson and LaPierre, and he wanted to establish them right away. (Watson had succeeded John Drainie as one of the two hosts.) Troyer was useful for other purposes. Leiterman also wanted to demonstrate his autonomy from management. The phrase later used against him was that he had tried to build "an empire within an empire".

No one in Toronto was prepared to lose LaPierre. Therefore, Haggan had to report to the Program Council that there had been a misunderstanding. Having previously expressed a preference for Troyer, he now had to report that he had no choice but to agree to the use of LaPierre. Haggan created the fatal impression that he was not in charge and could not control Leiterman. He suffered a serious, perhaps irreparable, loss of face. On October 12th Hogg sent him a memo. "Since we are at a time of reassessment of staff performance", he wrote, "I would bring formally to your attention Management's displeasure..." Subsequently Haggan did not receive his annual salary increment because "his supervisory performance has not been up to expectations".[2]

It was an unpropitious beginning of the season. In one respect head office's dire predictions turned out to be well founded. In the hot-seat interview with Réal Caouette, the leader of the Créditistes, LaPierre indeed failed to respond to his guest in the cool, detached, professional manner of a traditional CBC interviewer. Caouette said the Liberal Party was about to impose conscription in Quebec to help the Americans fight the war in Vietnam.

LaPierre couldn't believe his ears. "Oh, my God", he exclaimed.

The invitation to appear on the hot seat had been extended to the five party leaders openly on the air. Only Caouette and Tommy Douglas (NDP) accepted. The remaining three declined. Prime Minister Pearson preferred to be interviewed on the more conventional public affairs show *The Men and the Issues*. He did not relish the idea of the hot seat, convinced that this was not a setting in which he would shine.

He never appeared on *Seven Days*. His press secretary Richard O'Hagan was at first receptive to the invitation but in the end negotiations collapsed. In late November, there was a crisis over the allegedly unfair editing of a hot-seat interview with the Minister of Justice, Lucien Cardin. After that it seems there was a cabinet order that henceforth no member of the government was to appear on *Seven Days*. If this was the case, it did not prevent Judy LaMarsh and Mitchell Sharp from coming on the show.

There was one memorable occasion when Haggan and Watson came close to persuading Pearson to appear after all. He was in Toronto for an official lunch, after which he withdrew to his suite in the Park Plaza Hotel for a rest. Haggan contacted his friend O'Hagan and asked whether he and Watson could call on the P.M. for a few minutes to discuss a possible appearance. O'Hagan checked and the two petitioners were admitted. Pearson lay on a yellow couch in a fetal position, fingering a rose. They had a pleasant relaxed conversation, discussing, among other things, the ground rules of a possible interview. He promised to think about it and let them know.

They never heard from him.

Rich Little, Stan Daniels: Satire

THE POPE SKIT

There was another reason why the opening program of the second season was unpropitious. It contained a satirical skit about the visit of Pope Paul VI to New York. The writer and performer was Stan Daniels.

INTRODUCTION: *Pope Paul VI is leaving the Vatican as we broadcast. He will fly westwards across the Atlantic to plead among the delegates of a hundred nations for peace on earth. This afternoon in Toronto a living rosary of Roman Catholics assembled in a football stadium to say prayers for the Pope's safety during his visit to the new world.*

A short videotape excerpt from the Holy Hour and Rosary in the CNE Stadium is shown.

Yesterday the Los Angeles Dodgers clinched the National League pennant. Now this is very fortunate because had the pennant race ended in a tie, there would have to be a play-off game tomorrow. This could have posed a very delicate problem.

NBC EXECUTIVE: *Hello? Yes, operator, I'm holding on. Hello. Is this the Holy Father? Good evening, Your Holiness. My name is Limbo. I'm an executive with the NBC Television Network. That's right, Your Holiness. The one with the peacock. To come straight to the point: we've run into a little snag here. You see, our network is wiping out all its regularly scheduled programs tomorrow, in order to give absolute blanket coverage to your visit to New York. . . .Bless you, Your Holiness. But the problem is: one of our rival networks—ABC—is planning to televise an important baseball game for part of the time, in competition with us. Now, I'm sure Your Holiness would agree that it wouldn't look very good, either for you or for us, if a baseball game would get a higher rating than the pope. So, with your indulgence, I would like to propose this little plan to you which we feel sure would guarantee you an overwhelming share of the viewing audience. Now, at eight thirty p.m. tomorrow Your Holiness is going to celebrate mass at Yankee Stadium. Right? Since we're going to be at Yankee Stadium anyway, we thought it would provide just that little added attraction for the viewers if immediately before the pontifical mass we have a*

*ball game, too. We're thinking at the moment of an
exhibition game between the New York Yankees and
in your honour the St. Louis Cardinals. How does
that grab you, Your Holiness? Yes, exactly. An ecclesiastical double-header. Now then, we feel Your
Holiness could attract an even greater number of
viewers, and, incidentally, win your way into the
heart of every single American, if you would consent
to just umpire a few innings of the game. Oh, Your
Holiness is too modest: I'm sure you'd make a ter-
rific umpire. No, no, I'm sure none of the players
would dare to question your infallibility. I'm sure if
anybody started to argue with you, you could not
only call him out of the ball game, you could excom-
municate him as well. How about it, Your Holiness?
I mean, from your angle what a dramatic way of
demonstrating the new ecumenical spirit. And from
ours, well frankly, I sincerely think it would be the
biggest thing since Barbra Streisand. You will?
Thank you, Your Holiness. Now, I know you have a
very busy schedule tomorrow, what with President
Johnson and the U.N., and then all the religious
leaders, but if there's anything I can do to make your
visit to New York more pleasant, anything at all—
yes? A couple of tickets to Hello Dolly? Well, I'll
certainly do my best. But to be honest, Your Holiness, I don't think you have a prayer.*

2,370,000 adults and teenagers, an estimated 26 percent of all
English-speaking Canadians with television, watched the program.

> Those who liked it commended it for being "well done", "a
> refreshing yet harmless treatment of a usually untouchable
> subject", "good satire", etc. The main criticism, however, by
> 19 percent of all those who saw it was that it was in bad taste,
> insulting, disrespectful, rude, an attack on the Catholic
> Church, irreverent and so on.[1]

Few people seemed to have noticed that the skit was not really
about the pope at all. It was about the vulgar way in which the
American networks were exploiting the pope's visit to New York.

Rumours began to circulate that Pearson was also among those
who disliked the skit. Donald F. Theall, professor of English and
director of communications at York University, heard about
these rumours and referred to them in a speech.

> A low point in the assessment of Canadian humour was
> reached when the prime minister observed he didn't want to

appear on *Seven Days* because it had shown a skit on Pope Paul. Perhaps some of the backlash of a humourless Puritanism is a great danger to our developing successful mass communications today.[2]

Perhaps Pearson changed his mind when he had a conversation with the Archbishop of Ottawa, the Most Reverend Marie-Joseph Lemieux. The archbishop told him that he had enjoyed it immensely and saw nothing wrong with it. For many years, he had said, efforts had been made to humanize the pope; *Seven Days* had at last succeeded.

Ouimet took the position that the Corporation had no right to offend 19 percent of the viewers "for no other purpose than to amuse 50 percent, and, perhaps, not amuse them very much. I could think of cases where we would have decided deliberately to offend and shock 19 percent of the population in order to inform the whole population of something. This was not anything to do with information, it was more in the form of entertainment. This applies to jokes about race, creed, as well as to jokes about people."[3]

On October 5th, Ralph Cowan, the CBC's most persistent critic in parliament, sent a telegram to Secretary of State Maurice Lamontage: "Only a public apology from the CBC could erase our memory of this insulting event". A Presbyterian, not a Catholic, Cowan was running for re-election as Liberal M.P. for York-Humber.

Vice-President Ron Fraser, assistant to Ouimet, replied, without having consulted the producers or middle management in Toronto, that the CBC was "guilty of an error of program judgment" in allowing the skit to go on the air. It "needlessly gave serious offence to the feelings of many of our viewers, Catholic and non-Catholic alike, and we regret the mistake."[4] On November 4th Cowan made the letter public.

When Watson found out about it, he "went through the ceiling like a skyrocket" and on November 5th sent off a strongly-worded wire of protest to Ouimet. However, he apologized to him a few days later for having been "precipitate and ill-mannered... Since our direct communications in the past have been so fruitful, I hope you will forgive the rudeness..."[5]

"All is forgiven", Peter Gzowski had written when he welcomed *Seven Days* back for the new season. A year earlier he had called it the disappointment of the season. This year it was one of the highlights.

It's lost its embarrassing on-air fascination with itself—its self-congratulatory gloating over the week's mail and telephone calls; its self-glorifying promotion of programs yet to come. It now seems happy to put what it has on the air and see how the viewers like it...Great journalism it isn't—I still don't think it has raised or clarified a single issue of importance—but it is *good* television.[6]

But forgiveness was not likely to be forthcoming after the bitterness generated by the opening program.

"SLEAZY"

One of the words in the arsenal of verbal weapons senior management used to attack *Seven Days* was that it was "sleazy". It was not hard to figure out what was meant. Leiterman had the circulation-building genius of a William Randolph Hearst. Titillation was a secondary ingredient in the *Seven Days* mix but it was an ingredient nevertheless and one not favoured by head office. This was not so because they were responsive to the sensitivities of exploited and abused women. In the mid-sixties the women's movement was still in its infancy. Betty Friedan's *The Feminine Mystique* only appeared in 1963 and probably had few readers on Bronson Avenue.[1] Head office was opposed to titillation not for her reasons but because it was populated by solidly respectable guardians of puritanical virtue.

"Sleazy" was a word which repeatedly came up at the parliamentary hearings in 1966. Leiterman took exception to its use and misuse.

> It has seemed to be the case that the word "sleazy" has been applied by senior management to a number of items which I think are more probably described as controversial and which, I hope, have not been sleazy in any case.

DAVID LEWIS: *What does "sleazy" mean anyway?*
LEITERMAN: *I am not quite sure what management means by it. But it certainly gives me an uneasy feeling.*[2]

The "sleaziness" of an item in the twenty-eighth program must have given many male viewers feelings which were not uneasy at all but extremely pleasant. It was called "The Art and Price of Andress" and featured the sex goddess Ursula Andress and some reasonably discreet photographs, taken by her husband, which had appeared in *Playboy*. She was interviewed by the star-struck and impressionable young Peter Pearson.

PEARSON: *Tell me, Miss Andress, there seems to be a fetish among young stars to appear nude in* Playboy. *Why did you do that?*

ANDRESS: *It is the opening of the picture I did with my husband. He took the photos.*

PEARSON: *Do you think it is necessary for a starlet to be nude before she becomes a star these days?*

ANDRESS: *It is not necessary. Why should it be necessary? It depends which films, which stories ... You go to the Cannes festival to get attention. It's all the journalists' fault.*

PEARSON: *Oh, it's not the starlets' fault?*

ANDRESS: *The girls know that the more they take their clothes off, the more they're photographed and appear in the papers. The papers wouldn't publish the pictures if the people didn't like them.*

Among head office's objections was that the program had given a free plug to *Playboy* and had therefore infringed the CBC's policies on the sale of airtime for advertising. "Some regional commercial acceptance people felt that their own local efforts were undermined."[3]

When Leiterman testified that management's use of the word "sleazy" gave him an uneasy feeling he went on to say that it probably meant program items such as the story about Carol Doda, the topless discothèque dancer in San Francisco, presented on December 12th 1965. It was produced by Ross McLean and tastefully directed by the man Dennis Braithwaite called "the esthete's esthete", Daryl Duke.[4] An article by Tom Wolfe about Carol Doda and her troubled family background had just been published in the *New York Herald Tribune*. Topless dancing was beginning to sweep California. Carol Doda was a pioneer "who takes injections of silicone to enhance nature's already liberal endowment".[5]

This was Dennis Braithwaite's comment:

> How ambivalent is *Seven Days*! How anxious it is to preserve a facade of dignity while serving up the gamiest video dishes it can find or get by its board of censors.
>
> The show's permanent, approved and certified image is Dinah Christie, a lass as square and sturdily Canadian as one could wish for. Her counterpart in dress, hairdo, manner and deportment could be found in any small-town public library in the land. Fine, that's apparently what viewers want, or are prepared to accept...
>
> What does *Seven Days* serve up, once the image has been established? Why, a bare-breasted go-go girl from Frisco...

Seven Days may try our patience, but, confess now, isn't it in so many unconscious ways a true reflection of our own square, hypocritical, frontier-conditioned psyche?[6]

Later, before a parliamentary committee, Leiterman would not admit that he had been trying "to stretch the limits of acceptability", an activity for which he and Watson had sought the Corporation's approval. This was his justification:

We exposed the pitiful emptiness of this woman's life and a kind of morally and physically sick person, and this came across to many people... I have two daughters, one seventeen and the other fourteen, who watched the program, and this was the main point they got.[7]

But that was not the point head office got. It complained that the program had failed to make clear its social relevance and its significance to Canada.

THE KU KLUX KLAN

On October 20th 1965 the House Committee on un-American activities in Washington had begun hearings on the Ku Klux Klan. The first witness was the Imperial Wizard of the United Klan of America, Inc.

What would happen, Doug Leiterman and Robert Hoyt wondered, if they staged in the studio, without giving the participants any prior warning, a dramatic confrontation between two of the Imperial Wizard's associates, Calvin Craig, the Grand Dragon of Georgia, and his colleague George Sly on the one side, and Reverend Jim Bevel, an ardent disciple of Martin Luther King, on the other? Hoyt knew Bevel. He was close to the civil rights movement. As a reporter, he had covered Martin Luther King's freedom rides and marches as early as 1961. He had been impressed by Bevel's single-minded devotion and spell-binding eloquence. Wouldn't such a confrontation be theatre of the highest order, the kind of happening that couldn't be done by any other medium? Weren't the risks minimal?

Unfortunately they were greater than Hoyt and Leiterman had anticipated. The Southern bigots, wearing pointed hats and white gowns, kept their composure with unexpected poise while the black man was thrown off balance. The Klansmen were

Robert Hoyt, two Ku Klux Klansmen in regalia

Hoyt, one Klansman, civil rights minister: not shaking hands

cunningly hypocritical and sanctimoniously reasonable and the experienced and passionate advocate of the black cause was intimidated and tongue-tied. This had not been foreseen and Hoyt, who acted as moderator, felt he had to help the good cause along. He was forced to reveal that he was not impartial between good and evil.

But not all was lost. When the Klansmen said that fifty percent of all crimes in the United States were committed by negroes who formed only ten percent of the population, Hoyt thought the moment had come to retrieve the show, and he was right. Wasn't this a suitable subject for a conference? he asked eagerly. Wasn't the connection between crime, discrimination and poverty an important matter for discussion between whites and blacks? Yes, the smooth Klansmen replied, they had asked for such a conference repeatedly. They had been in touch with the governor of Georgia and had even contacted the president of the United States. But no one had followed up on it. Well, Hoyt said, let us be optimistic and agree here and now to have such a conference. Why not shake hands on the deal?

Nobody moved. He repeated the question. Still, nobody moved. It soon became clear that under no circumstances were the Klansmen prepared to shake hands with a black man. The point was made. Hoyt had achieved at least one memorable theatrical effect.

"They told us," LaPierre concluded, "they rather liked this 'nigra fella' but they never did shake his hand."

The producers themselves were disappointed in the item. Still, seventy-two percent of the audience found it "very interesting", and of the six items on the show it had the highest "enjoyment index": eighty-eight percent.[1] The audience appreciated that the concept was enterprising and imaginative and may have sensed that no American network would have tackled the subject the way *Seven Days* had. If it did not come off the way it had been intended, the general public thought, the producers still deserved praise for having taken a legitimate calculated risk.

Head office thought differently. The feature was...

...gimmicky and lacked integrity in the way the negro was introduced...

Conclusion: suggest we should take special care to avoid even the appearance of unfairness and trickery. Criticism of the interview might better be traced to inadequate research in preparing factual material for hard-hitting questions, and mis-judgment as to the abilities of the participants.[2]

VICTOR SPENCER

On May 8th 1965 the Department of External Affairs announced in a press release that two Soviet diplomats had been caught engaging in intelligence activities and been asked to leave Canada. They had tried to buy information from two Canadians. One of these, a naturalized citizen, had gone straight to the RCMP as soon as he was approached and, on police instructions, allowed himself to be enlisted by the Soviets. The other, an unnamed civil servant, sold them information about pipelines in Western Canada and other economic data in Canada and the U.S. He was was ill with cancer and was not expected to live. Pearson said in the House that under these circumstances there would be no prosecution. To a friend he confided that he hoped the case would die with him.[1]

It did not. The summer passed. The still-unnamed civil servant had one lung removed. A week before the election on November 8th the enterprising Tom Hazlett of the *Vancouver Province* found him. He had just been released from hospital. His name was George Victor Spencer. He admitted to the reporter that he was the civil servant who had been mentioned in the press release. On November 28th Hazlett was on *Seven Days*:

> We set up quite a James Bond operation... We staked out his house... We also set up a radio car outside. The young man sitting in it was supposed to do something intelligent if we didn't come out again. However, Mr. Spencer was very shaken but very cordial. He realized who I was and that the game was up and invited me in for a glass of wine. I eventually sent my bodyguard away because he seemed so inoffensive.

Spencer, a mild-mannered postal clerk in Vancouver, was a decorated war veteran with vague socialist ideas. Neither in the post office nor anywhere else had he had access to any information which the Soviets might not have easily obtained elsewhere. Like thousands of others, including the government, he had favoured Soviet-Canadian friendship during and after the war. He was predisposed towards the Soviets and had learned a great deal from the way they treated illness. This had not only been of benefit to him but also to his aged mother.

On November 28th, following the interview with Tom Hazlett, the new Minister of Justice, Lucien Cardin, was on the *Seven Days* hot seat. He was normally a rational and cautious man who had served with distinction in the navy during the war and had been associate minister of national defence. But he was quite capable of losing his temper when he was taunted by Diefenbaker, with whom he had been conducting a long-standing feud. He had been appointed minister of justice on July 7th.

This was his first appearance on *Seven Days*. A few days earlier he had received an invitation from the CBC in Ottawa to be interviewed. He declined, because he was going home to Sorel, Quebec. The CBC caller said that was fine, he would be going through Montreal, wouldn't he? Perhaps he might like to drop in at the studio in Montreal and tape an interview? Cardin agreed. He was told the subject was Spencer and that Spencer would be mentioned by name. It seems Cardin assumed he was going to be interviewed by the news department. If he was told he was going to be on the *Seven Days* hot seat, the significance of this prospect had evidently not sunk in. He was not prepared for an inquisition.

Once on the hot seat, Cardin must have become increasingly aware that he was getting his government into serious trouble by the way he handled himself. He was nervous, he fumbled. After all, it was one thing for a reporter to name Spencer and quite another for a minister of the crown to finger a man as a traitor and identify him by name on national television. Cardin explained that the government did not have enough evidence admissible in a court of law to prosecute Spencer successfully. Spencer was no danger to the security of Canada, he said, because of the nature of the information he had been asked to give to the Soviets. He would remain under RCMP surveillance as long as he remained in Canada. If he wished, he could have a trial. Cardin ended by saying that the government had treated him with consideration and fairness.

> Neither I, nor Mr. Diefenbaker, nor any other lawyer, could possibly have come to a different conclusion. There is no question that he was in contact with Russian officials, and I personally have no sympathy for him.

In the House of Commons, Diefenbaker made the most of the public unmasking of George Victor Spencer by his old adversary. He was at his vitriolic best when he accused the freshly elected government of vacillation and incompetence.

Peter Newman described the consequences of the debate in his column.

> The prime minister's office managed to obtain a transcript of the studio interview with Cardin and compared it with the

severely edited version that went on the air. The results deeply dismayed some cabinet ministers. With his statement taken out of context, they felt Cardin was made to sound much more positive than he felt.[2]

In this case, it was not head office which took exception to an item on *Seven Days* but the government which had translated its embarrassment about Lucien Cardin's performance into a charge of unfair editing.

Four months after the interview, on March 6th 1966, Jack Webster interviewed Spencer on *Seven Days*. He wanted to find out what had motivated him. He was unusually gentle and compassionate with him. There was not a word of complaint from Spencer that he had been unjustly treated, though on December 30th he had been suspended from the Civil Service and on January 31st fired with his pension rights cancelled. He said the RCMP had been kind to him.

WEBSTER: *Were you, George Victor Spencer, the prize sucker of the Soviet embassy?*

SPENCER: *I guess I am, Jack. I've been a sucker all my life.*

On April 10th Watson played back a segment from that interview at the end of the show. Webster had asked Spencer what he would do next.

SPENCER: *I would like to go to Russia to see things, but I'd like to live in England. I can't speak Russian. I wouldn't enjoy it there for any length of time... I would like to see some of the scientific things they are doing, especially in the field of health... I would like to get away and go to some section of England where I could quietly retire for the rest of my life, amongst my friends and relatives.*

WATSON: *Victor Spencer won't achieve this ambition. He was found dead in Vancouver this morning at the age of sixty-two.*

GERDA MUNSINGER

On Friday March 4th Diefenbaker assailed and taunted Lucien Cardin beyond endurance, forcing him to retaliate in hot anger. "For the last fourteen years," Cardin exploded, "I have sat in this House and I have watched the hon. member pummel away at a chosen political opponent, heaping abuse, ridicule, scorn, accusations and insinuations of all sorts upon him with evident delight. Of course, he could be considered by some to be a great political debater, a great fighter, except for one thing. The right hon. gentleman has a glass chin. He can't take it. He cannot take the least possible criticism... Well, I can tell the right hon. gentleman that of all the members of the House of Commons he—I repeat he—is the very last person who can afford to give advice on the handling of security cases in Canada... I want the right hon. gentleman to tell the House about his participation in the Monsignor case, when he was prime minister of this country."[1]

There was too much noise in the House for the Hansard stenographer, nor anyone else, to hear the minister clearly. Or perhaps the minister did not remember the correct name. It was not Monsignor, nor Monseigneur. It was Munsinger, Gerda Munsinger, the alluring East German lady with suspect connections with whom some of Diefenbaker's ministers had associated.

At last, thanks to Cardin's blurting out the exotic name, Canada had a sex-and-security scandal as exciting as the Profumo case in England.

On Saturday afternoon March 5th Robert Hoyt was in Studio One, rehearsing the show, when the telephone rang. A "government source" was on the line telling him that what Cardin had in mind the day before was that the associate minister of national defence in the Diefenbaker government had consorted—while he was in office—with a certain Olga Munsinger (her real first name, Gerda, was not divulged until later), and had thereby put the security of Canada in jeopardy. His name: Pierre Sévigny.

Sévigny was now out of politics. He was a forty-eight-year-old stockbroker, with a distinguished war record, having held a hill against heavy attack at Falaise in 1944. During the war he lost a leg and received seventy-two shrapnel wounds. His father had been chief justice of the Supreme Court of Quebec and was a member of the Borden government during the First World War. Pierre Sévigny was a proud man who belonged to the best clubs in Montreal.

Hoyt told Leiterman. Leiterman phoned Troyer who was on assignment in Ottawa, editing. He asked Troyer to rush down to Westmount where Sévigny resided and ask him two questions: did he know a woman called Olga Munsinger? What was the extent of his association with her? Troyer happened to know that Sévigny had a teenage daughter (as a matter of fact, Pierrette Sévigny was nineteen, her two brothers were younger), and he did not think it was right to ask a family man questions of this sort in his own home. He would be delighted to film an interview with him in his office in the morning. "Why don't you send Larry?" Troyer suggested, half-joking. Larry, of course, was Larry Zolf. As he put the receiver down he thought Leiterman would fire him for this brazen act of disobedience. But he survived.

Leiterman accepted Troyer's suggestion and dispatched Zolf, together with a cameraman and an assistant cameraman handling sound and lighting. By now the *Toronto Star* had come out with an eye-catching picture. The lead story was written by Martin Goodman.

> The photograph shows a voluptuous blonde, nude, lying in bed with a man. Ordinarily, it might be just another picture. But the woman is Olga Munsinger, an East German who was considered a security risk by the RCMP. And the man was a minister in the Diefenbaker government.[2]

The *Star* had called a number of former ministers in the Diefenbaker government, Pierre Sévigny among others, who said he had never heard of Olga Munsinger.

Zolf was to act as interviewer and director. It was a cold, dark night. By nine o'clock they had set up the equipment outside Sévigny's red-brick Westmount mansion at 33 Rosemount Avenue. No attempt had been made to conceal it: it was set up in full view of the passers-by. Other television and press reporters, including a man from *Time* magazine, had already knocked at Sévigny's door and the former minister's telephone had been ringing all day. Zolf had strict instructions, whatever he did, not to take "no comment" for an answer. The camera would be rolling from the moment he rang the door bell. Madame Sévigny, a real estate executive, opened the door and said her husband was not at home. As Zolf was walking back to the station wagon, pondering his next move, he heard the door opening again. He turned around. He saw a hand beckoning him to come back. The camera was turned on again. Zolf went back.

Once he had crossed the threshold, Pierre Sévigny, aiming for his head, began to whack him with a heavy cane. Zolf ducked, taking the blows on the padded shoulders of his overcoat. In retaliation he used a few of the gutter expletives he had picked up during his formative years in North Winnipeg. The camera picked up picture and sound.

Sévigny pursued Zolf to the station wagon. Zolf had two good legs, Sévigny one. Therefore, Zolf was faster. While the crew assembled the equipment with lightning speed Sévigny flailed

Larry Zolf knocks on door

Mme. Sevigny: Husband not at home

A hand beckons Zolf back

A cane appears

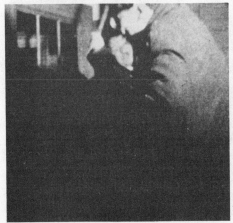

Zolf is whacked

Zolf ducks, retreats

the station wagon with his cane with unabated force. They drove off. Sévigny went back into the house and phoned the Westmount police asking them to recover the camera and film. If there was a police chase, Zolf and the crew did not notice it. At two a.m. they were back in Toronto. Zolf, much shaken and not laughing at all, reported to Leiterman and Hoyt. The lab was still open and the film went there for editing and processing, to be ready for showing the next evening. Once the editors started to work on it, the first thing they did was to clean up the sound track. They did this to protect Zolf in case Leiterman decided to sacrifice his reputation as a respectable journalist on the altar of show biz. The edited film then went under special security into the film library.

The next morning everyone agreed with a heavy heart that the film could not go on the air until the legal situation was cleared up. No solid evidence had as yet turned up to link Sévigny to Gerda Munsinger and there was danger of a massive defamation suit in case Sévigny's denials were justified.

A week later he invited the CBC to send cameras to his home. With his wife and daughter at his side, he first issued a prepared statement. Later, in response to a reporter's question, he said he had known Mrs. Munsinger "casually" and only had "a social relationship" with her.[3]

CBC management was highly critical of *Seven Days'* handling of the case. Their complaint was officially conveyed to Gauntlett.

> I must convey to you Management's displeasure over the way a *Seven Days* crew was briefed and assigned to interview Mr. Sévigny in Montreal on Saturday, March 5th, and over the events that followed.
>
> In my opinion, after considering the known circumstances, and against the background of my own previously-expressed concerns in somewhat similar circumstances, we invaded the privacy of a family who at that time was not in the public eye nor in the news except by unsupported rumour or report.
>
> Our action left the Corporation open to serious public criticism if not legal action, and in the event we put our interviewer in a potentially dangerous situation.[4]

Three weeks later, by which time "Gerda" had become a household word, *Seven Days* wanted to show the film. But management said no, even though in the meantime CBC lawyers in Ottawa had carefully examined the situation and come to the conclusion that there was no basis for any legal action. Zolf had not illegally invaded the privacy of his home. Sévigny had beckoned him in. Management objected on moral grounds.

It also said no to four other items *Seven Days* had prepared in connection with the Munsinger affair:

1. An interview Leiterman had conducted with James B. Donovon, the former head of the U.S. Office of Strategic Services and the man who had negotiated the exchange between the U-2 pilot Gary Powers and Colonel Abel, the most important Soviet spy caught in the U.S.;

2. A carefully written sketch;

3. A song with lyrics by Stan Daniels;

4. Man-in-the-street interviews.

Only an interview with a German friend of Gerda Munsinger was allowed to be shown, with a character sketch of her, and a sequence of interviews with boys of Upper Canada College. Two grandsons of former members of parliament expounded on the moral state of the nation, comparing it to the time their grandfathers were in politics.

A: *It's more evident now what's going on. I mean, it was suppressed before, I'd say. If there was any activity of this nature.*

B: *I can't really imagine my grandfather going around with Gerda Munsinger.*

A week earlier, Dinah Christie sang this opening song, with lyrics by Mavor Moore:

This hour has seven days
Of scandals, spies and sex...
Parliament is in a flap,
M.P.s are nervous wrecks.
To top it all our hockey team
Got beaten by the Czechs—
So here once more is *Seven Days*
So, sweethearts, clear the decks!

This hour has seven days
Of charges and denials.
Though Pearson recommends a probe
The Tories want no trials—
Because old Erik Nielsen says
It isn't in his files:
On *Seven Days*
Your weekly stock of smiles.

Hurray for Gerda Munsinger,
Who in the great tradition
Did what the Liberals couldn't do:
Laid flat the opposition.

Dinah Christie: Informal (inset), and formal

Hip hip hurray for Cassius Clay
An oddball he may be,
But in Toronto
He'll find lots of company.

Three days later, Robert Reguly of the *Toronto Star* scooped *Seven Days* by tracking down Gerda Munsinger in Munich. The scoop on March 11th made newspaper history. The banner headlines, normally reserved for declarations of war, screamed STAR MAN FINDS GERDA MUNSINGER. Roy Faibish, *Seven Days'* Ottawa editor, had nearly beaten Reguly, and so had *Time* magazine. The CBC news department was also hot in pursuit. *Seven Days* tried to block all telephone lines from Toronto to Germany to prevent their rivals from getting through. To rub salt in *Seven Days'* wounds, it was Norman de Poe of CBC News who finally obtained the television interview. It went on the air on March 15th.

There had been restrictions on the questions de Poe was allowed to ask Gerda Munsinger. Once the contract had lapsed, *Seven Days* wanted to do an unrestricted interview. By then her story had appeared in magazines and her price had gone down to a fraction of the original. Leiterman wanted to go ahead and submitted the interview to his supervisors for approval before it was aired.

Head office refused to agree to Leiterman's proposal.

STEVEN TRUSCOTT

During the week of March 20th the book *The Trial of Steven Truscott* appeared, written by the Toronto writer Isabel LeBourdais. Few readers were able to resist the force of her case against the conviction in 1959 on circumstantial evidence of the fourteen-year-old Steven Truscott of the rape-murder of his schoolmate in Clinton, Ont., the twelve-year-old Lynne Harper. Dan Truscott was a warrant officer on the R.C.A.F. station. The boy had been sentenced to be hanged but the Diefenbaker government had commuted the sentence to life imprisonment. The bill for the abolition of capital punishment came up in the House of Commons at the end of March and capital punishment was the one controversial domestic issue about which *Seven Days* made only occasional token efforts to be objective.

In addition to presenting an interview with the author, *Seven Days* commissioned Roy Faibish to do an interview with the boy's parents.

This was one of the few occasions when Faibish acted as on-air interviewer for the program. His main usefulness to *Seven Days* was not as a journalistic performer but as a political expert who knew—or at least knew about—all the main players on the political scene in Ottawa. A gifted young Westerner, he had been special assistant and adviser to assistant to Alvin Hamilton, the minister of agriculture in the Diefenbaker government. In 1963 he had responded to his friend Watson's suggestion to acquire television experience on *Inquiry* rather than accept Diefenbaker's invitation to become one of his economic advisers. Diefenbaker was then leader of the opposition.

Faibish was asked to interview Steven Truscott's father not because this was the kind assignment for which he had special expertise but because the Truscotts lived incognito in Richmond, just south of Ottawa, and time was of the essence. Normally, filmed interviews were ready for the dress rehearsal on Saturday afternoon, but in this case the interview could only be arranged for eleven o'clock on Sunday morning.

Leiterman had heard vague rumours that Steven had been estranged from his father and it seemed to him and Faibish that, if this were true, a conversation with Mr. Truscott might yield some illuminating revelations. Therefore, Faibish used up much of the film available on the interview with Mr. Truscott. But he turned out to be taciturn and tense. There were now only four hundred feet of film left for the interview with Mrs. Truscott. Faibish therefore decided to do something which he later considered inexcusable. In the little time available he was deliberately going to bring Mrs. Truscott to the edge of tears.

"I know exactly what I'm going to do," he told his cameraman. "I only have enough film for two or three questions. The moment you see tears welling up, cut."

The cameraman promised to oblige.

FAIBISH: *When you visit your son, does he say whether he's innocent?*

MRS. TRUSCOTT: *Well, he has said that he has just nothing more to say because he says "I didn't do it". What can you do?*

FAIBISH: *Are you able to be alone with him?*

MRS. TRUSCOTT:	*No, I believe there are six or eight tables, with four chairs around each one. And, as a rule, there are other people visiting.*
FAIBISH:	*Do you embrace your son?*
MRS. TRUSCOTT:	*Yes, I definitely have, and he knows this, and I write all the time. He knows by my letters that there is no doubt in our minds that he's innocent.*
FAIBISH:	*Is it hard not to cry when you visit him?*
MRS. TRUSCOTT:	*Sometimes.*
FAIBISH:	*Do you talk about your hopes for getting him out?*
MRS. TRUSCOTT:	*Oh, yes we have.*
FAIBISH:	*Does he know that you have never wavered?*
MRS. TRUSCOTT:	*He knows that if there is something we can do we'll definitely do it. We've written letters. My husband has. We just don't get too much response.*
FAIBISH:	*What moments are the most difficult? Birthdays? Christmas?*
MRS. TRUSCOTT:	*Christmas.*
FAIBISH:	*Cut.*

The film was not ready in time for the rehearsal. LaPierre saw it for the first time during the show. His voice was slightly hoarse, as though he had a lump in his throat, as he read the conclusion. After the word *hang* he rubbed both his eyes.

> Steven Truscott was sentenced to hang by the neck until dead. Although the sentence was commuted to life imprisonment doubts about his innocence, ladies and gentlemen, give urgency to the movement to abolish capital punishment. Next week in the House of Commons the abolition bill will get first reading.

One month later, during the *Seven Days* crisis, LaPierre's tear became a major issue. That is perhaps why in the CBC's 25th anniversary special on October 2nd 1977 three famous highlights were shown: the Coronation in 1953, Churchill's funeral in 1965 and LaPierre's tear in 1966.

Dave Broadfoot: Air farceur   Rich Little *as John Diefenbaker*

Don Harron: As Charlie Farquharson, satire

THE ORGY

At the end of April 1966 Ouimet received a call from John Bassett, chairman of the board of CFTO and a director of CTV. He was also publisher of the *Toronto Telegram*. Bassett warned Ouimet that his paper was about to publish an important story about the CBC. Ouimet thanked him for his courtesy and hung up.

The prime minister had just appointed a mediator in the *Seven Days* dispute and the parliamentary committee was in session. The *Toronto Telegram* had been waiting for almost a year to publish a story at a moment when it would be most embarrassing to the CBC and to the government. Bassett was a prominent figure in the Progressive Conservative party.

On May 2nd, the paper carried an exclusive story on its front page: THOSE SEVEN DAYS PEOPLE FILM TEEN BED SCENE.

> A seventeen-year-old girl has revealed to *The Telegram* that while under the influence of "a pill" she was photographed in bed with two youths by the rolling cameras of a crew from *THIS HOUR HAS SEVEN DAYS—DOCUMENT* programs.

> A film session last July—to simulate a teenage marijuana party—took place in a west-end Toronto apartment during the shooting of a segment of a planned documentary titled *Youth and Morality*.

There was a box at the top of the page.

> ...There's a certain code of ethics that the CBC must follow. The one thing we worry about and want to improve next year—and will improve next year—is the method of collecting information.

> CBC President Alphonse Ouimet
> in a closed circuit statement
> to all CBC employees last week.

The shooting of the scene which had occasioned this story had taken place on June 17th the previous year. The director was Beryl Fox. It had morally upset someone from *Seven Days* who alerted Sid Adilman, then a reporter for the *Toronto Telegram* and also correspondent of *Variety*. Adilman contacted Leiterman on July 19th and asked whether it was true that *Seven Days* had filmed a boy and a girl fornicating. Leiterman said of course not. If they undertook to film fornication, he added sarcastically, Adilman would be the first to know. Adilman accepted Leiterman's word and did not print the story. Leiterman was in hospital at the time, recovering from the broken legs and severe burns he had suffered while shooting a scene with the motorcycle gang for the same documentary.

As soon as he was out of hospital, he screened the bedroom scene which lasted less than a minute and decided it was of no value. He had it destroyed lest it fall into malevolent hands. It was not in any way pornographic, he thought, a good deal less so than many current art films. But he did not want to take any unnecessary risks.

The *Toronto Telegram* spared no effort and expense to locate the seventeen-year-old girl in question—she was sixteen at the time of the filming—and found her in Kamloops, B.C. They flew her to Toronto where she told her lurid tale to Frank Drea and Fred Cederberg, the authors of the story.

On May 2nd, Erik Nielsen (Yukon) rose in the House of Commons.

> Mr. Speaker, my question is directed to the secretary of state and is based on a world copyright story in the *Telegram* today... Under whose authority was such a filming set up in the CBC? Would the minister inform the House whether the RCMP or Department of Justice had been requested to investigate the possible use of narcotics in this case?

Hon. Judy V. LaMarsh (secretary of state):

> Mr. Speaker, I learned of this matter just before coming into the House. I am informed that the CBC is looking into the matter. I have a memorandum from the executive producer indicating, in his words, that the story is grossly inaccurate and in its essentials untrue. I would hope it is only a smear story and that the particulars are not accurate. However, I ask hon. members to give me a day or so to ascertain the facts, at which time I shall be happy to give them to the House.[1]

Two police forces were mobilized, the RCMP's Criminal Investigating Branch and the Metropolitan Police Department. Their report was completed on May 12th.

> There is no basis for charges being laid in connection with the alleged obscene or pornographic films. Insofar as the drug aspect is concerned, this is strictly an allegation by a 17-year-old-girl... and her story cannot be substantiated in any way. In fact, this point is strongly refuted.[2]

The exoneration did not help *Seven Days*. It had ceased to exist on May 8th.

PART THREE
THE CRISIS

Cartoon by Duncan Macpherson, Toronto Star Syndicate

'Well, that's showbiz.'

CHAPTER 6

MANOEUVRES

Never before had one program, either English or French, deflected top management—though not yet the president, Alphonse Ouimet—from its other duties as much as *Seven Days* did as soon as it was on the air. Without let-up, there were crises every week.

The man who held Frank Peers' position as General Supervisor of Talks and Public Affairs during the *Seven Days* crisis was Reeves Haggan. He had joined the Public Affairs Department just before the *Preview Commentary* affair as program organizer on business and labour. In 1963 he became General Supervisor, succeeding Bernard Trotter, one of Frank Peers' two deputies, who had left to join the staff of Queen's University.

Haggan was a different type from his predecessors. He had been a lawyer-businessman, not an academic. There were several members of the department senior to Haggan who might have been considered but they were too much in the mould of the old adult education specialists. Toronto management thought it was time for a change in the direction of populism.

When Patrick Watson produced *Inquiry* in Ottawa in the early sixties, Haggan was Public Affairs Area Supervisor in Ottawa for two years and they became friends. He had an excellent manner with politicians of all parties. He treated them all with the same slightly formal bonhommie. His relationship with Prime Minister John Diefenbaker was just as good as with the Leader of the Opposition, Lester Pearson.

In the fall of 1963 the annual Talks Conference took place at Clevelands House in Muskoka. For Haggan it was the first time he presided over the whole national department. The rank and file knew nothing as yet of the plans for *Seven Days*.

These gatherings combined solemn stock-taking, addresses from distinguished outsiders, evening performances or roastings and skits, as well as pious resolutions for the future. On this occasion, there was acute tension as the old guard of the Frank Peers era confronted the new regime. It was a raw occasion, memorable for two reasons. Haggan made a speech in which he questioned the wisdom of being unduly addicted to the virtues of objectivity. This raised many eyebrows. And secondly, an evening's performance of satirical skits went out of hand and some of the offended senior people left the room in a huff. They had looked for Haggan to keep a lid on the proceedings and when he failed to do so they concluded with grave forebodings for the future that he was not likely to assert firm authority over the new generation of producers who were social activists in a cause very different from that which had animated them in their formative years.

Born in Belfast, Reeves Haggan had joined the Royal Engineers in 1941 at the age of nineteen, studied law after the war and became a member of the English bar in 1950. His family had extensive connections in Canada and it was perhaps no coincidence that in London he had made friends with a number of Torontonians, mainly from Trinity College at the University of Toronto, who had gone there after graduation. Many of them remained his close friends. After an unsuccessful wartime marriage he came to Canada. He spent eight years with the Imperial Tobacco Company in Montreal as executive assistant to the president and in the advertising department. For the first time he came into contact with the world of the media. He became interested.

Rotund, imperturbable and sociable, he had the self-confident and self-indulgent manner of the successful, expensive, slightly rumpled barrister. He had a first-class legal mind and a gift for succinct, lucid expression. Some of his friends thought he would have advanced quickly in the Anglican church as a worldly priest. The worldliness was to some extent a façade: hidden behind it was a pronounced sense of social responsibility. Once in the CBC, he understood quickly that being in public affairs was discharging a public trust. In fact, that may have been one of the reasons why he had crossed the floor from the private to the public sector. At the same time, he was very much aware of who was a "person of consequence"—an expression he often used—and who was not. His own ambitions were not clearly defined, except that, in order to feel fulfilled, he required a sense of power and influence.

"Without power I feel naked," he once confessed to an amazed colleague late at night over drinks. (His ability to recuperate after late nights with little sleep was astounding.)

An amusing conversationalist and bon vivant, he had a much larger circle of friends outside the Corporation than most of his

CBC colleagues, including some from his postwar years in London who belonged to the circle around Lester Pearson.

In the moral, not the hierarchic, sense Reeves Haggan considered the position of General Supervisor of Public Affairs the most powerful in the Corporation. He had learned from his experience as an officer in the British Army and as an executive in a large private corporation that the way a man earns respect depends less on the organization chart than on his natural authority. He was not an organization man, and was too proud and too Irish to be a courtier. Since he had not come up from the ranks and was a newcomer to the CBC there were some who found him presumptuous and arrogant and regarded his agile lawyer's brain as that of a man not to be trusted.

He later explained his attitude:

> Let me say that loyalty to management is not a matter of any interest to me whatsoever. I think employees have confidence in management or they do not. Loyalty, to me, seems a totally misplaced word. It has been my experience, not only in the CBC but in other institutions with which I have worked, that a demand for loyalty is usually an admission that confidence does not exist.[1]

No organization takes easily to employees who pick and choose their loyalties.

•••

In 1960, without Ouimet's approval, Captain W.E.S. (Ted) Briggs was appointed executive vice-president of the CBC by the Diefenbaker government. The appointment was made at the recommendation of George Nowlan, the minister of national revenue through whom the CBC reported to parliament. Only the president and the executive vice-president were directly appointed by the cabinet.

Briggs was not the type of man Ouimet would have chosen.

His father had come over from England and settled on a fruit farm near St. Catharines, Ont. The family made considerable sacrifices to send the boy to prep school at Clifton in England and later to Upper Canada College. In 1920, when Briggs was fourteen, he travelled alone to England to begin three years as a naval cadet. He returned to Canada to work in advertising and joined the CBC as an announcer in Ottawa in 1937. Forty-eight hours after the outbreak of war he became a sea-going officer in the Royal Canadian Navy. In 1942 he received the D.S.C. for "bravery, resourcefulness and devotion to duty" and for "rendering excellent and invaluable service with convoys generally". In the previous September, while in command of the corvette *Orillia*, he had taken in tow the torpedoed oil tanker *Tachee* and pulled ninety-five survivors from the sea.

Briggs was an excellent broadcaster because he loved the English language and was a natural actor. His specialty was royal tours. The recording of his remarkable *ad lib* description of the arrival of King George Vl and Queen Elizabeth on the *Empress of Britain* in 1939 had been used as a model to train announcers for many years. It was one of the first ship-to-shore broadcasts ever done by the CBC. In 1957, when Briggs once again covered a royal tour, he said: "I can see Her Majesty across the room, looking rather tired as she smiles at all the dignitaries here, probably thinking how good a stiff belt of scotch would taste at this moment."[2]

One of Briggs' lasting services to the CBC was his discovery, and subsequent support, of Max Ferguson, the literate and witty Halifax announcer who created *Rawhide*, which for many years had a large daily audience on CBC radio. In his satirical programs Ferguson often referred to the strutting old captain with loving affection and gratitude, and wrote about him later as a memorable figure. When Ferguson had joined the staff as an announcer at the age of twenty-two, Briggs told him "In my region you can make any mistake in the book—*once!*"[3]

Briggs had been regional director for the Maritimes for fifteen

W.E.S. Briggs: Executive Vice-president, CBC, at left. H.G. Walker, above.

years when he was appointed CBC executive vice-president in 1960. In Halifax he was famous, or notorious, for running "a tight ship". He was neither Liberal nor Tory, but Nowlan had chosen him to succeed Bushnell, who had left in 1960 in the wake of the *Preview Commentary* crisis. As a Maritimer Nowlan, who was the M.P. for the Nova Scotia riding of Digby Annapolis Kings and a consistent supporter of the CBC, knew Briggs and thought of him as a no-nonsense type who would bring some order into the chaotic system and help make the Corporation slightly less *embarrassing* to his government and get Diefenbaker off his back.

During the three remaining Diefenbaker years, Briggs continued a casual drinking relationship with George Nowlan. Alphonse Ouimet did not approve of drinking, least of all with cabinet ministers. On one occasion, when the Corporation needed the minister's help to shake some millions out of the Treasury Board, Briggs took the reluctant Ouimet to Nowlan's office during a short parliamentary recess. Briggs and Nowlan cheerfully consumed a great deal of scotch in a very short time while Ouimet sipped a soft drink. The Treasury Board remained adamant. The experience confirmed Ouimet's unshakeable belief that there was nothing to be said for a close personal relationship with a politician.

Ouimet had little use for the Old Salt's endless story-telling at the end of the day, nor for the garrulous lunches downstairs in the cafeteria with all ranks. Nor he did he see the point of dressing up for dinner like an Englishman in the jungle.

For Ouimet, the temptation to find a way to move Briggs sideways once the Liberals took over in 1963 must have been overwhelming. But such a move would have exacted a heavy price. All the directors on the CBC board had been appointed by Diefenbaker. The term for most of them ended in 1964, for the remaining ones in 1965. With all these—including some recently appointed members—Briggs had an excellent rapport. They would have objected vigorously.

Moreover, Briggs had a considerable following among the staff, with the exception of the "intellectuals" for whom he had no use and who naturally had no use for him. The regional directors were friends from the time he was one of them. Therefore, in 1963, instead of making a frontal assault, Ouimet limited Briggs' responsibilities to the essentials of his job. His term came up at the end of 1965 in any case and Ouimet knew that it would not be renewed.

Haggan was skilled in dealing with Briggs. From his days in the army he understood the military—and naval—mind. The few meetings they had were pleasant. Haggan thought of Briggs as an "aging dunderhead" and considered it tactically wise to play up to him. Indeed, while only in his late fifties, Briggs was aging quickly and was increasingly crippled by painful arthritis.

While he was sensitive to Ouimet's feelings Briggs held no grudges. Once he had moved to the sixth floor of the Bronson Avenue headquarters in Ottawa and decorated his executive suite like a ship's cabin, he was unswervingly loyal to his boss. There were four rules in his code of honour. Always play the game. Never foul another man's nest. Be loyal, polite and respectful. Always lay your cards on the table.

On one occasion he laid his cards on the table for Ross McLean. McLean had produced a documentary which, while having pleased most others, had displeased Briggs. McLean was summoned to Ottawa, ushered into Briggs' office and given a mean, barbaric chewing-out. If he was acting, McLean did not notice it.

But Briggs did not always play Captain Bligh. Many of his former subordinates remember him as a compassionate friend who listened patiently to staff grievances. On his attitude towards *Seven Days* one of his former associates remembers:

> The Old Man, in the face of avant-garde happenings whether in broadcasting or in the performing arts, always trotted out this phrase: "There's really nothing that cannot be heard or seen (by the public) if presented or aired when the time is right" ... I know that Ted Briggs never objected to the airing of *Seven Days* as such, but he was greatly disturbed by its cavalier handling (to put it mildly) of people, the means to sensational ends, perhaps. Yet, perturbed, even angered by some of the goings-on, the Old Man would never have been vindictive.[4]

Briggs was rarely involved in direct confrontations with the *Seven Days* producers but he played an active and powerful role backstage in the unfolding battle. In the testimony before the parliamentary committee in 1966 it was made clear that from the beginning he had been the program's severest critic at head office. He had grasped instinctively that if he summoned Leiterman and Watson to Ottawa, had them piped into his office and given them a court martial, it would have been useless.

••••

The man Alphonse Ouimet had appointed to be directly responsible for running the English networks was H.G. (Bud) Walker, the Vice-President and General Manager of English Network Broadcasting. He reported directly to Briggs.

Leiterman and Lefolii: Absorbed in meeting

Ouimet liked Walker but was not unaware of his limitations. His choice of candidates, however, was limited. He thought of Walker as an all-round program man, on good terms with Toronto, a man of common sense endowed with a natural grasp of elementary journalistic ethics. The fact that no one could call him an intellectual was an added bonus. If anybody had a feeling for the whole country, Ouimet thought, it was Bud Walker. The "creative people" in Toronto were too self-centred and self-indulgent to worry much about the hinterland.

Walker had become an announcer in 1930 on station CKGW at the age of twenty-three. Once in the CBC he became studio supervisor, manager of CBL, and regional representative for the prairies in Winnipeg. When an administrator was required to set up and run the Dominion network, to meet commercial commitments which the main Trans-Canada network was no longer willing to absorb, he was available and duly appointed. Throughout the first decade of television Walker was useful to Ouimet in his efforts to assert head office's administrative authority in Toronto. In 1959 Ouimet persuaded him to come to Ottawa and be responsible for running the English networks from head office.

Walker did not believe in Ouimet's centralizing policies in the area of programming. The man in charge of English programming, he told Ouimet, should reside in Toronto, not in Ottawa. But he moved to Ottawa anyway, against his better judgment. Affable and conventional, he was not the man to refuse a promotion, nor was he capable of standing up to Ouimet. He was an organization man who did what he was told. His temperament was easy-going but at times he could be gruff and autocratic.

Walker was to play a key role in the coming struggle with *Seven Days*. Briggs put him in direct charge of the program and held him personally responsible for it. From his quarterdeck he treated him with humiliating condescension. There was little love lost between them and Briggs made few efforts to conceal his low opinion of him. He was constantly demanding information and Walker tried to oblige. At first, Briggs wanted to know on Tuesdays what was coming up on the following Sundays. When he was told that in a topical program the line-up was bound to change until the last moment he concluded that there was deliberate insubordination in Toronto. Or worse, attempts to outwit him.

Ouimet did not know at the time the extent to which Walker was being harassed by his immediate boss and how much he resented it. He only found out about it later. However, Walker was far from being a mere messenger boy for Briggs, nor were his actions primarily motivated by fear of the Old Man. He made many of his moves on his own initiative and in accordance with his own standards and convictions.

Ted Briggs and Bud Walker were not the kind of men Gérard Pelletier had had in mind when he suggested to Alphonse Ouimet in 1958, just before he assumed the presidency, that he should surround himself with a brains trust on whose advice he could rely.

••••

The men at the top never knew in advance what kind of trouble *Seven Days* had in store for them. Far from knowing on Tuesdays what was being planned for Sundays, as Briggs had demanded, Ottawa often didn't even know on Sunday mornings. They may have received telexes with (more or less complete) lists of the subjects the program planned to cover but that did not really tell them very much. The scripts were usually written throughout Saturday night and changed their shape constantly under conditions of semi-controlled chaos until the dress rehearsal which finished just before the show hit the air. Ottawa's fate was entirely in the hands of local management. Unless Walker could have confidence in it he could not exercise the kind of firm authority which Briggs constantly demanded of him.

It did not take long for head office to realize that *Seven Days* had raised grave questions of policy for the CBC. There was no policy against inventing an original "mix", nor against presenting serious subjects in an entertaining manner. But there was an overall policy upon which, in head office's view, *Seven Days* was infringing. It provided the intellectual basis for its battle against *Seven Days* from the first day to the last. Three weeks after *Seven Days* went on the air, E.S. Hallman, Vice-President of Programs, the senior policy expert at head office who, however, had no executive authority, wrote this guideline:

> The Corporation policy which should govern this series is simply stated. No program or series of programs can be permitted to adopt an editorial point of view or take a position in matters of public controversy. CBC journalism is free to gather and present the facts of controversy in a systematic and unambiguous form. It is free to report and to reflect the significant points of view in matters of controversy. CBC programs should avoid the drawing of conclusions which the documentary information presented does not itself support. Comment on the issues under discussion by program staff is not permitted by policy.[5]

The day before this memo was written, the CBC was subjected

to an unusually severe pounding in the House of Commons.[6] This was only partially due to *Seven Days*. John Diefenbaker was upset by the "communistic infiltration of the French network" and H.A. Olson, the M.P. for Medicine Hat, demanded drastic action, spurred on by furious indignation about the avant-garde program *Quest*. He said the whole moral structure of the CBC had "deteriorated to such an extent that the members of this House have not only the right but the obligation to have a good, hard look at who is perpetuating this kind of thing". He cited the *Declaration of Canadian Women*, which insisted on "an end to the domination by a minority who misuse the CBC to spread propaganda for perversion, free love, blasphemy, dope, violence and crime". The signatories included the president of the Ontario section of the Catholic Women's League, a former U.N. delegate and CBC director, a Quebec senator, the president of the Ontario division of the Canadian Mental Health Association and a member of the Toronto Board of Education. Olson cited Dennis Braithwaite, the columnist of the *Globe and Mail*, who asked how it was possible that "the usually circumspect CBC had managed to alienate so many of those who should be its friends and supporters".

Douglas Harkness, M.P. for Calgary North and a former minister of national defence in the Diefenbaker government, asked what had happened to the recommendations of the Glassco Commission which, in January 1963, had pointed out the need for an extensive reorganization of the CBC to secure efficiency and economy in its operations. He chastised the Corporation for taking for granted an annual increase in its parliamentary appropriations and pointed out that apparently the board of directors exercised very little control. Its powers should be increased so that it could be in a better position to lay down policy and see to it that it was carried out. But even more serious, he said, was head office's ignorance of what was going on and its inability to control programs.

The only member who came to the rescue of the CBC was Stanley Knowles (Winnipeg Centre). It was his view, he said, that in the main the CBC was doing a good job.

> I want to congratulate the CBC for being the subject of controversy. If there were no controversy surrounding the CBC, if nobody complained about anything which appeared on CBC programs, it would not be worth five cents of public money...I believe it is perfectly proper for members of Parliament to voice their criticism in a debate such as this, provided we do not dictate to the CBC what it should do. But my main point is

that with everybody else expressing negative criticism, I thought there should also be an opportunity for someone to express positive criticism.

This was not much consolation. Head office was deeply stung by the charge that it was not able to exercise effective control of programs. Ouimet had tried hard to centralize programming supervision at head office. It now appeared obvious that more effective measures had become necessary.

Action was taken in two phases, the first in early December 1964 and the second at the end of season in the spring of 1965.

In the first phase, the news and public affairs departments were put under one director, both in Montreal and in Toronto. This move had been contemplated for some time. It was not a merger of the two departments but merely a device to shorten the reporting lines. The two new heads were no longer to report to their respective network managements but directly to Ottawa.

In Toronto William (Bill) Hogg, the Chief News Editor since 1953, was put in charge of both departments, on top of Reeves Haggan. The appointment was an indication that head office did not grasp what powerful social forces the new program had unleashed, both inside and outside the Corporation.

Hogg was a small-town Ontario newspaperman, gentle, patient, fair-minded—and ultra-conservative. Highly respected by the community of news professionals, he was puritanical about objectivity and a stickler for detail. Before 1941, the year he joined CBC News at the age of thirty, he had been a political reporter for the *London Advertiser*. Leiterman and Watson liked and respected him. They thought he was "a man of dignity". Haggan, too, was rather fond of Bill Hogg. But the warmth of his affection cooled somewhat in 1965 when he discovered that Hogg had started building a file on him, no doubt at head office's instigation. The dossier was designed to justify firing him if and when that should become necessary.

Haggan took this discovery with stoicism. "You really shouldn't associate yourself with that kind of thing, Bill," he told him sadly.

Hogg's appointment as the man in charge of both news and public affairs must be seen against the background of the old rivalry between the two departments. From the perspective of the news department, its members were expected to provide the bread and butter, objective reporting, while public affairs added the jam, opinion and analysis.

The natural tension between news and public affairs was a

crucial element in the way the Corporation functioned and one of the main reasons for its moral and intellectual strength. It made it possible for the public affairs department, which was not tied to the hectic routine of covering the news, to give concentrated thought to fundamental questions of the long-range purposes of the Corporation and the overriding requirement of maintaining high standards of social responsibility.

This tension became particularly acute when *Seven Days* arrived on the scene. The news department, too, had its own esprit de corps, and it, too, had no sentimental attachment to the Corporation as such. Since the end of the war it had become more and more ambitious and expansive and had developed a number of first-class professional correspondents who demanded time on the air. *Newsmagazine* had been on CBC television since its start and went far beyond being a mere newscast. The department as a whole was anxious to stretch the definition of objectivity and produce interpretive documentaries of its own.

Reeves Haggan explained the situation to the parliamentary committee in 1966.

> When I first joined the Corporation in 1958 there was a strain between News and Public Affairs because this was a period in which News was pressing forward and Public Affairs was perhaps falling behind. At every Public Affairs meeting I attended there were continual complaints about the News Service; that they were doing documentaries, that they were taking over this or that, and this was a major preoccupation of Public Affairs.[7]

Once *Seven Days* was on the air, Public Affairs was no longer falling behind, far from it. Both departments tried to deal with topical events, often the same events. There was friction from the beginning and collisions were inevitable.

On one occasion, Dennis Braithwaite, usually one of *Seven Days'* sharpest critics, sprang to its defence in his column in the *Globe and Mail*:

> A delegation of CBC newsmen, feathers ruffled, filed into management yesterday to complain once again about encroachments by *This Hour Has Seven Days*. What makes this running jurisdictional dispute more than intramural is the news reporters' curious notion that news belongs to them and that *Seven Days*, being a public affairs show, should leave it alone... Nothing can stop *Seven Days* from covering the news, and no one should even try to stop it. Within the CBC it's merely filling a vacuum created by the News Department's lack of aggressiveness and imagination.[8]

Sometimes the war between news and public affairs had its

cloak-and-dagger aspects. One Saturday night in early December 1964, some intrepid *Seven Days* burglars broke into the news department's locked library in the television building on Jarvis Street and stole some film the show needed. When the theft was discovered the newsmen lodged a protest:

> The Guild demands that these wanderers of the night, these semi-professional merchants of the strong-arm method of film procurement, these pilferers of pictures and slap-happy exponents of the sly lie, be forbidden access to the third, fourth, and fifth floor offices occupied by the News Department.[9]

This protest may well have been the most eloquent in the history of Canadian labour.

••••

In December 1964, in the first phase of the reorganization to tighten head office's control over programming, a number of staff changes were made in Toronto designed to strengthen Bud Walker's authority. The powers of Doug Nixon, the director of programs, were severely curtailed. He was deprived of his responsibility for public affairs programming—Haggan had reported to him—and his jurisdiction was henceforth confined to the entertainment side. Keith Morrow, the director of English Networks and Toronto Area, who, like Nixon, had played a decisive role in the creation of *Seven Days*, was removed altogether. He was appointed "Special Assistant on Management Studies" at head office. Robert W. McGall was appointed the senior man and made assistant to Walker. Marce Munro was named the new head of television. McGall and Munro were to play major roles during the last phase of the *Seven Days* drama.

In the exercise of authority certain words were taboo. For example, head office could not admit to wishing to "control" the production centres. What was required was "better communications".

This is a sample memo from H.G. Walker to Keith Morrow. It was written two months before Morrow was relieved of his position.

> My criticism as General Manager is that in our honest desire to give freedom of program expression to our producers there has been just too much evidence that in doing so, communication has been lost as between management and programming. We have put management in the precarious position of being out of touch.
>
> At the risk of being misunderstood, I express the view that producers in general do not have an appreciation of, nor a particular interest in, total management responsibility. They

live only for the opportunities of artistic expression, unencumbered by management authority. The last part is the rub, of course, and has no place in a responsible national organization such as ours.

At various times when we have...become involved in a difficult program situation, I frequently hear our program people referred to as "responsible" in whom we must have "confidence"—a general hint to management probably to keep its warm breath off the necks of program people. Communication is another thing...I am determined to see that communication lines are truly working down to our program output so that management guidance, where necessary represented by your General Manager, reaches down through your supervising people to program planners and producers.[10]

Very soon after Hogg's appointment it became clear to Walker that Hogg was the wrong man "to establish better communications" with *Seven Days*, even though a month later he reported to Briggs that a good working relationship between him and Haggan had been established, and that was perfectly true.[11] But it was irrelevant. The problem, Walker began to think, was Reeves Haggan. Up to then, *Seven Days*' misdemeanors were blamed on Nixon and Morrow, and Haggan was thought to be doing his best to keep the two dynamic producers in check. Hogg's appointment had been intended to strengthen supervisory controls rather than to undermine Haggan's authority. But when Walker began to lose confidence in Hogg's ability to establish firm authority, he decided to devise a strategy to neutralize Haggan. This was the second phase of the reorganization.

The strategy was designed to take *Seven Days* out of the public affairs department of which Haggan was the head, on the grounds that it was too different in character from traditional public affairs programs to fall into that category.

There was a box on the organization chart ready to receive it— "Special Programs". Four days after the last program of the season, Walker recommended to Ouimet and Briggs that *Seven Days* be taken away from Haggan and placed under a newly appointed "Senior Supervisor" in Special Programs, to report directly to Hogg. The program had been "too demanding on the time and attention of Reeves Haggan and his departmental officials", anyway. Of course, he had to be prepared "for something less than a happy reaction from Haggan".

It may be a question of pride, or he may feel Senior Management seriously questions the supervisory guidance and authority he has applied to *Seven Days* (indeed in some measure I do). Haggan himself, however, has admitted that he has not been at all satisfied with the way things have gone this past season in his (he says) earnest efforts to guide and properly control Leiterman and Watson. Also he admits that many other important activities of Public Affairs have not had the kind of attention he, as the Senior Officer, should have given them.[12]

It was true that Haggan had some difficulty discharging his many responsibilities. His attention was far too much absorbed by *Seven Days* which, after all, was only one of many programs in radio and television he had to look after. Many producers, especially the radio producers, resented this preoccupation and also the fact *Seven Days* ate up a large chunk of the departmental budget. Sometimes, while screening—or playing back on radio—some of their programs for him, hoping for praise, he dozed off and began to snore softly. One of his friends tried to explain this to the hurt and indignant producers: "This is what Reeves always does when he's concentrating!"

While Walker was right about Haggan's over-extension it would have been unreasonable to expect him to have any insight into the nature of Haggan's authority over Leiterman and Watson. He could not know that Haggan was often quite firm with the "tiresome" producers and asked them on numerous occasions not to tackle a particular story which had appealed to them. "If you want to do that," he told them irritably, "start your own television network."

The man Walker had in mind for the job of Senior Supervisor, Special Programs, was Hugh Gauntlett, who had been assistant program director of the TV network in Toronto. Born in London, England, he had been in the RAF from 1945 to 1947, serving in Signals Intelligence in the Far East. For a time he was interpreter in Japan. From 1947 to 1950 he studied history at Balliol College in Oxford, where he received a first class honours degree. In 1951 he came to Canada and worked for four years for various business publications. A man with a natural talent for administration and good political instincts, he could have had a successful career in the academic world, in the civil service or in journalism. But in 1955 he joined the CBC, where he slowly worked his way up in program administration.

Haggan was delighted to agree to Gauntlett's appointment. They happened to be good friends. Haggan talked to Hogg and Hogg talked to Walker. Haggan said it would be a good idea to have Gauntlett as a full-time supervisor, *but of course under him*. As a matter of fact, it would be a great help. It would take some of the pressure off him, especially since Peter Campbell, the general supervisor for current affairs who had spent much of the first year on *Seven Days*, found the task somewhat less than satisfactory. Leiterman and Watson, though they liked Campbell, still preferred to deal directly with Haggan, especially in emergencies.

Haggan did not have much difficulty in agreeing to a formula which saved Walker's face. Gauntlett's title was to be "Supervisor, Special Area (Public Affairs)". On the point that mattered he prevailed. Gauntlett was to report to him, not to Hogg, though he did not have to go through Haggan when dealing with Hogg.

On June 4th Walker wrote that it would be unwise after all arbitrarily to "remove *Seven Days* from the Public Affairs departmental identification". He had changed his mind. He did not want to "apply corrective surgery only to lose the patient".

> I sense that every move we make is considered alongside the still rumoured "management is taking over" etc. It does seem possible that the removal of *Seven Days* from Public Affairs would be regarded as an act of management to penalize *Seven Days* for its sins and to adjust organizationally to allow for direct management control.
>
> I fully expect that under the new regime conflicts will be more easily avoided and resolved and cooperation increased. [13]

Gauntlett was the *deus ex machina*. Not only was he to keep Haggan in check, but also—this was of even more vital importance—he was to be groomed as his successor. [14]

●●●●

Throughout the first season Ouimet had not been directly involved in the battles over *Seven Days*.

Early in the summer of 1965 Patrick Watson met Ouimet in Watson's capacity as president of the Toronto Producers' Association. He described the meeting later:

> He's very good, you know. He's so intelligent and sharp...We got briefly on the subject of *Seven Days*. We got all wound up. He was on his way to the airport and we climbed into a cab and went tearing out together to finish the conversation. I sat with him at the airport until his plane was called and he said he was sorry we hadn't been able to talk more about *Seven Days* and I said I was, too. There was a lot of misunderstanding and I hoped we could clear it up some time.
>
> So I wrote to him the next day and proposed that the next time he was in town he try to make some time to see Douglas and me, because I would like to tell him about a lot of things that were on our minds. I guess it was fairly soon after, three or four weeks anyway, that he called and said he'd be at the

Westbury on such and such an afternoon; he was going to bring Bud Walker with him and would we come over. We spent five hours together, really knocking it out, and there were times when I was just astonished because he had to cut Walker off and tell him "You don't understand what they're saying". And this is the strange thing, because Ouimet supports Walker and has given him a lot of power and there were intimations that the president does at least dig what our intentions are, even if he doesn't seem very sympathetic to them. But Walker doesn't get anywhere close.[15]

As the beginning of the second season approached Ouimet wrote to Leiterman in reply to some information Leiterman had sent to him.

Dear Mr. Leiterman,

Your letter of July 8th was brought to my attention on my return from holidays.

It brought back to my mind the far-ranging conversations Bud Walker and I had with you and Pat Watson earlier this year on general ethics and CBC's journalistic policies.

I am sure that the fact that *Seven Days* has so well maintained its popularity gives you a lot of satisfaction which I share with you.

The goal of the Corporation and for you personally in the coming season will be to maintain that popularity without any compromise of the Corporation's journalistic policies and principles. It is a challenge worthy of your talent and it is with this thought in mind that I extend to you my very best wishes for a most successful 1965–66 season.[16]

This letter was written exactly two months before the new season opened with the battles over the pope skit and over the coverage of the 1965 federal election.

CHAPTER 7

THE STORM GATHERS

One of the reasons why Ouimet had kept aloof of the *Seven Days* battles during the first season was that he had to deal with the Fowler Committee, formally called the Advisory Committee on Broadcasting.

The new Liberal government, not much happier with the CBC than its Conservative predecessor had been, had announced the formation of the Committee on April 6th 1964, six months before *Seven Days* went on the air. Throughout the following year the Committee held informal hearings.

Headed by Robert Fowler, the Committee was not a full-fledged royal commission but merely a commission of enquiry. It had the power to call witnesses but there was no opportunity to have any of their testimony rebutted. Fowler had been chairman of the royal commission which made its far-reaching recommendations in 1957.

Ouimet's relations with the Committee were strained from the beginning. He was excellent at testifying before formal commissions and parliamentary committees but in informal one-to-one dealings with inquisitors he often appeared to them to be proud and prickly and occasionally gave the impression of holding back information or, worse, deliberately obfuscating.

On September 5th 1965, a month before the second season of *Seven Days* was launched, the Committee's report was tabled. It was almost as long as the royal commission report of 1957 and formed the basis of a White Paper which eventually led to the Broadcasting Act of 1968.

The report's critical attack on the competence of CBC head office was to have an enormous influence on the manner in which the *Seven Days* producers were to conduct their assault on senior management in the spring of 1966. In fact, it virtually gave them quasi-official encouragement.

When the report was published—a month before the election of November 8th 1965—CBC management was stunned. No one had expected quite such a severe indictment. Its tenor was clear from the famous first sentence: "The only thing that really matters in broadcasting is program content: all the rest is house-keeping". While praising the Corporation for the overall quality of its programs, it had little good to say about the way it was run. "We gained the impression," the Committee summarized, "that the CBC lacks cohesion, unity and esprit de corps."

The criticism of CBC head office on Bronson Avenue was particularly sharp. There was nothing in the building, the report said, to indicate to a visitor that it was a broadcasting organiza-tion. Besides, it was too remote from the city and there were no videotape viewers anywhere. The network people, it went on, described their relation with head office in terms of "we" and "they". Senior officers should have their feet in the cultural soil of Canadian life and the general manager should have under-standing of, and sympathy for, the creative process. Above all, there was need for fresh blood.

There was comfort, however, in a few aspects of the report which the Corporation welcomed, above all the recommenda-tion that there be one mixed public-private system regulated by one strong board, and not two systems governed by two boards, the existing state of affairs which the private sector preferred.

Still, the report greatly impaired Ouimet's prestige and it was widely assumed that his seven-year term, which expired on November 10th, would not be renewed. During the campaign, rumours were floating around Ottawa that Ouimet had refused the offer of a one-year extension, just long enough to give the government a chance to study the report. There was much speculation that new broadcasting legislation might eliminate the position of president altogether and that therefore it did not matter at all whether he received a full term of not. However, in the last cabinet meeting before polling day, with most ministers opposed to Ouimet away campaigning, it was decided to reap-point him for another full seven-year term.[1] Now, even more than before, Ouimet was determined to demonstrate to the world that he was a vigorous, efficient president.

The announcement was made on October 15th 1965, just before parliament was dissolved. It was a lively election cam-paign. In the hope that the Quebec wing of the Liberal party would be revitalized, three wise men—Trudeau, Pelletier and Marchand—were persuaded to run.

While on the hustings, the ministers had other things to do than worry about the CBC.

The secretary of state in the new government was Judy La-Marsh. That was bad news for Ouimet.

A former defence lawyer from Niagara Falls, LaMarsh was articulate, pugnacious, highly partisan and notoriously tactless. Tommy Douglas said of her that "the only time she doesn't put her foot in her mouth is when she's changing feet." She was the delight of cartoonists who portrayed her with warm affection as a dowdy, frog-like loudmouth. The most outspoken and activist of Pearson's ministers in the previous government, LaMarsh and Walter Gordon had been the leaders of the progressive forces. As minister of health and welfare, she had masterminded the Canada Pension Plan, one of the most innovative pieces of social legislation of the sixties, as well as Medicare.

In politics LaMarsh was a middle-of-the-road Liberal, by no means always on the side of the fashionable causes. She firmly

Judy LaMarsh, Alphonse Ouimet: A rare happy moment, inspecting new CBC Montreal headquarters, 1966

Canapress Photo Service.

opposed total abolition of capital punishment, probably because as a criminal lawyer she had come across some particularly abominable crimes against women and children for which she thought death the only appropriate punishment. Therefore, she was one of the few "hanging judges" in the cabinet and objected to Pearson's single-minded determination to abolish the death penalty. This was the reason she declined the portfolio of solicitor-general. She did not see how, as solicitor-general, she could have been responsible for legislation of which she did not approve.

An activist secretary of state was the last thing Ouimet needed. She was bound to spell trouble. The thing to do, therefore, was to make sure the door to the prime minister's office was always open to him. Ouimet liked Pearson—everybody liked Pearson—but he was not entirely sure where he stood with him. Pearson always said he would fix things up and then you didn't hear from him again. Still, he was the prime minister and it was certainly better to deal with him than with Judy LaMarsh.

For Ouimet the perfect minister through whom the Corporation reported to parliament was an impersonal channel, as faceless and selfless as possible. In his many years of public service only one secretary of state with whom he had to work met these criteria adequately: G.Y. Halpenny, by profession a pharmacist, who was the last secretary of state in the Diefenbaker cabinet from August 1962 to April 1963. Never having had any ambitions in the area of communications and culture he was easy to get along with. Even a solid CBC supporter like George Nowlan had too strong a personality to be entirely satisfactory. It was Nowlan who had imposed Briggs on Ouimet, for which he was hardly grateful.

Just after being sworn in as secretary of state Judy LaMarsh confessed to Watson and LaPierre on *Seven Days* that she thought she had made a great mistake going into politics.

WATSON: *Are you serious? Why?*

LAMARSH: *You become a target in politics. You completely lose your privacy. This is the price that no one realizes before, and no one who hasn't lost his or her privacy has any idea how high a price it is.*

WATSON: *This isn't a recommendation, but why don't you get out of it if it's so unpleasant?*

LAMARSH: *Well, you don't always do what you want to do. ...An election comes along. You run. You have commitments to your constituents, to the people who work for you, to your party. If I told them that I want to go home and practise*

> *law, they would scoff at you. They would ask: what is the*
> *real reason?*

LAPIERRE: *Would you have entered politics if you were married and
had children?*

LAMARSH: *I don't know. I doubt I would have been nominated...*

WATSON: *You're typecast as violently partisan, undiplomatic.*

LAMARSH: *Uncultured.*

LAPIERRE: *Uncultured, and things like that. What are you going to
do?*

LAMARSH: *What am I going to do?*

LAPIERRE: *Except bleeding.*

LAMARSH: *Well, I bleed inside, I hope, not publicly. I'm going to do
what I did before... Time proves that I can get things
done... I think I'll just go my own way.*[2]

LaMarsh was determined to make a splash as a reform politician and all her instincts were on the side of the "creative people". Moreover, she had a deep-seated hostility towards whatever she considered institutional rigidity. She had no natural penchant for the cultural field. Her tastes were traditional. She preferred *Bonanza* to *Festival*, the high-culture program of CBC-TV, and she knitted while she watched hockey.

LaMarsh's relations with Pearson were tenuous. They were destined to become terrible. She considered her appointment as secretary of state a demotion.[3] She thought Pearson was weak and spineless. She particularly held it against him that when Guy Favreau, whom she worshipped, was in trouble Pearson failed to come to his rescue. Pearson found her uninhibited, unsophisticated style crude and tiresome. Since he was interested in broadcasting, he never left her alone after she became secretary of state.

In her autobiography LaMarsh described her first meeting with Ouimet.

> I found him soft-spoken, pleasant, but quite uninformative.
> He stressed... the importance of working closely with him as
> the source of the most expert opinion for the development of a
> new broadcasting policy. He promised complete cooperation
> from the Corporation. He also informed me that the govern-
> ment could have his resignation any day it wanted, and that he
> had so informed the Prime Minister. That, at our first meeting,
> was the first time he was to refer to the Prime Minister and to
> his ready access to his office—but it was far from the last.[4]

LaMarsh thought her relationship with Ouimet should be based on a simple equation: I will battle for you and you open up for me. She was prepared "to catch the tomatoes" for him in parliament —these are her executive assistant William Neville's words—provided he gave her full information and told her the truth. While Ouimet never told anything other than the truth he firmly believed that the less of the truth he told a politician the better. He was conditioned to keep them—all of them, even the Corporation's closest friends—at arm's length. That is why he had built his headquarters on Bronson Avenue on the outer fringes of Ottawa, physically as remote as possible from dangerous and time-consuming contamination.

LaMarsh became increasingly irritated by his reluctance "to open up" and developed an extensive network of informants within the Corporation. From her point of view these contacts were entirely proper. It was her duty to know what was going on. The president didn't keep her informed, so what choice did she have?

> I have had a great many discussions since assuming this portfolio because I conceive it as part of my responsibility to keep as well informed as I can on matters within the agencies for which I am responsible or for whom I report to Parliament... You cannot do that by getting formal submissions from CBC management. You have to use all your contacts, all your friends and former friends or acquaintances. As I have said in other places, I know a great many people who work in the CBC, or have before, and many of them I have known over a long period of time. I have no doubt that anyone who had a similar position or who had similar conversations with similar individuals could reach anything but the same conclusion.[5]

It was good for her to know, early in 1966, that Ouimet was talking about resigning. Incidentally, the reference in her memoirs was not quite accurate. Ouimet offered his resignation to Pearson in March 1966—a month before the *Seven Days* rebellion—and the subject is therefore unlikely to have come up at their first meeting.[6] Pearson asked him to stay on until the government had introduced the new legislation.

By March LaMarsh had formed a firm opinion about Ouimet. She never disliked him personally and she never wavered in her support for public broadcasting. But she thought he lacked the necessary social and political sensitivity to be able to restore the CBC to its rightful place in Canadian society. She found it difficult to accept that he seemed to feel he knew better than the Glassco Commission and the Fowler Committee and his own internal study group how to run the CBC and that he resented enquiries and criticism as unwarranted intrusions. What was required was a younger man with better political sense, preferably a program man. After all, didn't the Fowler Committee report say that the only thing that should matter to the CBC was programs—all the rest was housekeeping?

••••

The second season of *Seven Days* had begun on October 3. Management was confident that its precautionary moves to tighten controls gave them reasonable assurance of a quiet fall and winter. Patrick Watson had succeeded John Drainie as co-host. It was evident from the beginning that he and LaPierre, in conjunction with the beautiful Dinah Christie, were going to be a memorable combination. Since Watson was now a performer, and therefore no longer a producer, the troublesome Leiterman-Watson axis, it was thought, was at last broken. This, in Ouimet's eyes, gave head office additional reason to assume that the program would be much easier to manage. Watson's production duties were confined to the monthly *Document* films.

The very first program proved them disastrously wrong. When Leiterman tried to establish his own authority over the way the party leaders were to be interviewed, defying corporate procedures and traditions—and when he prevailed, otherwise LaPierre would have resigned—it was obvious that even more serious challenges were to come. The row over LaPierre's role as an interviewer of party leaders was the most bitter test of strength during the entire two-year history of *Seven Days*.

This was also the occasion—right at the beginning of the season—when senior management became convinced that, once the chips were down, it could not count on Haggan to control the producers. All this was exacerbated by the conflict over the pope skit, which was also presented in the first program.

Then there was a clash over the word "homosexual" in a literary spoof on James Bond movies, presented on the second show of the season. Leiterman gave in after many days of discussions.[7] This may, or may not, have been the occasion when Briggs said that the word "homosexual" was unintelligible in Saskatchewan because there were no homosexuals in that province and, anyway, homesexuality was not a Canadian problem.

This was followed by a battle which was pure farce. The rival CTV network had scheduled the *Miss Canada Pageant* for November 14th. The exclusive rights to it were held by Cleo Productions, which had a contract with Baton Broadcasting Limited, that is, CTV. But *Seven Days* took the view that these rights did not include rehearsals and other preliminary behind-the-scenes activities and dispatched Larry Zolf and a crew to gather material for a mini-documentary. Later, he did some filming at a press conference at CFTO, having duly signed the book at the door. Since everybody knew Zolf there could not have been any suggestion of false pretences. But suddenly the climate changed. Some of the people in charge at last realized what was going on. Zolf and his crew were thrown out and an ex parte injunction against the use of the film was obtained. In the evening, Zolf gained admittance to a suite at the Royal York Hotel where many of the beauty queens from out of town were getting ready for the night, wearing pyjamas and curlers: perfect material for *cinéma vérité*.

Ottawa heard about this in two ways. The well-known broadcaster June Dennis was employed by Cleo Productions as a matron. As soon as she saw Zolf she phoned her old friend Bud Walker.

But Briggs was informed by telegram.

> This is to advise that your crew from *Seven Days* has gone beyond all bounds of decency and reputable journalism by persisting despite repeated requests and demands by us to refrain from harassing Miss Canada contestants in bed clothes at 12.45 a.m. in restricted area of the Royal York Hotel. Unless immediate action forthcoming charges will be laid.

No charges were laid. But the injunction was the basis of a lawsuit, not on the question of whether the contract with Cleo Productions included rehearsals and other background material, but whether an agent of the Crown, that is, Larry Zolf, could be restrained by court action.[8]

Walker sent a telegram to Gauntlett's home:

> This will confirm that *Seven Days* is to refrain from using film footage or any associated program material of any nature directly or indirectly associated with the *Miss Canada Pageant* including events or rehearsals leading up to the contest... This is my decision on advice of legal counsel.[9]

Watson later explained the implications of this battle from the producers' point of view.

> We were of course obeying the injunction but wanted to put on some other material that night relative to beauty contests in general. They wouldn't let us because they said it would contravene the injunction, which was legal nonsense. But in this case they said if we went ahead and did it they'd pull the program off the air and this all went on on Sunday afternoon during rehearsals. And in that case we decided that we'd better yield and we did. That's one of the few cases in which arbitrary irrational censorship has prevailed.[10]

On the Monday morning after this hassle LaPierre spoke to students at the University of Manitoba. The subject was French-English relations. During the first hour he stuck to the subject but then there was a question-and-answer period. An account of the event appeared in the *Winnipeg Tribune* under the heading HE BITES HAND THAT FEEDS HIM.

> The entire higher echelon of CBC executives should be fired because of the "gigantic failure" of the network to put the two languages of Canada into communication with one another, said controversial CBC personality Laurier LaPierre Monday...
>
> "They will have to go," Mr. LaPierre said. "...They are costing us millions. There are nineteen supervisors on *This Hour* alone. It's a miracle the show goes on at all. I guess it is very indiscreet of me to say this. They are always trying to censor *This Hour*."[11]

After LaPierre's return to the east Haggan was asked to have a little talk with him. Haggan duly made his report to Hogg.

> The remarks attributed to him in the *Winnipeg Tribune* arose out of a freewheeling discussion with the students after the formal proceedings were over. Laurier was not aware that the press was represented and indeed it is his opinion that the news report was the work of an enterprising student.
>
> He very much regrets the critical tone of some of the things he said, but points out that his judgment was not at his best since the day before had seen the difficult matter of the *Miss Canada Pageant*. He points out that the report contains a number of gross distortions... For example, the reference to the nineteen supervisors was a reference to a brief presented by the French producers to the Fowler Committee and was not in any way connected with *Seven Days*. He told me that the chitchat with the students was 'good-natured tomfoolery'.
>
> Without any prompting he offered to send an apology to the management. I replied that management had been generous enough to leave the matter to me to be settled, that in view of this fact I did not think any such action on his part would be necessary.[12]

This was Walker's reply:

> "The regrets" of Laurier LaPierre... add up to utter drivel as far as I am concerned.
>
> Anyone who is in the public eye knows perfectly well that anything he may say may be picked up and used at any time.
>
> LaPierre is a professor—he is used to public speaking—he is well known (courtesy of the CBC). He is fully aware that as a television personality he is fair game for a quote.

If he was under stress as a result of the "difficult matter of the *Miss Canada Pageant*" situation, I shudder to think what his judgment would be like if he ever had to face up to a real problem.[13]

A fair comment.

••••

By now six weeks had elapsed since the beginning of the season. Management's hopes for a quiet time were shattered. Walker was consistently confronted by attitudes which he could not help but regard as insubordinate. His authority was treated with indifference, if not contempt, and he was given the minimum of information, often at the last minute. It had become impossible for him to defend the program to Briggs and to maintain that the control mechanism he had so carefully constructed was working.

On the day LaPierre spoke to the students in Winnipeg, Walker wrote a memo to Briggs:

It is my considered view that we have reached the turning point in the life expectancy of *Seven Days*. And its span of life is for us to determine—now.

Entirely apart from the serious strain the program has imposed on senior officers at a variety of supervisory and management levels, we must look at the audience size it has achieved, and assess this against the "fire-fighting" attention the program will call for as long as it stays on the air.

Basic to the problem is the fine line between "fearless journalism", that is more or less in keeping with the stated objective of the program, and what might be identified as illegal, unethical or—at the very least—unpalatable planning and programming. This kind of program always will walk the thin borderline.

My personal attitude thus far this season has been hopefully to allow a controlled freedom for the producers subject to, what I believe to be, an attempt at responsible and firm supervision. If, within these terms, we avoid pre-judging the broadcast material, then of course we must be prepared to apply discipline where necessary after the fact—discipline commensurate with the degree of error when one occurs.

Of greater concern to me is the manner in which *Seven Days* people gather material. There have been altogether too many occasions (quite a few of which we have contained before reaching management ears) when it seems film directors have gone out under order to get a story no matter how. This has led to arrogant, threatening approaches to people; almost a suggestion of blackmail.

Very often access to a situation is gained by a "buttering-up" process, with what at first, to outside people, appears to be collaboration on a program item. Disillusionment sets in quickly when our program people are found to be going well beyond suggested terms of reference.

I cannot help but comment, as many of us have before, that the program is altogether too close to yellow journalism to be part of the Corporation's program service. In fairness, violent reactions to *Seven Days* enquiries can be expected from people in the news who, for their own private reasons, choose not to recognize any form of the right of access to stories behind the news.

An example of the foregoing occurred in the few days leading up to this past weekend when the people behind the *Miss Canada Pageant* were determined that it not only be a financial success, but that it be looked upon as dignified, important Canadian event (in spite of some of the highly controversial failures of the past, here and in the United States as well). This brought about immediate and violent clashes with our *Seven Days* people who were trying to look behind the scenes—not as irresponsibly, it appears, as the pageant people would have management believe. But any suggestion of editorial control by outside people is a fighting challenge to *Seven Days*.

I put the question to all of us then—can we go on any longer with this program and its arrogance; its determination for absolute journalistic (yellow?) freedom; its preoccupation with sensationalism; and, yes, its large audience?

My personal view is that the program eventually would kill itself anyway. Already its special kind of inquisitive audience may be tiring, but the tune-in habit still is there. But can the Corporation's reputation for integrity, fairness and responsibility as the national service stand much more of this program and its behind-the-scenes operations?

I think not. I feel we must seriously consider terminating this series within the next few weeks. And, of course, we must be prepared, if this is the decision, for the consequences. Obviously some of the criticism that would follow could be off-set by the kind of program that replaces *Seven Days*, but we cannot mount anything of real substance for a number of weeks—and perhaps not even this season.

May I suggest this calls for a special meeting today. I believe the President would want to be involved.[14]

●●●●

If Ouimet had accepted Walker's recommendation he would have spared himself and the Corporation endless agony. He would have acted like the BBC's director-general Hugh Greene who, in November 1963, had snapped his finger and put an end to *That Was The Week That Was* at the height of its popularity.

Ouimet's response to the situation confronting him in November 1965 was very different from Greene's two years earlier. Greene was a professional journalist, a former radio and television correspondent, a program man. Ouimet was not. He was a cultivated engineer, a man of high intelligence whose probity no one questioned, highly creative in a field other than programming. He had built the most extensive television system in the world. Most other large public broadcasting organizations were headed by high-level mandarins rather than programmers. It was Greene, not Ouimet, who had unusual qualifications for a top position in broadcasting.

The brother of Graham Greene, Hugh Carleton Greene had been chief correspondent of the *Daily Telegraph* in Berlin in the thirties and had been much impressed by the cabarets of the Weimar period. In May 1939 he was expelled from Berlin, became a Warsaw correspondent, and then reported the first year of the war from Poland, Rumania, Turkey, Holland and Belgium. After a stint in the RAF he became chief of the BBC's German service. In 1945 he took charge of German broadcasting in the British zone of occupation, with headquarters in Hamburg. In 1960 he became director-general.

His many achievements at the BBC included new directions for the drama department. He brought to the BBC the Canadian Sydney Newman, the former head of CBC drama, one of John Grierson's earliest disciples at the National Film Board. Under Greene's guidance Newman created a new "kitchen sink" tradition for BBC drama.

It had been Greene himself who had conceived TW3, together with Kenneth Adams, the director of television. Having fathered TW3, Greene stayed out of its way and permitted "an amiable conspiracy", as Adams called it, "to keep reference upwards as minimal as possible".[15] He preferred to defend the program afterwards to censoring it beforehand. He could do this because he had confidence in the producers and he was extraordinarily persuasive with his nervous but faithful board. When apologies had to be made they were restrained: "The BBC regrets that viewers were offended by..." He never admitted an error in judgment. When Sir William Haley, a predecessor of Greene's as director-general, attacked the BBC in a series of lead editorials in *The Times*, of which by then Haley was editor-in-chief, Greene cunningly replied with a statement Haley himself had made in 1950 in his former capacity:

If no overwhelming abiding good can be done by a single

broadcast, it is also true that one single broadcast, however bad, can do little abiding harm. As a matter of fact, far too much fuss is made about the occasional bad broadcast.

In November 1963, while TW3 was at the peak of its popularity, Greene was in bed with the flu and had more time to think than usual. He had become increasingly aware that TW3 in its second season lacked the originality and sparkle of the first year.

> During its first season the Board of Governors had backed it to the hilt, even though it caused offence to many people. They had, however, been worried by what they thought of as occasional schoolboy smut. In the second season, partly because the original spark was somehow missing, this aspect began to make them move, and I became aware that Sir James Duff, the very much respected (including by me) vice-chairman, was getting close to resignation on the issue.
>
> In addition to what the governors considered "smut" (though it seems pretty harmless now) there were a number of rather shrill and ill-directed attacks on individuals at the beginning of the second season which undermined support for the program. In fact, it had gone rather out of control.[16]

After his recovery from the flu, Greene told the board at its final meeting that he had decided to take the program off the air at the end of the year instead of keeping it on until the end of the winter.

> There was a certain sense of relief. The public reason we gave was that there was bound to be an election in 1964 . . . and that the sort of pre-election balance could not possibly be maintained in a program of that sort. That was true but not the whole truth. There had been no political pressure to take the program off. Indeed the parties hastened to announce that they had nothing to do with my decision. That was perfectly true, though no one believed them.[17]

"It was in my capacity as a subversive anarchist," he said in a speech at the end of 1963, "that I yielded to the enormous pressure from my fellow subversives to put TW3 on the air and it was as a pillar of the establishment that I yielded to the fascist hyena-like howls to take it off again."[18]

●●●●

Ouimet had no intention of following Walker's advice and cancelling *Seven Days*. He firmly believed that the political consequences of a mid-season cancellation would be catastrophic for the Corporation. Such a move would be interpreted as repressive and cowardly rather than competent and responsible. What was now required was to make sure that the producers toed the line. If they didn't, then other producers could be assigned to produce *Seven Days*. He did not grasp that without Leiterman, Watson and LaPierre *Seven Days* would not be *Seven Days*. He was certain that suitable people could always be found, usually within the organization, to perform necessary functions.

The presidential meeting took place. As a result, Walker was authorized to proceed to Toronto and present an ultimatum to Leiterman. Unless in future he accepted management's instructions without challenging them, and stopped talking to the press, the program would be taken off by the end of the calendar year, that is, in six weeks' time. Furthermore, the hot seat was to be supplanted by a more conventional round-table discussion format.

In the morning of November 18th Walker presented this ultimatum to Leiterman in the board room of "The Kremlin", the vernacular for the CBC Toronto headquarters on Jarvis Street, in the presence of McGall, Hogg, Campbell and Gauntlett. Haggan was in Halifax at the time. Leiterman was asked to give his reply by the end of the day. In the afternoon he met with his producers. It was agreed that they had no choice but to accept.

Leiterman later testified:

> I personally felt it was a dishonourable acceptance. I examined my own conscience at great length and with great concern because, you know, there comes a point where you either have principles which you believe in, or you do not, and there is always the danger, as several of my colleagues felt, that if you keep on accepting this kind of thing and telling yourself "Do not worry about it, because it is only a minor point," it is only one of a series of points and eventually you get to the point that you do not have a program that is worth producing and where you have sold out your own principles.
>
> We decided, however, that we really had no alternative. We had forty people working on the program. We felt we had a public trust to the people who believed in the program, and we thought the best thing to do was to accept what was demanded of us and do the best we could, with the hope that the process of department responsibility would bring about a swing back eventually; and we hoped that Haggan and Gauntlett and his supervisors could finally bring management to a realization that something would have to be done and that the program would have to be restored to the kind of controversy that it had always had.[19]

During the coming weeks Toronto was buzzing with stories about the forthcoming cancellation of *Seven Days*. Dennis Braithwaite wrote a column about these rumours in *The Globe and Mail*:

In response to goodness know what bureaucratic law, rumours of *Seven Days'* demise have begun to circulate at the precise moment of the show's apparent triumph over all. It is not just other CBC producers who are spreading the evil word; *Seven Days'* own top men are speculating gloomily about the chances of their program's coming back next season. Reeves Haggan, the head of public affairs, won't come right out and deny the rumours, for no show is ever really safe and it is too early to discuss renewals; besides, a little insecurity never hurts smart young fellows like Pat Watson and Doug Leiterman. There had been, in Haggan's droll phrase, internal dialogue about *Seven Days* and intense discussion of the show between him and his Ottawa superiors; nothing like a crisis, though. Are Watson and Leiterman spreading the story to create a climate of martyrdom? Certainly some of the things they are saying are ridiculous—that Alphonse Ouimet hates the show, for example. The CBC president can't afford the luxury of hating any program. My impression is that the brass is very pleased with *Seven Days*; they should be, it has put them back on the map at a time when the Corporation's image has begun to disappear into an ocean of banality.[20]

Leiterman was upset when he read this column. He immediately composed a memo to go "up the line".

We happen to consider Mr. Ouimet one of the most important backers of *Seven Days*, and we are of course thoroughly aware that without his support the program would not continue as it has.

When Vice-President Ron Fraser, assistant to Ouimet, was asked whether it was true that the president hated the show, he replied that it was "the funniest thing he had ever heard."

●●●●

A man more sympathetic with the peculiar personalities of program people than Ouimet, and more familiar with the way programs were produced, might not have chosen to keep the program on the air. It was, after all, fairly clear by now that the producers of *Seven Days* were unwilling to submit to management directives without challenging them, at a time when they had a success on their hands and were convinced the public was supporting them. They also knew that the criticism contained in the Fowler Committee report had gravely impaired Ouimet's prestige throughout the country. Still, Ouimet would not have made the decision to carry on with *Seven Days* if he had not thought he could enforce it. He was determined to prove to his critics that he was an efficient administrator who was going to avoid, if at all possible, depriving Canadians of a program towards which they had developed strong proprietary feelings.

Ouimet's course of action raised both structural and internal political problems. The structure forced him and Walker to play a direct role in programming. They were about to determine who was a suitable host and who was not—an area traditionally within the production centre's competence and not head office's. When in 1959 Bushnell had decided without consultation to take *Preview Commentary* off the air, his act would have been considered an improper interference into the prerogatives of the public affairs department even if his reasons had been acceptable.

The internal political question was equally sensitive. The programmers lived in an intellectual universe dramatically different from head office's. Only rarely was there a meeting of minds. That was as true in Montreal as in Toronto. The programmers in the French network bitterly complained of Ottawa's increasingly oppressive "interventionism", but there the situation was complicated by the all-pervasive suspicion of "separatism in the French network".[21]

Just before Christmas, Walker sent a personal, confidential memo to Hogg, confirming a previous conversation. He wrote that there were enough "compelling reasons not to renew *Seven Days* next season".

> It is possible that a program of this kind which spends much of its time with conscious non-conformism—with shooting down the establishment, with journalistic crusading, and so on—might begin to wear thin after two years. Please plan on wrapping up the series permanently at the end of this season— mid May.

He continued by asking Hogg not to renew Watson's contract.

> Watson is particularly qualified to be associated with the kind of program *Seven Days* has been, and with its termination I see no place in our organization for him in relation to current planning for the future. This is not a permanent write-off. Depending on the shape of future programming for which Watson with his special abilities might be qualified, we could perhaps consider some kind of association later on.

Leiterman's contract, too, should be brought to an end as close as possible to the termination of *Seven Days*.

> Leiterman, I feel, is at his creative best in the documentary field, and I would like to see a new contract drawn up associating him with us in the production of a certain number of documentaries, the subject matter of which will be clearly spelled out in the terms of the contract.

With the termination of *Seven Days* LaPierre, Roy Faibish,

perhaps Zolf, maybe Lefolii, and others, should be dropped. In the case of Faibish, *Seven Days'* Ottawa editor, there was a possible reason for his being on the list. He had taken leave of absence in May, June and July 1965 to work as a researcher for the Fowler Committee which had been highly critical of CBC top management. As for Haggan, Walker confirmed that he should not receive a merit increase in his salary.

> While public affairs, under Haggan, has done many good things, my feeling is the respect for public affairs recently has not been quite the same as it was—say, under Peers. I mean in terms of the former years of absolute integrity, recognized and respected internally and, I believe, externally as well. Additionally, I have been hearing altogether too much comment about unrest within the department, as well as some criticism from the regions. You are aware, of course, that some of Haggan's own people have charged him with disloyalty to the Corporation. Then, too, I must charge Haggan in terms of final responsibility for not having applied sufficiently firm Management attention to the *Seven Days* problem—this most certainly could be said of last year. All in all I feel it would be unwise to grant a merit increase at this time. In fairness to the man we must watch his performance most carefully over the next few months, and come to a constructive conclusion in his interests as well as those of the Corporation.[22]

Before the end of the year Hogg told Haggan that *Seven Days* should not be renewed for the 1966–1967 season. Consequently, Haggan, Campbell and Gauntlett had "long and solid discussions" about another program.[23] But in January Hogg told him something else. He told him that the program *would* come back, but without Watson, LaPierre, Zolf and Faibish.

Haggan never conveyed this information to Leiterman or Watson, nor did Hogg—nor anybody else—ask him specifically to do so. Haggan felt he could not have done it in mid-season without destroying the morale of the unit. Either management made the decision to take the program off the air immediately, which it had every right to do, and swallow the consequences, he thought, or it had to wait until the end of the season to announce the decision that it would come back in the fall, but with different personnel. Moreover, Haggan was far from certain that what Hogg had told him was the final decision. In his observation, senior management had rarely stuck to its guns. And indeed, throughout the next three months he heard no more about the proposal.

Ouimet was firmly convinced that it was Haggan's job to convey the information to Leiterman directly.

This was his testimony when later cross-examined by David Lewis in the parliamentary committee:

OUIMET: *It was the job of Haggan to do it.*
LEWIS: *To do what, sir?*
OUIMET: *To advise his people. He knew the wish of management. You may say that in some way it was not passed on. It was his job to do it. It is certainly not my job to talk to Leiterman.*[24]

When Haggan was asked about this at the parliamentary hearings, he replied he was not "a drain pipe through which things flow".

> I pointed out to Mr. Hogg that the public affairs department would take the traditional stand on this matter. Changes of this nature in programs, or program personnel, are carried out only because there are grave, definable program reasons for doing so, and I personally failed to see any program reason, and certainly none was adduced at that meeting, except the question of Mr. LaPierre's tendency to let his opinions show...

In another passage, he referred in more general terms to communications he received from Ottawa.

> If complaints come to me from above, which is frequent, normal, expected, and received as cheerfully as possible, I, of course, immediately try to discover what really happened. These things inevitably come sometimes fourth, fifth, and sixth hand. Somebody at a cocktail party in Ottawa says something to somebody else, and eventually ten days later I am told that *Seven Days* did this or that *The Public Eye* did that.[26]

●●●●

Although neither LaPierre nor Watson knew in the early months of 1966 what was in store for them, neither was happy. LaPierre said in an interview,

> I don't think I could last in *Seven Days* much longer. This year the show doesn't seem to *care* as much. It's falling into the same trap as all CBC public affairs shows: it's losing concern with matters of real social consequence.[27]

Watson, too, was feeling discouraged. Like many other members of the team, though not Leiterman, he was exhausted. The gruelling strain of the constant battles was beginning to take its toll. This is how he described his mood at the time:

> We're not as mischievous. We are more inhibited. We're a little sad. Because one thinks that having achieved what the program has achieved for the Corporation it would be awfully nice if it could be supported. And there's so much bland, blah talk

coming down from the top about how we're all in this enterprise together and how we must all support each other and so on, but in fact we're not supported and it's clear that what we do we do in spite of them. And that's sad. That's depressing.[28]

He and Leiterman were as close as ever. But Leiterman occasionally gently suggested to him that he was not paying as much attention to the monthly *Document* films as he should. After all, he was executive producer of the series. He thought probably Leiterman was right.

But Watson was not depressed for long. Soon he was in the throes of a new enthusiasm.

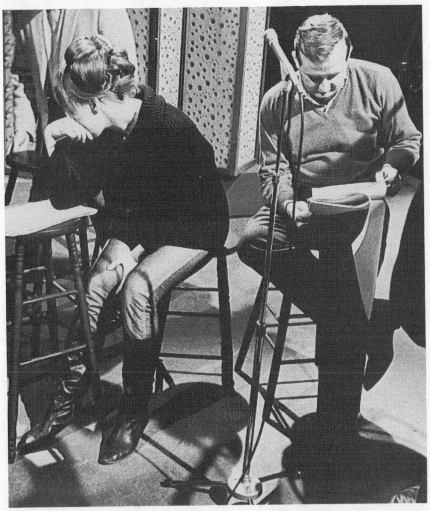

Dinah Christie and Laurier LaPierre: Can anything else be as exciting?

CHAPTER 8

TO THE BARRICADES!

No wonder Watson was excited. For the first time in the history of the CBC there suddenly arose a real chance of producing a joint English-French program of considerable proportions and he was to play a key role in it. The occasion—the centennial year of 1967. It was now March 1966.

The tensions between Quebec and English Canada were becoming critical. If any institution was designed to build a bridge between the two camps it was the CBC. The CBC's inability to "bring the two languages into communication with one another" had prompted LaPierre's outburst against top management in Winnipeg the previous November. He had called it "a gigantic failure".

Two years earlier, on February 24th 1964, an attempt had been made on the highest corporate level to bring the leading news and public affairs people from both English and French networks together at a two-day conference in the Seigneury Club in Montebello, Quebec. No man was better equipped than Ouimet to take this initiative and the speeches and the discussions about the CBC's responsibilities in this crucial area were excellent. But they had led nowhere. Even the very incarnation of biculturalism, Alphonse Ouimet, could not knock English and French programming heads together because producers on both sides were chronically disposed to respond to their own inner voices rather than to directives emanating from Ottawa. In both camps there was deep-seated resistance among producers to making propaganda for the employer's cause and a solid conviction that audiences were bored by lectures about the need to love one another. But among the best in both camps there was a strong desire to do whatever they could to prevent English-French relations from becoming ugly. Nationalist bigotry was the common enemy.

In middle management, too, there was more interest than there had ever been for some sort of *rapprochement*. Reeves Haggan talked frequently with his opposite number in Montreal, Marc Thibault, one of the wisest and most skilful supervisors in the system, a superb tightrope walker between the exigencies of the federal establishment and the Quiet Revolutionaries within Radio Canada. As time went on, another element was added to the Haggan-Thibault conversations: their growing grievances against vice-presidential encroachments.

Thibault was a good friend of Gérard Pelletier, a regular host of public affairs programs on the French network and one of the *trois colombes*—the three pigeons—who had flown to Ottawa a few weeks earlier. Thibault never concealed his sympathy for the Montreal producers' strike of 1959 and he was not trusted by head office. In particular, relations between him and Vice-President Marcel Ouimet (Walker's French counterpart, no relation of Alphonse) were strained.

In the middle of the winter 1965–1966 Haggan and Thibault had a brainwave. What about starting on an entirely new tack? they wondered. Why don't we suggest to management that they should let us gather together at some pleasant place a few of our best bilingual producers and supervisors and just leave them alone, with lots of delicious food and unlimited drink? Mightn't that generate sparks? Instead of pontifications about the Plains of Abraham and its lamentable consequences, why not stage an alcoholic happening in the Laurentians? The proposal to management was not exactly couched in those terms but that was the general idea. The eight to ten bilingual celebrants from each solitude were to form a "study group"—Watson was a member of the English contingent—and the purpose of the orgy was "to examine possible fruitful areas for co-production, assess different techniques for versioning and to consider establishment in Montreal of a pilot unit made up of French network and English network production personnel."[1]

The happening was staged at Mont Gabriel from March 9th to March 11th 1966. For everyone who was there the three days were unforgettable. The talk was boisterous and funny and extremely fruitful. Every few minutes the language switched. Nothing in Canada forms as close a bond between two groups as their natural hostility to their common enemy in Ottawa. But in this case there were additional elements to bind the two groups together: the challenge as *producers* to do something which was almost impossible—to make substantially similar but not the same programs in the two languages. This had never seriously been tried before. Usually it had been assumed that if a script was translated or dubbed and the language gap was bridged, the problem was solved. But even more serious than the language gap was the culture gap. What was significant, moving, funny or sad to one culture was by no means automatically significant, moving, funny or sad to the other.

After one long happy lunch Watson went up to his room with Jean Lebel, one of the producers of *Le Sel de la Semaine*, the hour-long magazine show on the French network which Watson admired. They had only met once or twice and did not know each other well. Watson had brought along a portable typewriter. In about an hour and a half they hammered out a plan. Four programs a year—one every three months—were to be produced with the general intention of telling Canadians how the country was doing. The working title was to be *Quarterly Report*, until a better title came along. Two program units would live side by side for a time and share staff resources, researchers, technical people, secretaries. Two independent executive producers would determine the program content for his unit according to his objectives. The arrangement would inevitably lead to socializing. There was only one obligation, to let each other know what they were doing and to regard all the material gathered as common property.

It was the perfect answer. Each group was to be left alone to decide for itself what was right for its audience, within the institutional framework of a common infrastructure. Haggan and Thibault endorsed the project wholehearted and promptly made their joint report to Ottawa:

> The unit should be established without delay to permit programming to commence in the late fall and thereby to be identified as the Corporation's most significant centennial project.[2]

Senior management was delighted with the project. At last the program people were responding to their leadership. But at the same time they must have been aware that there was danger for them in the Haggan-Thibault axis. The alliance between the two strong-minded supervisors might thwart their efforts to centralize programming in Ottawa. Moreover, neither of them was trusted. Walker had already put on paper, in a confidential memo to Hogg, that questions had been raised about Haggan's "loyalty to the Corporation", and, as to the tightrope walker Marc Thibault, he was thought to be uncomfortably close to the separatists.

For head office, there was one particular reason for exercising supreme caution. Haggan recommended that Watson be the executive producer on the English side. Obviously, no one could deny that Watson was an excellent candidate. There were not many producers of his calibre and professional competence in English Canada who were capable of undertaking the assignment. He spoke excellent French, which few of them did. He was universally liked and admired. There were other advantages. Last year's attempt to break the Leiterman-Watson combination appeared to have failed: the two of them seemed still to be far too close. At last, they would really be separated.

But, head office wondered, was he really the right man? Wasn't it he who had kept alive, with LaPierre, that aura of irreverence—no, impudence—which had made *Seven Days* so objectionable? And didn't he submit, as head of the Producers' Association, a brief to the Fowler Committee which was acutely critical of management? Was he really loyal to the Corporation?

Time was pressing. The CBC board of directors was to meet in Halifax on April 20th. Plans for the centennial year were on the agenda. A decision had to be made. But Ouimet did not want to be overhasty. Before making up his mind he asked Walker to to fly to Toronto—the date was Tuesday April 5th—and have a personal man-to-man talk with Watson, with all the cards on the table, and report back. Haggan was to make the arrangements for the meeting.

It was this man-to-man talk which unleashed the *Seven Days* crisis.

●●●●

Walker considered Watson a friend. After all, he thought of himself as a straightforward no-nonsense program man from Toronto who knew how producers' minds worked and he assumed that Watson knew his and LaPierre's contracts would not be renewed. In any case, it was not *Seven Days* that was on the agenda —there were only four more shows to go before the end of the season—but the exciting plans for the centennial project *Quarterly Report*, which was to start in the fall. He hoped Watson would pass the test and he was looking forward to the talk. When he had lunch with his assistant general manager, Robert McGall, just before meeting Watson in "The Kremlin", he refrained from having a drink. He wanted to have a clear head.

Watson approached the meeting in a very different frame of mind.

Haggan had told him that Walker wanted to have a personal

chat with him and that he, Watson, would have to make some major decisions. He did not indicate that, whether or not *Quarterly Report* was going to come off in the fall, he had been informed in January that the contracts for Watson and LaPierre as hosts of *Seven Days* would not be renewed.

Instead of trying to anticipate what Walker was going to ask him, Watson prepared himself for another battle about *Seven Days*. He had met Walker several times. He regarded him as an enemy. He felt he was dangerous because he was an over-promoted little man who lacked the capacity to use the power properly which Ouimet had so incomprehensibly placed in his hands. The previous spring, when meeting Ouimet together with Leiterman in the Westbury Hotel, Watson had observed that Ouimet and Walker were rarely on the same wavelength and that Ouimet had cut him off several times during the long discussion on journalistic policies. In a battle of wits obviously Watson would score against him and he had every intention of doing so.

While the prospect of the French-English enterprise in the fall was exciting, that was in the distant future and Watson was still totally involved in *Seven Days*. He would vehemently resist any attempt to destroy, as he put it later, "the most important artifact I had ever made." Any wrong move on Walker's part would be used against him and he took pad and paper with him to make notes for possible use later. Watson was president of the Association of Television Producers and Directors CBC Toronto, henceforth to be called the Producers' Association. He was to relinquish his duties two weeks later—and he was aware of protocol when talking to the general manager. There were strict limits to what the general manager could legitimately say to a producer without going through the proper channels—in this case Reeves Haggan. Most of the *Seven Days* people had by now accumulated so much anger against senior management and were so certain of massive public support that they were looking for any match with which to light the powderkeg. But Watson personally was not anxious for total war.

Walker opened the meeting by saying he was going to come straight to the point and be blunt and direct. "I'm arbitrarily severing the relation between you and *Seven Days*," he said. (He did not notice that Watson was jotting things down on the pad on his lap).

Two weeks later Watson described the encounter to the parliamentary committee:

There was a new program to be developed in Montreal which

he understood had originated at least in part with me—the idea for it had—and if he were able to overcome certain questions he had in mind and the management had in their minds about me, it might be possible for me to participate in the development of that program. If he were unable to overcome these questions in his mind, or to resolve them, there would be no future permanent employment for me with the CBC, but the Corporation might be prepared to consider some purely occasional contracts for the production of documentary films.

He said that management had total confidence in my professional capacity and in fact felt that I had served it extremely well and that I was one of the best producers in the Corporation, but that the reasons for separating me from *This Hour Has Seven Days* were that it was thought I had a chip on my shoulder towards management; that I was anti-management, disloyal to management, perhaps anti-Corporation, anti-president, and he said he had some questions in his mind about my attitudes.

David Lewis, a member of the parliamentary committee and subsequently leader of the NDP, then asked Watson if his words were actual quotations.

I have my notes, Mr. Chairman, which contain some quotations if the Committee requires them: "anti-president, anti-management, perhaps anti-Corporation, anti-CBC, we believe you to be 'not one of us'". And later: "We are afraid you are not with us, and I do not want anyone in the CBC who is not with us".

On the subject of my attitude towards Canada, he clarified that by saying "I do not know whether you believe in Canada or not; you have got to believe in Canada if you're going to take on such a project as we're now discussing, and I have to clarify my mind on that.

He said that my association with *Seven Days* had brought out the bad side of Patrick Watson and that he was also convening this meeting between the two of us to see whether or not he could change his mind about the bad side of Patrick Watson...

It was the management's intention to preserve the best of *Seven Days* and that meant the "thoughtful, gutsy parts"— and that is a quotation—but that the trivia would have to go... Considerable changes were planned, including the removal of LaPierre, whose feelings showed too readily; "he's clearly not with us either, and we cannot afford the luxury of a person whose feelings are worn on his sleeve"... He gave my colleague and executive producer Douglas Leiterman a vote of confidence and said he hoped he would continue with the program.[3]

As Walker talked, "a sweet sense of calm" descended on

Watson, he recounted later. He knew "he'd got him". But he gave no indication, by word or gesture, that he was going to make use of his words to "destroy him." There was doubt that he was "totally deceptive" in the manner in which he conducted himself. The interview ended on a friendly note. Walker gave him permission to report the conversation to his superiors and colleagues. As they parted they shook hands.

Walker flew back to Ottawa. Ouimet was still in the office as he arrived from the airport. Walker put his head in the president's door.

"Al," he said, "Watson's going to do it. There's no better man around for *Quarterly Report*. He's really a great guy. Sometimes we misjudge these people. We should really see more of them."

••••

The question has been asked why Haggan did not hand in his resignation the moment he heard about the man-to-man talk, call a press conference and denounce management for having made a decision affecting the personnel of a public affairs program without the supervisor's consent. During the *Preview Commentary* affair, just after Haggan had joined the Corporation, Frank Peers had first resigned, was soon joined by the whole public affairs department, then carried the fight to parliament and the press and scored a total victory.

But this situation was different. Haggan was a lawyer by training and had sound political instincts. Before resorting to a public fight he would have to feel that all possible internal means of redress had been exhausted. This was far from the case. In rare moments of optimism he told himself that he had established a good relationship with the president. They had had a number of long conversations. True, that was some time ago, before management's hard line had pushed Haggan closer and closer into the *Seven Days* camp and, in the eyes of management, put his usefulness as a supervisor in grave doubt. Still, some time the previous fall, after he and Ouimet had had lunch at the Cercle Universitaire in Ottawa and were putting on their rubbers on the way out, Ouimet had said something to him which he later thought was significant:

"Make some mistakes, Reeves," he had said jovially, "that'll make it easier for Bud. Don't always defeat him."

Clearly that meant that Ouimet, however much he respected Walker as a manager, was not blind to his flaws. Ouimet had also put his finger on the flaw in Haggan, namely that Haggan had not found the right way to deal with Walker, that he was showing his contempt too openly. Surely it was not beyond Ouimet's means at this stage, nor beyond Haggan's own, to devise some ingenious face-saving formula to extricate himself from the mess into which Walker had landed him. Haggan did not know that Ouimet was a party to Walker's personal diplomacy.

For the moment, the thing to do was to spell things out. Eight days after the Walker-Watson encounter, Haggan drafted a memo which he discussed with his departmental supervisors and sent to Ouimet.

> The Department accepts without question the right of head office to determine policy governing public affairs programming and to assess its performance. Only chaos can result, however, from attempts by head office to undertake detailed direction of particular programs and their personnel. This breaks the established lines of responsibility extending from producers through supervisors to head office and generates widespread uncertainty and distrust amongst producers which in itself compromises program control.[4]

Four weeks later Walker replied to this point:

> We do not agree that only chaos can result from detailed direction from head office. There is no need whatsoever for head office to undertake detailed direction of programs and program personnel provided the overall objectives of the Corporation are being observed and properly administered by its officers. When this is not the case, the Corporation's principal officers must exercise their final authority... If you had violent objections to the non-renewal of the co-hosts, why was this not protested up the line to me at the time the decision was made?[5]

The answer Haggan would have give to the last point is that he did not bother to do so because he did not really believe at the time that management would stick to its guns. It was by no means a foregone conclusion, he thought, that in a power-fight between head office and the supervisor of the most successful program the Corporation had ever produced he would lose. On many previous occasions head office had yielded under pressure.

But Haggan knew that his situation was very different from Frank Peers' during the *Preview Commentary* crisis. The public affairs department had stood unanimously behind Peers. Haggan knew that they were not likely to stand behind him. The department was divided. There was much criticism of his preoccupation with *Seven Days* at the expense of other programs. There was jealousy of *Seven Days'* success and criticism of its seamy side, especially by the "old guard", the adult education wing, and by the radio people.

Furthermore, Haggan understood that in the case of *Preview Commentary* the ideological issue had been clear. The CBC appeared to have yielded to attempted government interference. This time the ideological issue was not at all clear. *Seven Days* had not been arbitrarily cancelled. True, it was unprecedented that a decision had been made by top management relating to a departmental program without the consent of the supervisor. But surely this was an internal bureaucratic dispute rather than an ideological matter on which to go public and carry the country with you. It was a serious lapse but not a capital crime. Besides, if Haggan had lined up the man-to-man talk with Watson, and had known about Walker's intentions beforehand, was it really true that Walker had been "jumping lines"?

By Thursday April 14th, eight days after the man-to-man talk and the day on which Haggan sent his memo to Ouimet, Leiterman was back from Florida. The key *Seven Days* figures assembled in Robert Hoyt's house for a strategy meeting. Haggan was not among them. If the subject of mass resignations came up, it was quickly dismissed. There were four more programs to go before the end of the season. It was crucial to remain on the air. After that, there would be the summer hiatus. To give up now would hand victory over to management without firing a shot. Ottawa would cheerfully hand over the Sunday night spot to somebody else in the fall, perhaps to the news department. No, the thing to do was to "go public", to stay on the air and fight with every available weapon. Watson was uneasy about the decision but went along. Hoyt knew a great deal about the way political campaigns were conducted in the U.S. As a newspaperman he had covered the Eisenhower-Stevenson campaign in 1956 and the 1960 Kennedy-Humphrey primaries and he had travelled with Kennedy in the election campaign. In the fall of 1964 he had worked on the re-election campaign of U.S. senator Stephen Young of Ohio. Now he quickly emerged as the key strategist. Leiterman had faith in his political experience and judgment.

Once the decision was made, they contacted George Bain of the *Globe and Mail*. Leaking the story to the press was designed as a deliberate act of defiance and a decisive move to make their dispute public. At three a.m. Leiterman called LaPierre in Montreal. He told him that the morning's edition of the *Globe and Mail* would carry the story of his dismissal. LaPierre took it stoically. He told his wife that he had just been fired from the CBC and calmly went back to sleep. He only became angry later.

The next morning the story appeared on the front page.

CBC PLANS TO DROP WATSON AND LAPIERRE BUT SEVEN DAYS TO STAY.

Top management of the Canadian Broadcasting Corporation which has been uncomfortable with its successful but sometimes controversial public affairs program *This Hour Has Seven Days* has decided not to renew the contracts of the show's co-hosts Patrick Watson and Laurier LaPierre after this season.

Word of the decision so far has not become property even within the Corporation, but it may be the intention to extend knowledge of it at least to a limited circle when the CBC board of directors meets in Halifax next Tuesday.

....The apparent reason behind the dismissal of the co-hosts is to de-fang the program by removing the people who are most closely identified with it in the public mind.[6]

It was the first day of the *Seven Days* War.

Margaret Penman, Warner Troyer, Peter Pearson, Jim Carney

CHAPTER 9

THE CONSTELLATION OF FORCES

Cocktail party speculations that Patrick Watson might make an excellent president of the CBC had been circulating in Ottawa even before LaMarsh was appointed secretary of state. At a reception in the Rideau Club on October 15th for the publication of Richard Gwynn's book *Shape of Scandal*, just before Ouimet's reappointment to another seven-year term, there was talk "that some of the younger members of the Pearson cabinet favoured the appointment of *Seven Days* host-producer Pat Watson (or someone with his nerve and flair) to the job of running the CBC under the new broadcasting act".[1] Once Judy LaMarsh was secretary of state and looking openly for candidates, even though Ouimet had just been appointed for another seven-year term, it was inescapable that Watson's name should come up again.

He had first met her just after her election in October 1960 when he put her on *Inquiry*. He picked her up at the House of Commons in his Jaguar, an occasion for some merriment for her. She liked media people and they liked her. Over the years they met a few times in the studios. Watson made a point of not socializing with M.P.s and they only saw each other on professional occasions. The subject of his candidacy probably did not come up between them until after the *Seven Days* crisis had erupted.

To Watson, however, the idea was suggested much earlier, first perhaps by some imaginative technical producers or camera or lighting men in the studio with whom he got on well and who had their own quarrels with management. Half-kidding, they would say to him during a break, over a cup of coffee, "Patrick, you'd make a perfect president of the CBC," and he would laugh.

Then others suggested it to him. Gradually, the idea ceased to be a joke, especially when he sounded out his wife and close friends, who were enthusiastic about it. He did not discuss it with Leiterman until much later. Leiterman also encouraged him but apparently not very forcefully. He was skeptical about it. He couldn't really imagine that Pat could pull it off. When Hoyt, who was not close to Watson at all, heard about it after the rebellion had broken out, he was furious. He thought the personal ambition of a key member of the group was bound to cast an entirely wrong light on the campaign he was masterminding.

No doubt Watson was driven by personal ambition but he did not think of it that way. He had a romantic notion of the CBC presidency. He thought he knew what was wrong with the Corporation, had constituencies in Toronto and in Montreal, and was convinced, as was everyone else in his crowd, that it was time for a change. He actively disliked Walker and Briggs but Ouimet he liked. He had no personal rancor against him at all.

One day, probably around March 1966, he invited LaMarsh to dinner. They reminisced about the occasion ten years later on CBC radio's *Morningside*:

WATSON: *We were an unmanageable group... We ran the show, not the CBC.*

LAMARSH: *It was said that you were after Ouimet's job yourself.*

WATSON: *What do you mean "it was said"? You remember I took you out to dinner at La Flamberge on Kent Street and put it to you when you were minister in charge.*

LAMARSH: *And my reaction?*

WATSON: *You asked me whether I chased boys and got drunk a lot, and was otherwise clean or dirty, because that was the first consideration. You couldn't even talk about it if I had any blackmail chinks in my armour. Then you asked me to prepare a long extensive proposal and do some lobbying, to see if I could pick up any support in cabinet. Which I did. Thank God I failed, by the way. Since then I've thanked you silently, and Lester Pearson. I guess I have to thank Paul Martin a little bit, too.*

LAMARSH: *Did you think I was was supporting you as president?*

WATSON: *I didn't know at the time what your reaction was. You played it pretty cool.*

LAMARSH: *I didn't know either... Do you remember my begging you to stay out of the mess... for your own good, for your own future? What I meant was that you could not aspire to be president if you were an assassin.*[2]

Watson followed her advice to lobby in the cabinet. This was a sobering experience for him. He went to see Maurice Sauvé and Paul Hellyer. They asked him a few specific questions about his intentions once he was president. He couldn't answer them convincingly. Moreover, he heard that there had been some discussion about his candidacy in cabinet and that he had little support. For Lester Pearson and Paul Martin the idea was too absurd to waste time on. Also, a friend gave him some books by Peter Drucker about management. He browsed through them, shuddered, and decided that perhaps he wasn't cut out to be president after all.

Still, Watson soon became the third or fourth on LaMarsh's short list of candidates for either the presidency or the executive vice-presidency of the CBC. On the top of her list was Stuart Griffiths, the brilliantly imaginative and visionary broadcaster who had been the first program director of CBLT in Toronto and was largely responsible for choosing the first generation of producers who created "the golden age" of CBC television in the fifties. Griffiths had seemingly inexhaustible energy and high ambitions but he ran afoul of CBC bureaucracy in the late fifties and, after a spell with Granada in London, joined Ernest Bushnell at CJOH-TV in Ottawa. Bushnell had formed a high opinion of him in the forties and fifties when he was CBC program chief. Watson was embarrassed, on one occasion, when LaMarsh pumped him with indiscreet questions about Griffiths' suitability for the top job in the CBC.

One of her techniques was to throw out questions and ideas whatever the consequences, and, as Tommy Douglas had observed, tact was not her strong suit. At one time, she invited her other strong candidate, Mavor Moore, to Ottawa. He was then general director of the St. Lawrence Centre in Toronto and had been head of production under Griffiths at CBLT in Toronto. Pearson favoured him but Moore was not interested in the job and strongly backed Griffiths. Subsequently he was to develop great respect for LaMarsh, especially during Expo, but their first serious conversation had a painful beginning.

They had met once at some function in Toronto for less than a minute and naturally addressed each other formally as Miss LaMarsh and Mr. Moore. One day he received a telephone call from her secretary. Would he come to Ottawa, the minister would like to consult him on various matters. She would be delighted if he could have dinner with her in the House of

Commons. The best thing would be to come to her office first, at six.

Moore was there, on time. Her secretary asked him to wait for about ten minutes, the minister had someone with her. About five minutes later the door was flung open. LaMarsh greeted him as though they were old friends.

"Hiya, Mavor," she said. "I've got a friend of yours in here."

Moore went into her office. A subdued Alphonse Ouimet was sunk deeply in an armchair on the opposite side of her desk.

She handed Moore a scotch, sat down, put her foot on the desk, and said, looking straight at Ouimet but addressing Moore:

"All right, Mavor. What are we going to do about all those queers in the CBC?"

For Ouimet it was not Watson, or Moore, or Griffiths who was the menace, or any other conceivable candidate who may be on a short or long list, but Judy LaMarsh.

●●●●

During the parliamentary committee hearings Watson was asked directly whether he had been lobbying for the president's job. In answering the question the absurdity of the idea may suddenly have become apparent to him. Moreover, he may have felt that a bluntly affirmative answer might have betrayed the cause of *Seven Days*.

> I will say that recently, within the last few weeks, or a couple of months, I have heard my name used in this connection. I have not asked the government to give me the job and fire Mr. Ouimet.
>
> I have been asked by some friends of mine, not connected with the CBC, to produce ideas that might be useful and that might go with the job, and have given some thought to a few ideas in that direction.
>
> In fact, as I said before, any ideas that I might have to propose to the president have been available to the man who now holds the position and have been offered to him, and occasionally asked for by him. That has not been unusual for me or for any of my colleagues. They have produced ideas in that connection for the president and have volunteered them in reply to his request about how the presidency should be conducted.[3]

Eight years later, Michael Enright interviewed Watson on CBC radio's *This Country in the Morning*.

ENRIGHT: *When I was going over some biographical material last night there was one point where you were suggested as a possible president of the CBC.*

WATSON: *I suggested myself as a possible president.*
ENRIGHT: *Did you put your name in?*
WATSON: *Sure, I went down and lobbied on behalf of me.*
ENRIGHT: *How do you lobby for a job like that?*
WATSON: *Well, you go and see the people who are going to have to make the decision, which in that case were the secretary of state Judy LaMarsh and some of her colleagues in the cabinet. And I wrote up some sort of prospectus about how the CBC might be managed.*
ENRIGHT: *Why on earth would you want the job?*
WATSON: *Well, I thought it was in such a miserable state at the moment that it really couldn't be done worse and that it maybe ought to be done for a while by somebody who understood programming and cared about programming and program makers.*[4]

●●●●

On Saturday April 16th, the day after George Bain had broken the story of the non-renewal of Watson's and LaPierre's contracts in the *Globe and Mail*, the historian William Kilbourn called a press conference at the Four Seasons Motel on Jarvis Street in Toronto and said he "represented a very informal committee of citizens formed to express concern over the apparent interference with creative freedom". A respected public figure, well known for his criticism of large institutions, he was acting on his own initiative and did not pretend to be familiar with the details of the dispute. But he was an old friend of Haggan's from his days in London after the war and moved in similar social circles. Kilbourn explained his position at the press conference.

> If one of the creators of the program and two of the hosts leave the program is finished. This may be the last edition of *Seven Days*. I expect a number of resignations. I assume something will break on this soon . . . Otherwise the CBC is going down the drain.[5]

The twenty-one-year-old *Seven Days* story editor Stephen Patrick was the chief organizer of the *Save Seven Days and the Integrity of the CBC* committees. That weekend he and his colleagues and friends made five hundred calls from campaign headquarters in the Four Seasons Motel, across the street from the CBC, and six hundred people phoned in to give their support.

All leading *Seven Days* players made personal donations to pay for the rent. Afraid of exacerbating the situation, management did nothing to prevent staff and contract employees from working for the committees on company time, nor were steps taken to stop them from using CBC facilities, including making long distance telephone calls.

Among those who immediately allowed their names to be used were senators Wallace McCutcheon and Grattan O'Leary, René Lévesque, Marshall McLuhan, Maxwell Cohen, Dalton Camp, Douglas Fisher, Frank McGee, Pierre Berton, W.L. Morton and Leonard Cohen. More than a thousand people agreed to call, write or send telegrams to their M.P. or to the president of the CBC. Within twenty-four hours similar committees had been set up in other parts of the country. In Quebec City, Gilles Vignault and some well-known Laval professors came out to support the local committee. All over the country committees received pledges of support from many hundreds of people.

This is how Dennis Braithwaite described the committees in his column:

> Anglican bishops in gaiters and frock coats in the far-off Kootenays are called from breakfast (it's noon in Toronto) by a persuasive young phone-nick. The British are coming, he says smoothly, or words to that effect. A gangling professor in the red-soiled Anne of Green Gables country also gets his coded message: Gauntlett hates Overlord, or something... The organization is not only thorough - scouting names from old faculty lists, ban the bomb and end the war in Vietnam rallies—its operatives are heartlessly persistent... All these professors, United Church clergymen, deans of art and deans of law, experts on bee culture, rabbis, farm quarterly editors, girl school principals, publishers, with here and there a chartered accountant whose wife is on the local arts council—all these good and earnest souls aren't really such red hot fans of *Seven Days* ("I don't get much time to watch TV," they'll plead) but they are not the kind to turn down a chance to strike a blow at the Philistines. The great trick of the *Seven Days* crowd was getting the CBC identified in the academic mind as the Enemy: that same old CBC that has always counted on the professors' love and fealty as trustingly as John Diefenbaker relies on the solid good sense of the prairie farmer...
>
> Vociferous support from the open-line crowd would have been an embarrassment in this crusade; the academics had to be rounded up to give the thing the right tone, real class, something to spook those plow jockeys in Parliament.[6]

One day Stephen Patrick called the secretary of state, Judy LaMarsh. She did not particularly like *Seven Days*. But the decision not to renew the co-hosts' contracts "offended her respect for free speech and she sided firmly with the producers".[7] Therefore, she encouraged the rebel leaders to keep in touch with her.

Patrick told her Leiterman would very much like to see her alone, and she agreed to meet him.

> I picked him up on the corner near the CBC Headquarters Building in Toronto and asked where we should go to talk as I was due back soon in Niagara Falls. He suggested I just keep on driving. It wasn't long before I noticed that we were being tailed by a rather noticeable automobile. It was a car that was following us to pick him up whenever our conversation had run its course. In retrospect I can't think of anything sillier than a Cabinet minister driving an employee of a Crown corporation slowly down the Queen Elizabeth Highway, to be free to discuss, in privacy, a matter of public concern.[8]

The matter of public concern was the strategy Leiterman and his associates were pursuing in their campaign to have the hosts reinstated. The question very much on both their minds was how long Ouimet was likely to remain in office. Obviously, if LaMarsh could engineer a departure quickly, that would be vital information. LaMarsh was unable to give Leiterman the assurance he sought.

"Not before the fall," she told the rebel leader before dropping him just outside Hamilton so that Stephen Patrick, the driver of the automobile tailing the minister's car, could pick him up and drive him back to campaign headquarters.

●●●●

The first casualty in war is truth.

Judy LaMarsh was not the only Canadian who thought the issue raised by the rebellion was free speech. That was the way the campaign managers presented their case: they were fighting for free speech, for the right to have controversy on the CBC, against repressive, tyrannical management which was denying it. It was Ouimet's task, during the weeks to come, to try to convince the nation that this was the opposite of the truth, that it was the policy of the Corporation to extend the right of free speech to all responsible parties and that it was *Seven Days*, not management, which had broken policy by engaging on many occasions in one-sided and crusading journalism and had often used improper methods to gather information. This, he said, was incompatible with the mandate of a public institution.

Another argument the *Seven Days* people used to mobilize opinion was that the Corporation had yielded to pressure from the government to curtail the program. Among those whom Stephen Patrick approached was George Grant, professor of religion at McMaster, an old family friend whom he had known since childhood. Grant had been appalled by the interview with

Mrs. Truscott and thought Leiterman and Watson would do "anything for a good show". He had been convinced that there were certain things the CBC, as a national institution, would not do. Deliberately to set out to make this lady cry was one of them. Still, he allowed his name to be included among those who supported the campaign.

On April 18th he wrote this letter:

Dear Mr. Ouimet,

This letter is a letter of apology. In the *Globe and Mail* of this morning I see my name connected to the fuss of *This Hour Has Seven Days*. A member of the staff of that program rang me and told me that the situation was one of interference by the government with the corporation. I now recognize from this morning's paper that this is not the situation, and I am thoroughly ashamed of myself for allowing myself to have been misinformed. I think the top management of the CBC obviously has a right, and indeed a duty, to control this program.

I am particularly ashamed of this action on my part because I have long since thought that *This Hour Has Seven Days* transgresses the limits of morality, let alone good taste. Two weeks ago I refused to appear on the program to discuss theology because I did not trust the people who ran it. Its popularity arises from the fact that it appeals to the lowest instincts of the gladiatorial show.

This letter of apology is particularly necessary insofar as I should have gathered that there was something wrong with employees of the program organizing "independent committees" in their own defence.

Yours sincerely,
George Grant

●●●●

Another casualty of war is civility and good judgment. Hatred and fear take over. On April 18th Haggan and his national supervisors from radio and television were asked to come to head office in Ottawa to state their position. This was one of two tense meetings between the national public affairs department and senior management during the crisis. On both occasions news-hungry reporters were beleaguering the front door so that they had to sneak in through the parking lot at the back. These meetings were conducted like confrontations between hostile powers. The public affairs people freely expressed their feelings about the authoritarian manner in which senior management had conveyed their communications to the department in recent weeks and deplored the deterioration in a formerly civil relationship. The frigid manner in which these representations were received compelled those members of the department who were strong critics of *Seven Days*, and of Haggan's leadership, to back him unreservedly in public. Outwardly the department preserved its solidarity.

When Haggan went to Ottawa for a private talk with Ouimet this opportunity was denied to him. Instead

> ...He found himself seated in Alphonse Ouimet's office facing a semi-circle of three chairs on which sat the president and two other top officers, Vice-President W.E.S. ("Captain") Briggs and Vice-President H.G. ("Bud") Walker, General Manager of the English networks.
>
> The three men hurled accusations at Haggan for more than an hour. They spoke as if there had been no discussion of *Seven Days* before, or if there had, they had not been listening.[9]

During the two weeks following the outbreak of the rebellion on April 16th some executives on Bronson Avenue were afraid that a terminal disaster might be in store for them. They imagined that a combination of producers and politicians, English and French, with Judy LaMarsh in the lead, supported by public opinion, might force the government to take immediate action against Ouimet and his associates and arrange for some sort of interim administration until a successor is named.

Ouimet never believed for a moment that this might happen. For him the dominating fear was a repetition of the traumatic Montreal producers' strike.

Some of Ouimet's associates strongly advised him to try and come to terms with the rebels. Robert McGall, the senior man in Toronto, was one of them. Many roads were open to Ouimet. He could have formed some sort of joint producer-management committee to examine the matter until *Seven Days* was off the air. Then, *Quarterly Report* would be planned, Watson and perhaps LaPierre (who might be deflected to it in some way) would operate out of Montreal. In any case, preparations for the centennial year would absorb everybody's attention. Moreover, there was some evidence that Leiterman might have trouble mounting a third season. Maybe, as Walker had suggested, the natural life-span of a program like *Seven Days* was two seasons and no more. Had a grievance procedure been in place, as there was in Montreal, the conflict would have been contained automatically. But even without such formal machinery, any number of holding operations customary in labour-management disputes could have been devised. But Ouimet spurned them all. For him the first priority was to reassert the Corporation's authority. He had no doubt that he would carry his board with him.

••••

Ouimet, as chairman, set the agenda for the board meetings and kept the directors informed on CBC matters throughout the year. He did this formally, through letters and briefs, and informally, by telephone. Briggs, as executive vice-president, was also a member of the board. The other members were laypersons, appointed by the cabinet from the professions, the universities and business. They received an honorarium of a hundred dollars a day while attending the meetings, which usually took three days, every two months. (During the *Seven Days* crisis, the board met three times, at the end of April, May and June.) In effect, this meant that they were performing their duties at considerable personal expense. Normally the board consisted of nine lay directors, but at the time of the crisis there were three vacancies. One director had recently died, and the other two vacancies had not been filled when the three-year term of the incumbents had expired.

The most vigorous member of the board was Edmund Boyd Osler of Winnipeg who, apart from being director of several financial institutions, was active in the Winnipeg theatre and the author of a book on Riel. He was, even more than the other members of the board, wooed by the *Save Seven Days* committees and Leiterman made a particular point of keeping in touch with him.

The others were Dr. James Beveridge, president of Acadia University in Wolfville, N.S., the father of seven children; David M. MacAuley, dean of men at Mount Allison University, in Sackville, N.B., an intelligence officer during World War Two; Dr. Stephanie Potoski who practiced medicine with her husband in Yorkton, Sask., and in 1961 had been a Canadian delegate to the World Union of Catholic Women in Rome; André Raynault, the director of the department of economics at the University of Montreal, who was adviser to the commission on bilingualism and biculturalism; and, finally, John G. Prentice from Vancouver. Born in Vienna, he had come to Canada in 1938 and become president of Canadian Forest Products, Ltd., as well as president of the Vancouver Theatre Association and the Playhouse Theatre.

The board had considerable admiration and affection for Ouimet, but they were, in various degrees, independent thinkers and not shy about expressing critical views about CBC management. But they unanimously shared with management a feeling of hot indignation when on April 21st the dispute was put on the agenda of the parliamentary committee and when, ten days later, Prime Minister Lester Pearson appointed a mediator.

Osler remembers:

> I think we could have solved the problem, but the moment word came to our meeting that this had been referred to a parliamentary committee, our backs went up just like that... Every single one of that group had the attitude that they didn't care a damn about anything other than their job and I think every single one of them felt sabotaged by the government... It's very nice being on the CBC board but it's a waste of time unless you can express yourself and do something.[10]

During the three board meetings in which they considered the *Seven Days* dispute—especially the last one, at the end of June—the members made ample use of their opportunities to express themselves.

••••

Throughout the crisis Alphonse Ouimet was prepared to make minor concessions, but on the central point—the non-renewal of the two co-hosts' contracts—he consistently refused to negotiate. Since Watson certainly, and perhaps also LaPierre, were going to be involved in *Quarterly Report* anyway, it should not be too hard, he thought, to stick adamantly to this matter of principle. He remained firm on this point to the end.

For Haggan, Ouimet's intransigence was acutely depressing. Haggan was at his best in small meetings, not on the barricades. He had no faith in the open battle and did not think *Seven Days* could win. If the *Seven Days* ship was doomed, he preferred to go down with it, his self-respect fully intact. He found Leiterman increasingly tiresome and had little patience with his humourless self-righteousness. At the same time he considered him something close to a genius, a uniquely superb practitioner of his craft, and he knew that good men were invariably hard to live with. He knew that if one wanted to achieve something, one simply had to put up with difficult people. That was the price to pay, it was part of the job. There was no other way.

Haggan believed *Seven Days* was an important achievement, a significant step forward in broadcast journalism, and an expression of something important that was happening in Canada. But it wasn't his creation and he didn't really like it very much. Nor, for that matter, did he have any real enthusiasm for any other radio or television program. He was not an enthusiast by nature. There was much in *Seven Days* that was below his aesthetic and moral standards, though nothing, in his view, which could conceivably justify management's attempt, in George Bain's phrase, "to de-fang" it. To him that was the action of an insensitive technocrat who had surrounded himself with philistines. In the interest of the CBC it was time these people left.

If Haggan had no clearer war aims, this was partly due to the increasingly heavy emotional strain under which he lived. There were too many late nights and too much gloom. With the important exception of his memorable appearance before the parliamentary committee he did not exercise much leadership between April and July when the final curtain fell. Going down with the ship with honour was hardly a process which permitted much forward movement. With an ever-increasing sense of revulsion he allowed events to take their course.

He saw clearly that this was not an ideological battle on the issue of free speech. The issue for him was management's competence. From the beginning, he had considered management's handling of *Seven Days* grossly inefficient. Only a president who was tone-deaf to the requirements of program-making, he thought, would have expected a man like Walker to exercise final editorial judgments in a journalistic enterprise light years removed from the universe in which he lived. Ouimet's failure to create a climate of confidence between his people and the program people in Toronto seemed to him an incomprehensible, fatal act of omission. That Haggan himself had contributed to this bad climate by not making any effort to develop a technique to deal with Walker did not occur to him at all. That would have been an easy thing to do, but he thought life was too short to have bothered with it.

Haggan considered himself in the straight line of succession from Frank Peers, the "Mr. Integrity" of the *Preview Commentary* affair, and assumed the role of the "Conscience of the Corporation" without having Peers' scholarly, austere personality. For head office, Peers' intellectual and moral qualities had at times been a little hard to deal with but Haggan's self-indulgent conviviality was anathema to it and so was his lack of attention to bureaucratic detail and hierarchic protocol. While he was far too experienced an organization man ever to disregard a direct order, there were few direct orders to disregard and he did not conceal his contempt for his superiors other than Ouimet. He thought they were not only second-rate but also confused and cowardly.

Another matter which worried senior management was Hag-

Stuart Keate: mediator

gan's relationship to politicians. During his years as area supervisor for public affairs in Ottawa he had become acquainted with many of them. His successor and close friend was Bernard Ostry, one of the most skilled lobbyists in the capital.

Eleven years earlier, in 1955, Ostry had made a splash on the Canadian academic and political scene with a sharply critical book about the rise of Mackenzie King. He had written it jointly with Henry Ferns, the Canadian professor of history at Birmingham University. Originally from Flin Flon in Northern Manitoba, handsome, elegant and a little aloof, Ostry was not the sort of man whose back one was tempted to slap in a smoke-filled room. Ostry was socially ambitious and fascinated by the political process. But he was too much of an outsider to seek political office for himself. The CBC's Ottawa job was perfect for him.

Like Haggan, he made a distinction between his duties to the CBC and his duties to CBC management. In management's mind the two were the same.

From the perspective of Bronson Avenue, Ostry and Haggan—and, of course, Roy Faibish—were moving in the shadowy and sinister world of political intrigue and conspiracy. No doubt it was true that Haggan and Ostry were giving their views on the shortcomings of CBC top management to a lot of people. For head office, that was bad enough. But to go further and solicit support from politicians or media people for an anti-management position in an internal dispute was deeply offensive to them. It was one thing to have young Stephen Patrick of the *Save Seven Days and the Integrity of the CBC* committees phone people like George Grant and tell them that they had better come out and protect the Corporation from government interference but it was quite another to have seasoned, well-connected, public affairs officials suggest to politicians of all parties to take a position on this issue. That was intolerable, unforgivable. The current joke was that *Seven Days* people —not Haggan or Ostry—phoned members of the government and asked them to come out and protect the CBC from government interference. A joke is only funny if it is at least half true.

If Haggan was deeply pessimistic, Leiterman was the opposite. He was an adherent to an optimistic religion which denied the reality of obstacles, pain and death. He was confident he would win and his confidence grew as the battle became more bitter. Nothing was further from his objectives than to topple Ouimet. His rebellion had only one aim—to preserve *Seven Days*. Ostensibly his aim was to have the two enormously popular hosts reinstated. That was a concrete issue which everybody could understand and for which he could rally popular support and —this was of great tactical importance—the support of his fellow producers. But actually he had already faced the possibility of losing Watson to *Quarterly Report* and was also prepared to yield LaPierre. However, it would have been fatal to say so publicly at this stage. In any case, he hoped that *Quarterly Report* would establish some working relationship with *Seven Days* as well as with *Le Sel de la Semaine*. When management found out about that intention it thought it was a diabolical plot. But a strong practical argument could be advanced for these connections. Both programs had existing resource-bases which *Quarterly Report* had not.

There was no question that at every step Leiterman was willing to make concessions. He was prepared to do without "sleazy items". He had already surrendered the "hot seat" which the public department had never conceded. He was in fact more conciliatory than the department. Watson and others kept urging him to be more "cunning" in his strategies. He seemed to them too naive, too straightforward.

Leiterman was convinced that the only way to preserve *Seven Days* was to engage the public in the resistance movement. He did not believe there was a chance any longer, using normal internal channels, that he or anybody else could persuade Ouimet to give in. To Leiterman, Haggan's point that management was incompetent did not seem an argument that would rouse the nation. Only the freedom issue had the required appeal.

Unlike Haggan, Leiterman had some of the attributes of a demagogue. Demagogues deal with moral black-and-white issues, not with questions of bureaucratic competence. It was he and his colleagues, he thought, who were the real servants of the CBC mandate. Management was an aberration, betraying it. Leiterman felt like Martin Luther fighting Pope Leo Xth, the head—in Luther's opinion—of a hollow, secularized, power-hungry, self-perpetuating, corrupt bureaucratic church which had become meaningless and lived off the proceeds of the original Christian message.

Only he, Leiterman, was the true Christian.

••••

On Tuesday April 19th Diefenbaker rose in the House during the debate on the budget to demand that parliament adjourn "in order to discuss a matter of urgent public importance, namely the crisis of uncertainty and chaos in the Canadian Broadcasting

Corporation culminating in the current dispute..." This was an allusion to an off-the-cuff remark Judy LaMarsh had made on Sunday on the "hot seat" at the Young Liberals Federation of Canada convention where she had described the row over *Seven Days* as "the tip of an iceberg", symptomatic of more fundamental problems within the Corporation.

DIEFENBAKER: I do not think there has ever been a matter which in so short a time has brought about so much antagonism in all parts of Canada. Indeed, I understand that 3,800 or more telegrams have been received by the CBC in this connection. I personally have received a greater number than in respect of any other matter in the last couple of years.

NDP leader T.C. Douglas supported Diefenbaker's motion.

There is a grave possibility of either mass resignations by producers and performers or the possibility of a strike by some of those in important positions within the Canadian Broadcasting Corporation.

The Speaker allowed forty-five minutes of debate and then ruled that there was no urgency. He ordered the budget debate to resume and continue until Friday. During the Question Period Gordon Fairweather asked the prime minister to convene immediately a meeting of the Standing Committee on Broadcasting, Films and Assistance to the Arts. Pearson replied that he would get in touch with the chairman of the committee, Gérard Pelletier, at once. LaMarsh supported him.

I took the opportunity of speaking to the chairman of the broadcasting committee when he arrived in Ottawa just before the house opened this afternoon. In view of the fact that he is a new member of the House I informed him that it was his responsibility, and he needed no direction from the government, as to when he called a meeting. I also told him he could call a meeting of the members of the steering committee as soon as he chose to do so, and that it was his right as a chairman of the committee to call before that committee any witnesses necessary.

I should add, Mr. Speaker, that there cannot and will not be any attempt by the government to restrain the committee from calling any member of the board of the CBC at any time.[11]

In other words, her message to Pelletier was: you may go after the CBC any way you like.

This was a key moment in the story of the *Seven Days* War. Pearson was under no obligation to pass the matter on to the broadcasting committee. On the contrary, he could easily have said that the dispute between CBC management and its producers was an internal matter to be solved through the usual internal processes by the Corporation, and that the committee, which traditionally was only concerned with broad matters of policy, was the wrong instrument to deal with delicate problems arising out of one specific program. He could have said that members of the committee were not CBC program directors, that it was dangerous to let them think that they were, and that an important principle was at stake, namely the integrity of Canada's public broadcasting system.

But he did not take that position. Politicians of both parties had been critical of CBC management for many years. The antagonistic mood had been intensified by the Montreal strike and the *Preview Commentary* affair and, more recently, by the recommendations of the Fowler Committee. No doubt Judy LaMarsh had suggested that the matter be dealt with by the committee. But he did not like her and it was improbable that her recommendation influenced him very much. He thought the committee was the perfect vehicle for backbenchers and men like David Lewis to let off steam and allow the issue to blow itself out. But the main charm of letting the Committee handle it was was that this would move the matter out of the reach of Diefenbaker's mischievous demagoguery.

The committee, which sat in the West Block, had thirty-two sittings and listened to half a million words from eleven witnesses.[12]

The chairmanship was Pelletier's first major assignment as an M.P. and he was anxious to make a success of it and catch the prime minister's eye. He had only come to Ottawa five months earlier. Born in Victoriaville, Quebec, in 1919, he had been active in Catholic youth movements in the thirties and forties and travelled widely in South America and post-war Europe. When he returned, he became a journalist and broadcast commentator, as well as editor of the trade union publication *Le Travail*. In 1961 he became editor of the Montreal daily *La Presse*. He had met Reeves Haggan at Couchiching conferences and he was a good friend of Bernard Ostry. When Pearson called him on Tuesday, April 19th, he immediately convened his sub-committee on Agenda and Procedure. They met in the evening and decided to recommend to the full committee that its first meeting be held on Thursday morning, April 21st. The first three witnesses were to be Judy LaMarsh, Patrick Watson and Laurier LaPierre. There seems to have been no opportunity to discuss the order of witnesses with Ouimet who was on his way to Halifax where the board was to meet the next morning at nine.

In Ouimet's eyes, Pelletier was a biased chairman. Ouimet thought Pelletier should have consulted him about the order of witnesses before the committee and that he would have chosen to testify *before* Watson, LaPierre and Leiterman. Some members of the committee agreed with Ouimet and said so. (Ouimet never made this charge in public, though one of the member of the committee did.[13]) A case, however, could be made that it was in Ouimet's interest to let the rebels appear first and let off steam, so that he could appear later and clear the air.

The first management witness was Walker who appeared nearly two weeks after the sessions began, on Wednesday May 4th. Ouimet was not called until Friday May 6th. By then everybody was bored to tears by the fuss. Watson, LaPierre, Leiterman and Haggan had appeared and received banner headlines across the country and plenty of coverage. Walker's and Ouimet's testimonies were greeted with nationwide yawns. When they gave evidence, the NDP leader David Lewis conducted his cross-examinations of them in the manner of a relentless prosecuting attorney.

There was another matter which Ouimet resented. Pelletier made a point of extending the hearing to cover the situation in the French network. (That, incidentally, was the only subject of interest to Trudeau, a member of the Committee, who turned up occasionally and asked a few questions about it. He was not interested in the *Seven Days* affair.) It was no secret that Pelletier was close to Marc Thibault, Haggan's opposite number in Montreal. If the world required visible proof of the close relationship between the committee chairman Pelletier and the witness Thibault who was bound to give anti-management testimony, the events of May 16th provided it. For some reason Thibault and his associates were unable to get on a plane or a train from Montreal to Ottawa. Thibault phoned Pelletier who happened to be in Montreal. Pelletier drove them up in his car in the morning. But there was radiator trouble and they were forty-five minutes late. For appearances' sake, they spaced their entries into the Committee Room a few minutes apart.

The majority of members were strongly committed to *Seven Days*, not necessarily because they liked the program but because their constituents did. One backbencher, Gordon Fairweather, who had no particularly warm sentiments for Ouimet's position, sympathized strongly with the beleaguered president.

He thought Ouimet was definitely the underdog. The few fellow members who were pro-management did not help Ouimet very much. They were Ralph Cowan, who had been the thorn in the side of the CBC for a long time, and Harold Stafford, M.P. for Elgin County, whose narrow, small-town lawyer's approach to the subject was often an embarrassment to Ouimet, and one or two others. The president could have done with more enlightened friends.

For management the hearings could not have been more painful. The committee's interference with the Corporation's internal affairs, together with Judy LaMarsh's mischievousness, was a far greater threat than the insubordination of producers. Ouimet was convinced that his dispute with them could have been settled easily if only the politicians had kept their hands off it. But while the committee was in session, he did not have any freedom of action for fear of being declared in contempt of parliament. That is why the CBC board, at the conclusion of its meeting in Halifax on April 23rd, took the unprecedented step to take the committee publicly to task:

> The Board stated the belief that the direct intervention of a parliamentary committee regarding a managerial decision has made more difficult its task and that of Management.

The nightmare had become true. Politicians were dabbling in the most sensitive area of all, public affairs programming, blindly unaware that, far from saving *Seven Days*, they were busily undermining the integrity of the CBC.

••••

Mobilizing politicians was considerably easier for the *Seven Days* people than rallying the support of professional colleagues. Their support was considered vital to legitimize the fight and to broaden it from the narrow issue of the two co-hosts to the fight for the program as such. The trouble was that most of them did not like *Seven Days*. Some were merely jealous of its success and budget. Others objected to it on aesthetic or ethical grounds. Very few were prepared to make even minor sacrifices to keep it on the air, let alone risk their jobs. On the whole, they liked Watson but had reservations about Leiterman. Hoyt was too much of an American campaign manager for them and they never warmed up to him.

The arena where the battle for support was to be waged was the Toronto Producers' Association, a gentlemen's club (including a few ladies) of sixty or seventy colleagues galvanized into sporadic action only in moments of crisis. The Association was proud of not being a union, in contrast to the vulgar syndicate in Montreal. The French called it a *club de pêche*—a fishing club. Of course it did not have the right to strike. Its proceedings were noteworthy for an aristocratic disdain for business-like formalities. Some members only discovered by accident that they held high office, such as secretary or treasurer. For others, it was a matter of principle never to attend meetings. No membership lists were extant and the minutes of past meetings, if they existed at all, were filed away in forgotten or inaccessible cabinets. Dues were collected capriciously.

Variety, drama, children's programs, sports and public affairs producers had little in common except the desire to be left alone to do their jobs with the maximum of budgets and facilities and the minimum of interference from the brass. Each considered himself or herself sovereign in his or her domain and they all had grievances of varying gravity against management. These grievances usually lacked a common denominator.

Watson's successor as president of the Producers' Association was Tom Koch, a former member of the *Seven Days* team, who was to become a pivotal figure during the crisis. He had been vice-president and was elected president on Tuesday April 19th when Leiterman and Watson succeeded in having a meeting of the Association called in order to persuade the members to take action in the matter of the firing of the two hosts, one of whom happened to be Watson. This, at least for the time being, disqualified Watson from the presidency.

Tom Koch, originally from Kamloops, B.C., had a quirky, original mind and a great deal of vitality. In 1958 he had called Ross McLean from a phone-booth in San Francisco and offered a piece for *Close-Up* on the beatniks in North Beach. Koch had taken a film course in California. With his trained nose McLean smelled an unusual talent, bought the item and subsequently imported him. Part of Koch's charm was his innocently pretentious use of English, which often made it difficult, if not impossible, for anybody to understand what he was talking about.

> Everybody is quoting Tom Koch-isms, those convoluted utterances of Tom Koch, the harassed president of the Producers' Association, and a kind of reverse Sam Goldwyn. "The question of forthwith has been exhausted," Koch said after one eight-hour meeting. Translation: this is taking longer than we thought... Asked whether he was going out to lunch, Koch replied blandly, "No, I'm eating internally today."[14]

Koch had done important work for *Seven Days*. But he was a slow, undisciplined and extravagant producer and early in 1966 he left the program to do other work in public affairs. His last show for *Seven Days* was a feature on LSD. There were rumours that he had taken it himself. It was to have been a ten-minute piece but the project grew and grew as he got more and more excited. Eventually Leiterman snatched the film away from him and arranged to have it completed under his own supervision. Watson was persuaded to devote an hour to it on April 24th in *Document*.

Leiterman had been worried about Koch's approach to LSD. This matter came up at the parliamentary hearings.

JOHNSTON M.P.:   *Mr. Leiterman, have you personally experimented with LSD?*

LEITERMAN: *No, I have not. I might add that it seemed to me essential that no one who was involved in that program undertake any experiments in that direction.*[15]

There was good reason for Leiterman to worry. To Tom Koch any activity which intensified awareness of the spiritual life, and any form of communication which enhanced a sense of the universal brotherhood of man, was to be encouraged. A good instrument for doing that was television, and his friends often teased him that his credo was "Redemption Through Electronics". Perhaps an even better instrument was LSD. Nothing was more natural than for Koch to be attracted to the possible spiritual benefits to be derived from it. Even in the final version of his program, in spite of the addition of large doses of cautionary advice from psychiatric experts on the lethal dangers of LSD, the overall impression the film left was that LSD offered unique opportunities for heightened spiritual awareness, for mystic experiences when "one's own essence merges with the essence of others", and for "a voyage into one's own body".

Whether or not Koch had personally had any LSD-induced mystic experiences he certainly had no experience in earthbound crisis-management. Soon he was to find himself on the national stage, the nation's eyes fixed on him. Within two weeks he was even going to spend a Saturday and a Sunday morning in the Prime Minister's Office. For this role he was totally unprepared. A few members of the Association, Richard Nielsen for example, knew something about labour disputes. But Koch did not. Nor had he or any of the other members of the Association's executive any talent for effective political action or for drafting concise documents. Consequently, they spent endless hours in the Westbury Hotel arguing, splitting hairs, posturing and play-acting, with reporters waiting at the door with their tape-recorders, grateful for any scraps of information. On several occasions Koch and his colleagues left by the back door to evade them. It was as though the opera society of Brandon, Manitoba, suddenly found itself giving a gala performance at La Scala in Milan, exciting and flattering no doubt but not very good for the nerves, nor likely to lead to very good results.

The *Save Seven Days* committees had been set up on Saturday and Sunday, April 16th and 17th. On Sunday (show-day) protesters outside the Jarvis Street studios carried signs reading SENSE NOT CENSORSHIP, WE WANT PATRICK, WE LOVE LAURIER, THIS HOUR HAS COURAGE, HANDS OFF—FREE SPEECH, WHO'S AFRAID OF LAPIERRE AND WATSON?, TALENT MUST HAVE SCOPE, and so on. Leiterman had given strict instructions that there were to be no references to the crisis on the program and there weren't. After the show, as usual, the public called in on the hot line. The Bell Telephone Company reported later that more than five thousand attempts had been made to get through to the studio, a hundred times more than usual. After taking as many calls as they could, Leiterman and Watson gave a late-night press conference. Leiterman declared that the producer had a historic right to decide who shall be host on his shows and that the status of every producer had been violated by the CBC action. Watson said: "My loyalty to the CBC has been in question. It damn well isn't. I'm totally committed to the CBC."[16]

At the first meeting of the Association, on Tuesday April 19th, it became clear immediately that on the technical point, the non-renewal of the two host-contracts, there was no argument. Management did not have a leg to stand on. It was an infringement of an agreement made in February 1965 between the Association and management according to which no changes in artists or performers were to be made without full consultation with executive producers or producers. The trouble with that agreement was that, if it was ever written down, no one could find it. Management (which also could not find the piece of paper) never denied its existence.

For the *Seven Days* people to obtain an admission of this technical breach by management was a mere start. The important thing was to win the support of the Association for their overall position. So they asked the members to pull out all the stops and threaten strike action. They agreed. In the days to come the members of the Association increasingly resented what they considered manipulative strong-arm methods used by Leiterman and Watson and some of their colleagues. Hoyt's attempted stage-managing and wire-pulling were especially considered out of place. For moderates like Koch and others, the important thing was to prevent the *Seven Days* lobby from dominating the proceedings.

In retrospect, it would have been wiser for the Association at the very first meeting to resist the *Seven Days* lobby's efforts to induce the membership to threaten strike action, rather than to yield to them. (The word "strike" was invariably used by the press though the producers did not have the right to strike.) After that it was too late. A smarter move would have been to suggest to management the formation of a joint committee to examine behind closed doors various possible face-saving formulas until *Seven Days* was off the air and tempers had cooled down. It might not have done them any good but it would have reflected more faithfully the real situation, namely that there was no consensus in the Association. It would also have kept the press out of their hair.

The threat was addressed to the president and the board and was phoned to Halifax on the evening of Tuesday, April 19th, the evening before the board met.

> We are sending this urgent appeal out of loyalty to the avowed aims of the CBC and out of concern for the future of public broadcasting in Canada.
>
> ... We acknowledge the right of management to manage, but good management should find it possible to admit mistakes. There can be no peace, nor can confidence in present senior management be established, unless prompt and positive remedial action is taken.
>
> We respectfully request a reply within twenty-four hours, with assurances of immediate negotiations.
>
> If a satisfactory settlement cannot be reached forthwith, the Association will be obliged to recommend that drastic measures be taken by its members including, if necessary, withdrawal of its members' services.

Seven Days had won the first round. It had made the fishing club act like the Teamsters.

CHAPTER 10

CRISIS CHRONICLE

Tuesday, April 19th

In Ottawa Ouimet faces the press. In his opening statement he declares that it is the CBC's intention to have *Seven Days* back in the fall schedule and that Mr. Haggan has been requested to ask Mr. Leiterman to carry on with the production. In many respects, he says, *Seven Days* has been a major achievement in Canadian television and management feels the show can continue to improve and be a better program with new hosts.

QUESTION: *Mr. Leiterman has said... that it has always been the business of the producer of a show to select the host of the show.*

OUIMET: *That is true and it is his primary responsibility. But on the other hand he must receive approval from those above him...*

QUESTION: *Were Mr. Watson and Mr. LaPierre disloyal to the Corporation or did anyone suggest that to them?*

OUIMET: *No. No. I don't know if anyone suggested it to them. All I can say is that I can speak for the Corporation and my own feelings on this matter. I don't like the word "disloyal" very much, by the way. It is emotionally charged. Let me say that we expect our people at all levels of authority to accept the directives that are given to them and not to challenge these directives. Now you can call that whatever you wish. This is normal behaviour in a well-organized corporation.*

QUESTION: *Where did the question of Pat's attitude towards his country come from?*

OUIMET: *I think this is a very interesting one. He was the one who said it, otherwise I wouldn't be discussing it now. You see... he was being considered to be the executive producer of this new program which has to deal with Canada and the problems of Canada. Now, you know how sensitive an area this is, and before we agree to making an assignment such as this, obviously we talk to the person about the field he's going to cover. It is a little bit like*

*choosing the head of our religious broadcasting... Well,
obviously we find out in the first place whether he is
interested in religion. There is no more to it than that..."*

Wednesday, April 20th

The CBC board meets in Halifax in an angry mood. The main
threat is not the internal rebellion but yesterday's referral of the
Seven Days dispute to the parliamentary committee.

Ouimet replies to the wire from Tom Koch, president of the
Toronto Producers' Association.

> The Board of Directors acknowledges receipt of your Associa-
> tion's telegram of April 19th dealing with situation in general
> and *Seven Days* in particular. The Board is actively considering
> the whole question and is studying your objections and their
> relationship to the 1965 understanding. The Board also con-
> firms the desirability of my meeting with you... at the earliest
> possible date. Will try to arrange for meeting next week. In the
> meantime, if you so wish, a preliminary meeting can be ar-
> ranged tomorrow with other CBC officials. You will be con-
> tacted separately on this.

Haggan and Leiterman are invited to meet with the board on
Friday April 22nd.

At McGill University LaPierre gives a press conference.

> I do not feel I owe loyalty to CBC management. I owe loyalty to
> a concept of broadcasting.

He is asked whether he was hired by *Seven Days* as "some kind
of performing bear or the CBC's French Canadian".

> I am not an exercise in Canadian unity. I am not a monument.[1]

Roy Shields of the *Toronto Star* interviews Faibish.

> I have a deep, deep conviction that the CBC top management
> became convinced Patrick Watson, Douglas Leiterman and I
> were lobbying for a coup d'état in the hope we could move in
> ourselves.[2]

Thursday, April 21st

Informal negotiations between the Producers' Association's
executive and two CBC officials, Robert McGall and Guy Coderre, vice-president of administration, begin in Toronto.
McGall allocates an office on Maitland Street to the association,
with keys "which might have to be withdrawn at some unhappy
future date".[3]

The Producers' Association meets at the Westbury Hotel to

discuss what position to take in the meeting with Ouimet planned for next week.

The parliamentary committee holds its first hearing. On Tuesday both Pearson and LaMarsh had urged the chairman Gérard Pelletier to meet as soon as possible. Pelletier acts at once. In the evening the sub-committee on agenda and procedure gathers and immediately decides to call LaMarsh, LaPierre and Watson as their first witnesses on Thursday.

Today, Thursday, David Lewis moves an amendment to add Leiterman to the first list of witnesses. In her testimony, La-Marsh reaffirms her intention to refer a White Paper on broadcasting to the committee during the current session. When asked about *Seven Days*, and more specifically about her observation that the dispute was "the tip of an iceberg" and that there was danger of a general explosion, she replies that what she has in mind is what the Fowler Committee referred to as a blaze. "Both are as likely, since they arise from the existence of combustible material."[4]

Watson begins his testimony, which will be continued on Monday and will take seven hours altogether.

Friday, April 22nd

It is fortunate that Leiterman does not have to appear before the parliamentary committee today because he and Haggan are in Halifax to explain their position to the CBC board of directors. Later, Leiterman writes a private note to Tom Koch, in which he gives a summary of his performance.

> I spent three hours answering questions from the board. The meeting was cordial and I had an excellent sense of support from several of the members. I was able to counter, I think effectively, just about everything that Alphonse said, and to point out most of the anomalies and contradictions in management's position.
>
> Ouimet made it clear that he did not intend to take Pat and Laurier back as hosts. He doesn't want Laurier at all, and he is set upon giving Pat the *Quarterly Report* program. I had hoped that perhaps my presentation which followed Reeves' may have moved the board to avoid supporting the president's action. After I left they spent another five hours in session and came out with a statement that is attached.

(Leiterman was referring to the board's statement issued at the conclusion of the meeting on Friday April 22nd supporting the president's actions and pointing out that there had been a serious breakdown in formal communications between management and the producers of *Seven Days* and that a shortcoming of the program had been its frequent departure from the Corporation's program policies.)

> This suggests to me that though we made some ground on the board, we didn't make enough to stop them confirming Ouimet, which they practically have to.
>
> I have a very clear sense that they intend to sacrifice Bud Walker. However, our position is not really improved and it is my feeling that the whole battle may be lost unless the Producers' Association can show enough strength to further scare Alphonse... They (the board) figure they can knock off a couple of hosts without trouble, but a strike is something that scares the hell out of them.

Leiterman's impression that the board intends to sacrifice Walker is corroborated by the *Toronto Star*'s Martin Goodman. He reports two months later, on June 28th, that, "according to informed sources", the board gave Ouimet until the end of June to replace Walker.

In his private note to Tom Koch, Leiterman does not mention that he said he was prepared to produce *Seven Days* without Watson and LaPierre. However, he evidently did acknowledge such a possibility.[5] He may have had in mind that he would not lose them altogether since their connection with *Seven Days* would have to be maintained if *Quarterly Report* was to get off the ground. It was April now—too late to construct an entirely new resource base for a major new program to be launched after Labour Day in September. *Seven Days*, as well as the French network's *Le Sel de la Semaine*, had such a resource base. To senior management, the establishment of such a connection between *Seven Days* and the new program appeared to be further evidence of Leiterman's efforts at empire-building. But to Haggan, Thibault and all the producers involved it seemed the only possible solution.

Saturday, April 23rd

After his return from Halifax, Leiterman declares to the press that he was astonished that the board supported Ouimet.

> If this means that Patrick Watson and Laurier LaPierre are not reinstated I have no alternative but to stop producing the program.
>
> Moreover, I expect the whole staff of *Seven Days* will walk out and that *Seven Days* will go off the air before completion of its season on May 8th.[6]

Sunday, April 24th

After a marathon session in the Westbury Hotel the Producers' Association passes a resolution by a vote of thirty-six to twelve to send a note to Ouimet on Tuesday, after seeking legal advice on Monday. The note is informally shown to Ouimet on Monday afternoon in Toronto.

> The recent action of the CBC Board of Directors appears to repudiate earlier commitments to the association to negotiate both existing disputes and operating procedures. Hence we now propose the following principles be written into the standard operating procedures of the CBC:
>
> 1. There shall be no program decision arbitrarily imposed by management with regard to performers or content without full consultation with the department and producers involved.
>
> 2. No producer shall be dismissed or subjected to disciplinary transfer without just cause.
>
> 3. Disputes arising from these principles will be settled by compulsory arbitration by a disinterested person selected by the federal minister of labour.
>
> We insist that the above provisions be adopted immediately and be binding on both sides in the existing disputes.
>
> The Association demands that they be acknowledged immediately as a basis of negotiations between the President and the Association.

Ouimet is to be advised that unless he accepts these principles the Association intends to recommend withdrawal of services.

Blair Fraser, Ottawa editor of *Maclean's*, summarizes press opinion about the crisis on CBC radio's *Looking through the Papers*.

> Pat Watson and Laurier LaPierre may be able to outnumber CBC management on the picket lines, but in the press management seems to have the edge. I haven't of course seen enough papers to give an exact numerical breakdown, but in general the producers are getting very little editorial sympathy in the fuss over *Seven Days*.

Monday, April 25th

On Friday, while Leiterman appeared before the CBC board, Watson continued his testimony before the parliamentary committee which made headlines on all the front pages. Today he concludes it.

He accuses senior management of lacking confidence in its supervisors and producers and of attacking all controversial programming "which is new and apt to arouse and provoke strong discussion".[7]

WATSON: I think there is evidence that what would be welcomed by
           the management is the return of the title of *Seven Days*
           and the popularity that goes with it...up to a point.
STANBURY: Without the misery?
WATSON: Without the misery. I do not see how anyone can say "Yes,
           we want the program back but we do not want back the
           people who make it," because basically the program is
           made by people just as the newspaper bears the character
           of a strong editor, or a novel bears the character of the
           author.[8]

●●●●

Ouimet, with Walker, Thibault and other representatives of
the French network present, meets Haggan and public affairs
supervisors in Toronto in the morning. The atmosphere is
strained. Walker apologizes for the mistake he made in violating
line authority. Ouimet observes that he regards the *Seven Days*
dispute as a symptom of a deeper conflict and appeals to the
public affairs department to help him diagnose and solve it. The
reception is cool.

In the afternoon, Ouimet and the executive of the Toronto
Producers' Association confer while a full meeting of the members is held at the Westbury Hotel. After long discussions about
the meaning of "forthwith"—the telegram to Halifax of April
19th had stipulated that if a satisfactory settlement could not be
reached "forthwith" the producers would withdraw their
services—they agree to recess the meeting without adjourning it.
Ouimet and the executive fail to devise a face-saving formula to
shelve the issue until after the last edition of *Seven Days*,
planned for May 8th, has gone off the air, but Tom Koch and
Vincent Tovell, the secretary of the Producers' Association, ac-
company Ouimet to Ottawa, continuing the conversations.
Leaving CBC headquarters Koch tells reporters, "We are splitting
up meetings between here and Ottawa... It's a mess." Exhausted, Koch and Tovell have soup and sandwiches with the
president in the cafeteria at the Toronto airport, carrying on the
animated and essentially friendly dialogue. Koch prepares a philosophical declaration about the "Renewal of the Corporation".
Ouimet appreciates the sincere efforts by the two moderate and
conciliatory producers' representatives to buy time but he cannot accept their proposals. Koch and Tovell return to Toronto in
the morning.

In the Commons Diefenbaker says the CBC board showed
contempt of parliament when it criticized the intervention of the
committee into the controversy over *Seven Days* and asks Pear-

son whether he had pointed this out to the publicly-owned Corporation. Pearson replies that he has seen a press report and has asked for a text of the statement.[9]

In the parliamentary committee, before LaPierre is called to follow Watson as a witness, committee member Bryce Mackasey also takes exception to the board's criticism of the hearings.

> I think we should point out to the board of directors that it was the wish and pleasure of Parliament that this problem be referred to this particular Committee. Whether or not the board of directors feel we are making their task more difficult is of no consequence.[10]

Tuesday, April 26th

A critical day. Ouimet issues a statement about his talks with the Producers' Association.

> We discussed future relations in terms of conditions of operations and these discussions have not finished. But there was one point they wanted in particular and that was the reopening of the Watson-LaPierre affair. I had to decline that request.[11]

DIEFENBAKER RISES IN THE HOUSE.

> *I direct this question to the Prime Minister. Has he had a report that the meeting which took place this morning between the president of the Canadian Broadcasting Corporation and the president of the Toronto Producers' Association has broken up and that a strike is imminent, the president of the CBC having declared that he would not consent to any arbitration and that the decision regarding the removal of the two producers of* This Hour Has Seven Days *is irrevocable?*
>
> *Further, will the Prime Minister say whether it is the intention of the government to use its good offices, without in any way infringing upon the act which sets up the CBC, to assure that there will indeed be arbitration with regard to this matter for the benefit of the Canadian people?*

PEARSON: *I have had no report on that particular meeting yet. As far as the latter part of the question is concerned, if the government can use its good offices in any way which will not constitute intervention in the affairs of the CBC, it will of course be glad to do so.[12]*

Pearson's delicate phrasing is due to his lack of jurisdiction in the dispute. The CBC is responsible to parliament, not to the government. But on a political level, if the prime minister is sure the public demands his intervention and if all parties agree, he thinks lending his good offices might speed up a settlement. This was also his press secretary Richard O'Hagan's advice. The Producers' Association had contacted him directly, asking him to attempt to persuade Pearson to intervene, in the hope that this would break the impasse in its favour. Moreover, Haggan was in frequent touch with O'Hagan, and so was Watson.

After a meeting of the Producers' Association a motion is carried which is immediately transmitted to Ouimet. The vote is forty-eight to four.

> The executive is authorized to recommend a withdrawal of services at a time and date to be determined by them, but such withdrawal to take place not later than 10.00 p.m. E.D.T. Sunday, May 1st, if by that date no action has been taken to eliminate the cause of our dispute with the Corporation as set out in our communications to the president of April 19th and 26th.

Ten o'clock Sunday May 1st is the starting time of the second to last *Seven Days* program planned for this season.

At three a m. Tom Koch tells the press "We want to renew the CBC, not to destroy it. If we really wanted to tear it apart, we could do it in five minutes." He says discussions with the producers during the last week have been confused because the question of producers' rights and the release of the hosts have never been clearly separated.[13] To Roy Shields of the *Toronto Star* he declares there is "a wall of non-perception". The producers are involved in "a tooling up for re-animation".

Leiterman begins his testimony before the Committee. With interruptions, it occupies nearly two hundred pages of Hansard.

Wednesday, April 27th

The parliamentary committee recommends:

> That the CBC producers and CBC management avail themselves of the good offices of the government, offered by the prime minister, to avoid the possibility of any work stoppage of CBC services.[14]

The chairman conveys this recommendation by telegram to both sides. A spokesman says that if both factions respond, this could result in the government appointing a person or persons to take the role of intermediary in the dispute. He says that if the prime minister feels the circumstances make it proper for him to do so he might himself take this role.[15]

It is, therefore, the committee rather than the prime minister which tries to persuade both sides to accept his good offices to avoid a work stoppage.

From the crowded board room of the CBC head office on Bronson Avenue Ouimet addresses the staff across the country over an hour-long closed-circuit radio hook-up at three o'clock in the afternoon. This was to be a private internal communication to the staff but it is recorded and leaks to the press. Case by case, he summarizes management's objections to *Seven Days'* transgressions against CBC policies on journalistic ethics. In Toronto the staff listens to Ouimet in Studio Seven. At a critical point during Ouimet's attacks on *Seven Days*, Peter Campbell (Haggan's second-in-command) rises—Haggan is in Ottawa—and dramatically leads other members of the public affairs department out of the crowded studio in protest against what they consider Ouimet's misuse of the Corporation's facilities to attack one particular CBC program, thereby causing senior officers—such as McGall and Hogg—considerable embarrassment.

Problems involving the show became so acute, Ouimet says, that at one point management officials decided to scrap it completely. They later reversed their stand and resolved to retain it but to eliminate some of its excesses. "But *Seven Days* must not destroy the CBC. If Parliament wanted the CBC to be more daring, Ouimet told the staff, they only had to say so.

As to LaPierre, Ouimet says he has not lived up to CBC policy requirements regarding the professional on-air conduct of hosts and refers sarcastically to his performance in the program about Steven Truscott. However, Ouimet has forgotten that it was Faibish and not LaPierre who conducted the interview with the boy's mother:

Ouimet gives his version of the interview:

> LaPierre asked Mrs. Truscott, "Wasn't it a terrible ordeal?
>
> She said, "It was a terrible ordeal".
>
> LaPierre said, "Wasn't is absolutely unbearable?
>
> She said, "Yes".
>
> LaPierre said, "Were you capable of not crying?"
>
> She cried.
>
> But she wasn't the only one crying. LaPierre was so moved that when the camera turned away he wiped a tear from one eye. Then he wiped a tear from the other eye.
>
> I could not believe it. He was wet under the eyes!
>
> This is a matter of policy. It must not happen.[16]

Ouimet concedes that LaPierre was "charming because he had the human failing of showing his emotions. However, it was just that failing which made him unacceptable as a host."

He later thought that he had been naïve in the way he spoke about LaPierre's tear, but he had no regrets about dealing with it honestly. He simply could not accept that the tear was genuine. Had he not made an issue of it, it would not have entered the history of Canadian television as one of the highlights.

Management could conceivably be challenged in its view that LaPierre's tear was a breach of policy. In 1965 Peter Campbell, in conjunction with Don Bennett, the Director of Program Policy at head office, had devised a new category of on-air performers, *The Permanent Program Personality*. These were allowed wider scope of personal expression than was permissible for ordinary hosts, though they would have been the first ones to admit that crying was likely to be construed as a somewhat extreme expression. LaPierre's contract specifically stated that he belonged in that new category. LaPierre had already said on April 25th to the parliamentary committee: "I understand the decision not to renew my contract was made...at the end of January or the beginning of February, and I did not weep until the middle of March."[17]

Watson and LaPierre send a letter to McGall, the senior man in Toronto, asking for equal time on the close-circuit hook-up. "In any dispute there are two sides," they say. "We believe the Corporation's management to be committed to fair treatment of the issue."[18]

Thursday, April 28th

Pearson tells the House that he has received a telegram from the president of the Producers' Association.

> It is addressed to the Prime Minister and informs me that the producers will abide by the expressed will of the parliamentary committee on broadcasting and will suspend their decision—quoting from the telegram—"to recommend a complete withdrawal of our members' services not later than ten p.m. eastern daylight time Sunday May 1st provided the officers of the Corporation suspend their decision in the matter of *Seven Days* hosts pending mediation."
>
> I am awaiting, Mr. Speaker, the reaction of the management of the Canadian Broadcasting Corporation to this telegram before I make any decision as to whether the government should intervene, and, if so, in what way.

Gordon Fairweather asks "whether we could be assured that in the exercise of good offices any mediator appointed would be chosen from outside either the ministerial ranks or the public service".

PEARSON: Mr. Speaker, if the government decides to intervene at all in this matter—and the government has to be very careful indeed in intervening in the affairs of the Canadian Broadcasting Corporation—but if it decided that government intervention will be helpful—I would like to consult with both sides as to the form which that intervention should take.[19]

• • • •

Haggan is self-assured and succinct as he testifies before the parliamentary committee. In his view, senior management is out of touch with the country. It is obsessed with organization and its influence on programming is totally negative.[20] Everybody's motives are suspect all the time. The most important consideration for management is caution. As to Haggan's own position, management's actions are designed to downgrade his responsibilities. This was a question of confidence which "operates both ways: I do not have confidence in them and they do not have confidence in me."

On the professional competence of LaPierre he has this to say:

If Mr. LaPierre or any personality on any public affairs program were, over a period, to exhibit a consistent editorial point of view, the public affairs department would move at once to get rid of that person. LaPierre has views on every subject under the sun, usually quite strong, while he holds them at least, but I think he has a patent honesty and people who watch the program know that he is reacting to what he is hearing and seeing on the program.[21]

On the subject of last week's statement of the board that *Seven Days* had serious shortcomings, Haggan is asked whether it wasn't good management to have fired him since he was responsible for program content. Why was this logical step not taken? Because, Haggan replies, it is a serious matter to fire the General Supervisor of Public Affairs. There had been strong but indirect suggestions that he vacate his position but he was determined to stay on. "If I were to consider my own health and peace of mind I would not stay."[22]

It is obvious that after the harsh things he has said it will be difficult, if not impossible, for Haggan to stay with the Corporation much longer.

Gordon Fairweather recounts later that Haggan's appearance before the committee was one of eight to ten great moments in his fifteen years as an M.P. He compares it to events like the resignation of Duff Cooper in the U.K., because "we rarely do things very well in parliament".

••••

On Thursday afternoon Ouimet calls Pearson from Montreal to tell him that he and his board will be considering the committee's telegram inviting "CBC management and CBC Producers to avail themselves of the good offices of the Government, offered by the prime minister", and in the evening he sends a message to the committee, with a copy to Pearson, that he would be pleased to meet at any time with the prime minister or with any other person or persons he may designate to discuss the present situation and its resolution. There is no reference to the producers' stipulation that the Corporation suspend its decision about the hosts.

Ouimet announces separately that he will set up an internal inquiry into the *Seven Days* controversy, to be conducted by Guy Coderre, vice-president of administration. Tom Koch responds that the Association welcomes "the timely offer of the president to commission a full-scale inquiry with mutually agreed terms of reference" but adds that the producers will suspend their Sunday deadline only if the Corporation's officers suspend their decision about the two hosts "pending the intra-Corporation inquiry".

In Montreal, Jacques Gautier, the president of the Producers' Association, announces that his group is unlikely to withdraw their services on Sunday. Such a move would have to be decided by a general meeting and no such meeting was scheduled. However, there was no intention to hamper the Toronto producers' strategy.[23]

During the Montreal strike in 1959 the Toronto producers did not support their Quebec colleagues.

Friday, April 29th

In Montreal LaPierre issues a two-page statement saying Ouimet and his spokesmen were using "the sneer, the innuendo, the half-truth and the lie" to uphold the dismissal action. He wanted:

> ...to declare solemnly that at no time have I resisted management...with regard to *Seven Days* and Mr. Ouimet has not been able to produce a single evidence to back his accusations... By his remarks Mr. Ouimet has demonstrated his complete ignorance of the very standards of the Corporation... It is the producer's responsibility to accept the contributions of the performers, hosts and interviewers, and to air

that contribution... The CBC should have fired Douglas Leiterman, executive producer of *Seven Days*, not the co-hosts.[24]

In the Commons Diefenbaker asks Pearson whether he is in a position "to make a statement in regard to the dispute between the CBC and the promoters or producers of *This Hour Has Seven Days*—I almost thought I might say fourteen months."

Pearson replies that yesterday he had two communications from Ouimet and that he was now considering what his next step should be. He was fully aware that the matter was of some urgency.

DIEFENBAKER: As I understand it, the representatives of the producers in Toronto have stated that they are prepared to post-pone their strike ultimatum date provided the stub-born attitude taken by the president of the CBC is at least diminished for the time being.

PEARSON: Well, Mr. Speaker, I cannot accept the characterization by the right honourable gentleman of the attitude of the president of the CBC. I would point out—

DIEFENBAKER: It wasn't diplomatic.

PEARSON: My right honourable friend says it wasn't diplomatic. That is not quite the same thing as stubborn. I would point out that the representatives of the producers, and the hosts in question, have appeared before the parlia-mentary committee and have had an opportunity to state their case, whereas the representatives of the Corporation have not yet had the opportunity, al-though it has been provided for.[25]

In the afternoon, the Association chooses three members of the executive to proceed to Ottawa to confer with the prime minis-ter: Tom Koch, Richard Nielsen (the producer of *The Public Eye* and head of the strategy committee), and variety producer Paddy Sampson. The choice of Nielsen does not please Leiterman and Watson. He is a rival public affairs producer and there is not much mutual trust.

In the evening Ouimet confers with Pearson at his residence on Sussex Drive for one hour. Pearson knows that Ouimet is under pressure and that his board's backing is not as strong as he suggests. Pearson has never been entirely comfortable with Ouimet—the feelings are mutual. In matters of broadcasting he is more drawn to personalities like Graham Spry, the founder of the Canadian Radio League in 1930, and in many ways the animating spirit of the broadcasting system that emerged.

Throughout the negotiations, Richard O'Hagan, Pearson's press secretary, is in close touch with Martin Goodman of the *Toronto Star*. Therefore, Goodman's account is likely to be accurate:

> Ouimet stressed that management's decision to dismiss the co-hosts...has been approved by the board of directors.
>
> He implied that the producers would not strike because they were more divided internally than their public statements indicated.[26]

At five o'clock, at a large gathering in Toronto's Royal York Hotel, Davidson Dunton, former chairman of the CBC and president and vice-chancellor of Carleton University, presents Beryl Fox with the Wilderness Award for her Vietnam documentary *The Mills of the Gods*, presented within the framework of *Seven Days* in the *Document* series. In her acceptance speech she says she is gratified to win the award "particularly when the program I work for...is under attack... It represents everything *Seven Days* stands for and I hope will stand for next year".[27]

Pearson is fighting a cold.

Saturday, April 30th

At four a.m. the CBC board member E.B. Osler makes a last-minute attempt to present an argument against mediation. He sends a telegram to Ouimet.

> I have been thinking. Regarding CBC's decision re *Seven Days'* hosts, producers' only ground for its being revised are that Leiterman was not consulted. But despite your statements committing the corporation before the board meeting, we refrained from upholding your decision until after the session with management and producer. At this session Leiterman stated to the board that he could produce *Seven Days* without Watson and Lapierre. Thus only after weighting management's reasons based on more adequate control against producer's artistic requirements was your decision upheld. This means consultation, or at least review, had actually occurred at CBC's highest possible level. Thus further outside review is tantamount to no confidence in CBC board and any claim that Leiterman was not brought into the decision-making process is specious. We also admitted breakdown in communications of which consultative process is part. Thus we remain open to discussions with Producers' Association... Surely this is the essence of what the responsible element of Producers' Association is concerned with. If the Association refuses to negotiate these points with management, I suggest their meeting with executive committee or full board would be preferable to outside mediation. If prime minister wants fresh approach, he

might bring board to full strength prior to this and request a cooling off period until he has done so. Is there any light here?

Apparently there wasn't. It was too late. Pearson was committed to mediation.

In the morning, the three members of the Association's executive —Koch, Nielsen and Sampson—meet with Pearson at Sussex Drive. Nielsen knew Pearson during his leadership campaign when Nielsen was in the labour movement. Pearson is somewhat puzzled, perhaps amused, by Tom Koch's unorthodox conversational style and by variety producer Sampson's habit of snapping his fingers while talking.

> Pearson tested the producers' determination....He asked them first to lift the strike deadline and second to delay a meeting that afternoon which was to give final approval to the strike.
>
> But the producers, sensing the need to impress the strength of their feelings on the prime minister, refused to budge. When Koch emerged, he told reporters "The situation is unchanged".
>
> Pearson did have their agreement, however, to hold off if an impartial review could be arranged. In his next conversation with Ouimet, Pearson emphasized that the producers were serious and that some formula to avert the stoppage had to be found.
>
> By this time it was clear that the prestige of the Prime Minister's Office was on the line...
>
> By the time he broke to address a twelve thirty meeting of the National Liberal Federation executive, he had agreement in principle to mediation.[28]

In a conference call at three in the afternoon Ouimet and Briggs discuss with members of the board the terms of reference for the forthcoming mediation. It is agreed that only the procedures surrounding the host decision are subject to investigation, not the decision itself. The board unanimously agrees that the producers' attempt to include "a provision for retroactivity regarding the non-renewal of the contracts of the co-hosts is totally unacceptable. The directors stress that the mediator be completely neutral and suggest some names for consideration."[29]

Pearson's cold gets worse. He cancels a Toronto speaking engagement for tomorrow, Sunday, night.

Throughout the afternoon and evening Richard O'Hagan and Pearson's special assistant Hal Dornan, working in their East Block offices, discuss terms of reference for the mediator with both parties. Ouimet has said the question of the hosts was not to be subject to mediation. The producers are committed not to agree to mediation unless that question is included. The *Seven Days* unit, back in Toronto, has a particular dilemma. Should they make it tough for the three negotiators and risk losing the Sunday night show? Would that not lead to a loss of public support? Or should the negotiators be flexible so that they can stay on the air for another two occasions and carry on the fight with full strength? As for the other producers, the spring season is just about over. Resolution is draining away. There is growing resentment of the *Seven Days* team's tactics at their meetings. After management's admission that its "jumping" of the lines has been a mistake and the general recognition that this sort of thing is not likely to happen again for a long time, it is no longer clear what they are fighting for.

Throughout the evening, O'Hagan frequently phones Pearson and Ouimet. In the end, Nielsen comes up with the compromise solution: leave out the specific instructions demanded by both sides and instead adopt the general instruction: "discuss the current dispute...with a view to making an independent and comprehensive review." This will permit the mediator to define his own terms of reference, and Pearson will once again be able to demonstrate his prowess as a diplomat. The assumption is that both sides are so anxious to avoid a work stoppage that they will accept the wording. In any case, there is no time to ask too many questions. The purpose of the intervention is to get a mediator appointed so that tonight's program will go on the air. His eventual "independent and comprehensive review" will of course be of little interest to anybody.

There is to be a public statement tomorrow but no written instructions are to be given to the mediator. All protocol is side-stepped.[30] For the executive of the Producers' Association it is not easy to convince Leiterman and his associates that this arrangement serves their interest, but in the end they succeed.

Pearson's two assistants keep dinner guests waiting at home while phoning various candidates. They don't return until after midnight and they are on the telephone for another three hours.

Sunday, May 1st

Stuart Keate, the publisher of the *Vancouver Sun*, returns home near midnight from a ten-day trip to Boston and finds a message to call the prime minister. It is three o'clock in the morning in Ottawa. Keate reaches Dornan, Pearson's special assistant, who once worked for his paper. Dornan asks him whether he is prepared to act as an informal mediator in the *Seven Days* dispute. If so, would he please call the prime minister at nine in the morning, Ottawa time, six o'clock Vancouver time. Keate accepts without hesitation and nine hours later is on a plane to Ottawa.

The Association agrees to his choice. Leiterman knew Keate in Vancouver.

At ten a.m. Ouimet and Briggs are again on the phone to members of the board. While on the line there is a phone-call from the Prime Minister's Office. The following draft announcement is read out:

> The Prime Minister has asked Mr. Stuart Keate, publisher of the *Vancouver Sun*, to meet at once with representatives of Management and producers of the Canadian Broadcasting Corporation to discuss the current dispute over the program *This Hour Has Seven Days* with a view to making an independent and comprehensive review which it is hoped will help to resolve existing differences.

There is some discussion. Some feel that the terms of reference are too restrictive. However, a majority of the members agree to the formulation.[31]

At one o'clock Pearson makes the announcement. The Association releases a statement:

> The president of the CBC has met our request for a full-scale review of the case of the hosts of *Seven Days* by a disinterested third party. Since this action has been taken by the prime minister, the executive of the Association has concluded that it is appropriate to suspend our decision to recommend a complete withdrawal of services at ten p.m.

●●●●

Pearson's diplomacy meets its objective: the May 1st edition of *Seven Days* goes on as scheduled. Before taking his chair in front of the cameras, two minutes before ten, LaPierre addresses the studio audience. "Feel right at home, ladies and gentlemen," he says. "Cry if you like."

When the show opens Warren Davis announces, as the camera swings back to reveal Watson and LaPierre, "Ladies and gentlemen, thanks to the good offices of the prime minister of Canada, THIS HOUR *HAS* SEVEN DAYS."

A minute later, after prolonged applause, Dinah Christie addresses her two co-hosts.

"With you fellows losing your jobs I feel so left out. I wonder what a girl has to do to get noticed in Ottawa?"

"Don't ask," LaPierre replies with lightning speed.

Wednesday, May 4th

Walker appears before the parliamentary committee. Now that a mediator has been appointed there is little tension.

He admits freely that there was a serious problem in communication.

> This being a communication organization, we should be experts in solving our internal problems of communications. But, gentlemen, you must take my word for it: it is a very large problem for us. There are physical and geographical reasons for its being a problem. Of course, the core of the Corporation properly is located in Ottawa. Let me at once say that any serious thought to move the core of the Corporation to Montreal or, indeed, Toronto in my opinion would lead to some kind of disaster.

He said this would be a giant step backwards for reasons "connected with biculturalism".[32]

Walker took a different view in the late fifties, before the Quiet Revolution, when he was the senior man in Toronto and resisted Ouimet's efforts to summon him to Ottawa and help him centralize program controls in the capital. But now, he says, a shift of power to Montreal would be a disaster. He suggests that, since such shifts in a federal institution have to proceed symmetrically, so would it be in English Canada.

While admitting problems in communication, he does not concede that the organization is inherently inefficient and rejects LaMarsh's iceberg metaphor categorically.

Inevitably, he is asked whether he used the word "disloyalty" in his talk with Watson.

WALKER: I have never used the word "disloyalty". I say that most emphatically; never in the context of—

BRAND, M.P.: Did you use the word in reference to Mr. Watson?

WALKER: No, not at all—positively not.

BRAND, M.P.: You realize that he has stated that you did say that he was disloyal to top management.

WALKER: I say as emphatically that I did not.[33]

David Lewis pursues Walker relentlessly. He thinks that if management was critical of *Seven Days* it should have fired Leiterman and not the two hosts and he tries to extract from Walker the reasons why this was not done. Walker's replies fail to convince him. Then he tries to get to the bottom of management's position that it was necessary to break up the Leiterman-Watson axis.

WALKER: It was my understanding that Mr. Watson was part of the editorial board.

LEWIS: Did you enquire from Mr. Leiterman?... According to my recollection he said "I often did not see him for weeks except during the Sunday rehearsal".

WALKER: Yes.

LEWIS: Did you ever ask Mr. Leiterman whether he was interfering with his work?

WALKER: No.

LEWIS: You decided on your own—without any evidence that Mr. Watson had anything to do with the things which you dislike on the program—that you would remove him?

WALKER: Yes.

LEWIS: And you think that is a right way to carry on a program?

WALKER: Yes, I do.[34]

Ron Basford, the vice-chairman, follows a different line of questioning. Walker said that he hoped Leiterman would stay and continue with *Seven Days* but he was aware of the possibility that he might not. In that case, Walker says, it might be possible to find somebody else, though that would not be easy.

BASFORD: Do I take it then that that is a vote of confidence in Mr. Haggan, as supervisor of public affairs, to supervise *Seven Days* next year?

WALKER: No, you may not take it as a vote of confidence in Haggan to supervise *Seven Days* next year.

The kind of supervision *Seven Days* required, Walker goes on to say, is under study.

WALKER: At the proper time a vote of confidence will be given to the people concerned, or, if you want to put it crudely, the axe will fall.[35]

Friday, May 6th

There is nothing crude in Ouimet's testimony today. (It will be resumed on May 30th and on June 2nd.) His magisterial opening statement, which covers twelve pages of Hansard, raises the level of debate to the high ground of philosophical principle. It is the first formulation in CBC history of a code of journalistic ethics, and in the classical purity of its case for objectivity and impartiality it has never been surpassed.

It is of first importance that the CBC provide a platform which others can use to influence public opinion but it must not mount that platform itself.

It is the Corporation's view that the CBC was not brought

into being to instigate or stimulate social changes. It was intended to use the communications techniques of broadcasting to help the Canadian people make their own choices of what their future should be. It presents and interprets significant events in Canada and the world at large, but it advocates no view. It must serve public opinion, but it must not directly mould it.

Our experience with *Seven Days* indicates that its people do not agree with the Corporation's views. Too often in past programs they have paid only lip service to the principles involved.[36]

Ouimet's testimony graphically provides the intellectual basis of the fight with *Seven Days*. His arguments are promptly challenged by Leiterman in an article for the Ottawa *Citizen* to which Keate is to refer in his report. First, Leiterman recites the achievements of *Seven Days*. Then he attacks Ouimet's position head on.

Television journalism of this calibre could not be aired without undermining the old myths of objectivity and "studious neutrality", the standard set by CBC President Alphonse Ouimet in his recent statement to the parliamentary committee.

These notions have never been more than myths.

The very process of editing, even the CBC National News, has always involved the subjective judgment of an editor, a director or even a stand-up reporter with his own evaluation for an "on camera" report.

But the conventional wisdom in high places has always been hidden behind comfortable myths. Not understanding the processing of hard news, some people in television understand even less the processes of vivid first-person TV journalism.

As long ago as 1954, when Edward R. Murrow effectively destroyed Senator McCarthy by a skilful edit of his speeches, the cognoscenti have been aware that TV journalism was a powerful tool. It could be used well, or badly. It could be used by honest and dedicated men, or by fools and knaves. The protection of the public lies not in trying to prevent the tool from being used. That would be as useless as pretending gunpowder had never been invented. The protection of the public lies in the choice of the men who use the tools, and in the public's shrewd and certain awareness when it is being hoaxed.

Only the bureaucratic mind can know the frustration of confronting a problem which defies corporate skill in drafting policy statements. To try to lay down policies or rules to cover the new-old journalism makes no sense at all.

There is only one way to do it, and every honest journalist of whatever medium has known it. You must be as honest and fair as you know how.[37]

Ouimet has anticipated these counter-arguments.

Admittedly, absolute fairness may be an unrealizable ideal, but it is one to which the CBC has traditionally dedicated itself as fully as human fallibility and the limitations of broadcasting allow.[38]

Turning from philosophical theory to actual practice, Ouimet deals at length with the recent behaviour of the *Seven Days* team.

It is an illuminating commentary on the conditions under which the CBC operates that a group of employees has been able, these last three weeks, to challenge corporate authority in a way that would not be tolerated in private enterprise for one minute... I know of no precedent in Canada or elsewhere for this challenge to corporate authority by employees who at the same time have continued to use the facilities and the financial resources of the organization they were challenging and, in so doing, have continued to enjoy their chosen work and to increase their public reputation.[39]

In his opening statement Ouimet had declared that, by supporting the Leiterman-Watson line, Haggan had put himself in an impossible position. Resignation normally preceded such action. Now he is repeatedly questioned as to what his intentions are regarding Haggan.

SHERMAN:	Could you state categorically—yes or no—whether, in your view, Mr. Haggan is now finished with the CBC?
OUIMET:	I am in the position of a man with a board to which he reports, and until this is discussed with my board, on which I have a vote, I cannot tell you what the decision will be.
SHERMAN:	Are you not chairman of the board?
OUIMET:	I chair the board meetings.
FAIRWEATHER:	Will his future be placed before the board?
OUIMET:	I think the whole situation will have to be studied very carefully by the board. You would not expect anything else in view of its responsibility to parliament for the conduct of the affairs of the Corporation.[40]

Later in the hearings David Lewis takes Ouimet to task for his statement that Haggan had "put himself in an impossible position".

LEWIS: I regard...the words as a threat to Mr. Haggan's position with the Corporation, and I want to ask you whether you seriously think that it is dignified and responsible for the president of the CBC to make this kind of threat which it clearly was not necessary to discuss or to issue before this committee, a threat you can make, as president, to Mr. Haggan in any private office. Why did you find it necessary to issue this threat in public?

OUIMET: I think because I have tried in all my appearances before this Committee to give you my full thought.[41]

Ouimet receives little press coverage. Now that the last show has gone on the air on May 8th, the country has become bored with the *Seven Days* War.

••••

But the last, the fiftieth, instalment of *Seven Days*, is far from boring. The pacing is fast, the editing smooth, and the camera work sophisticated. Any one who remembers the first program must be struck by the immense improvement in production technique. There is only one reference to the crisis.

"Would you believe it, ladies and gentlemen," Laurier LaPierre says at the beginning of the show, "Patrick and I have not yet made up our minds whether to come back next year."

The program contains two interviews about aircraft sabotage due to flight insurance. Captain James Foy, an Air Canada pilot and president of the International Federation of Airline Pilots, says that "one of the prime motivations of saboteurs has been flight insurance", and pleads for the removal of machines in airports which made the purchase of flight insurance easy. James Barret, executive vice-president of Mutual of Omaha, disagrees. His company sells thirteen million dollars worth of flight insurance every year. "In all our investigations in the last forty years we've found that the primary motives have been the the same age-old things which have bothered mankind forever: love triangles, greed, business failures, and it is only after that...that flight insurance comes in as a secondary motive."

Once again, the program presents a skit by the Second City Company, as it had in the first program, this time satirizing southern fundamentalist faith healers.

The skit's target is a Christian crusade against communism.

"The Good Lord needs *your* help in its never-ending struggle against the atheistic communistic conspiracy. He needs *your* financial aid... My friends, I ask you to send whatever you can, be it a penny, a dime or a dollar. Send it to KILL A COMMIE FOR CHRIST, Box 224, Totem, Oklahoma."

In the other skit on the program, Don Harron, playing his

familiar Parry Sound character Charlie Farquharson, is interviewed by Dinah Christie, and towards the end of the program Walter Gordon discusses his book *A Choice for Canada* in which he warns against excessive foreign ownership of the Canadian economy. There is also a short documentary about old-age homes in Toronto, containing interviews with patients waiting out their days in pathetically sordid establishments.

In retrospect, two other interviews are particularly memorable. The first one is with small, wiry man wearing a sari and appearing as a yogi, sitting on the studio stage with his legs crossed and performing, as he talks, extraordinary contortions with his body. His name is Alfred Schielewski and he speaks with a heavy German accent. First, he tells Warren Davis that he lives mainly on a diet of honey. Then they range over other subjects.

WARREN DAVIS: You speak of your ability to foresee events... What do you see in the future for Vietnam?

YOGI: The Vietnam situation is in a sense one attempt to virtually fling Western civilization into self-destruction.

WARREN DAVIS: What do you see in the future for Canada?

YOGI: If no divine miracle will happen, Canada will become a nuclear battlefield.

WARREN DAVIS: How soon?

YOGI: In less than ten years.

WARREN DAVIS: Who will drop the bombs?

YOGI: I am convinced that it will not be Russia that will start a nuclear war.

WARREN DAVIS: Do you watch the CBC?

YOGI: Very rarely.

WARREN DAVIS: What do you see in the future for the Canadian Broadcasting Corporation?

YOGI: Well, when the bomb falls, the tower will be molten.

The other guru on the program is Marshall McLuhan, who is interviewed by Robert Fulford. It is unlikely that it is a coincidence the producers had waited for the last program to present the interview. Many of McLuhan's thoughts have a direct bearing on the *Seven Days* dispute although it is never directly mentioned. This is Watson's introduction:

WATSON: Tonight we can report that our national image is changing. After years of exporting wheat and aluminum and newsprint and Lorne Greene and Raymond Massey we've finally come of age, and now we're exporting ideas. The man responsible is a tall, gangly ego who is professor of

English and director of the Centre for Culture and Technology at the University of Toronto. In the past year his name has become a password for the world of real and pseudo intellectuals. From New York to San Francisco, from Chicago to Atlanta, our own Herbert Marshall McLuhan has been labeled poet, philosopher, prophet. *Life* magazine has called him "the oracle of the electric age". His critics are almost as lively as his admirers. They call him a gadfly, a spellbinder, a word-merchant. But almost everyone agrees: no one can make sense out of more then ten percent of what the professor is saying, and that seems to include even the professor himself. Tonight he tells Robert Fulford—and you—how the world is going out of style, or maybe how it's coming back into style. Well, try and figure it out for yourself.

MCLUHAN: The planet is going to get a great new processing—from the meteorologists, and from all sorts of scientific therapists. It's going to be put in apple-pie order. So it'll be nice to come back to the old homestead from outer space every once in a while.

FULFORD: You've been writing about the mass media for a good many years and now are an object of the mass media. How has this changed your view?

MCLUHAN: Let me explain why this has happened. It's because the mood of North America has changed very drastically. Things like the safety car couldn't have happened ten years ago.

FULFORD: Why is that?

MCLUHAN: It's because people have suddenly become obsessed with the consequences of things. They used to be obsessed with mere products and packages and with launching these things out into markets and into the public. Now they've suddenly become concerned with what happens when these things go out on the highway—what happens if this kind of program gets on the air. They want safety air, safety cigarettes, safety cars and safety programming. This need for safety is a sudden awareness that things have effects. Now, my writing has for years been concerned with the effects of things, not their impact, but their consequences, after impact. TV, unlike the fantasy escape world of the movies, creates an enormously serious and realistically-minded kind of person, almost oriental in his inward meditativeness.

FULFORD: The teenager of today?

MCLUHAN: Yes, he's become almost oriental in his inwardness.

FULFORD: He's so thoughtful and serious?

MCLUHAN: Yes. Grim. Whereas the movie generations of the twen-

	ties and thirties were a coon-coated bunch of superficial types, had a good time, and went to college, but not for knowledge and that sort of thing. All is changed.
FULFORD:	And changed because of television?
MCLUHAN:	Television gave the old electric circuitry that's already here a huge extra push in this direction of involvement and inwardness. You see, the circuit doesn't simply push things out for inspection, it pushes you in. It involves you. When you put a new medium into play, people's sensory life shifts a bit, sometimes shifts a lot. This changes their outlook, their attitudes, changes their feelings about studies, about school, about politics. Since TV, Canadian, British and American politics have cooled off almost to the point of rigor mortis ...
FULFORD:	What kind of a world would you rather live in? Is there a period in the past, or a possible period in the future ...?
MCLUHAN:	No. I'd rather be in any period at all as long as people leave it alone for a while.
FULFORD:	But they're not going to, are they?
MCLUHAN:	No. So, the only alternative is to understand everything that's going on, and then try to neutralize it, turn off as many buttons as you can, and frustrate them as much as you can. I'm resolutely opposed to all innovation, all change. But I'm determined to understand what's happening because I don't choose just to sit and let the juggernaut roll over me. Many people seem to think that because you talk about something recent you're in favour of it. The exact opposite is true in my case. Anything I talk about it almost certainly something I'm resolutely against and it seems to me that the best way of opposing it is to understand it. Then you know where to turn off the button.

The program ends with a nostalgic review of *Seven Days* highlights.

WATSON:	It has been a year to remember for us and we hope it has been for you, too. Good night.
LAPIERRE:	See you in seventeen weeks. Well, maybe. Au revoir.

CHAPTER 11

MEDIATION

Less than twenty-four hours after Stuart Keate had agreed to act as mediator, he was in his suite in the Château Laurier in Ottawa, which was to serve as his office, going through files of newspaper clippings.

He arrived in Ottawa on May 1st and handed in his report on May 26th.

Publisher of the *Vancouver Sun*, former head of the Montreal bureau of *Time* magazine, member of the Canada Council and of the senate and board of governors of UBC, retiring president of the Canadian Press and good Liberal, Keate accepted the job as a patriotic duty. Besides, he considered the prime minister a friend. But he also took it on in the spirit of a journalist who is given a fascinating assignment.

Nathan Cohen was unhappy about the appointment.

> The spokesmen for the TV Producers Association in Toronto welcomed with exuberance Prime Minister Lester B. Pearson's intervention in their latest dispute with CBC management, and his appointment of Stuart Keate to mediate these differences. It is a development they will long rue.
>
> Mr. Keate's good faith and qualifications are beyond challenge. But the prime minister's involvement and the acceptance of his offer both by the producers and CBC management is a most dangerous turn of events.
>
> For thirty-three years...resistance to government interference in its affairs has been a cardinal CBC principle... A good many of the producers now screaming for management's scalp owe their jobs and have the latitude they enjoy on their programs because of CBC top-level opposition to political pressure... By their behaviour, their agitation and their ultimatums, the TV producers have laid the basis for real and continuing political interference in the CBC's affairs... A terrible thing has happened, and they will have to answer for it.[1]

On arrival in Ottawa Keate said he did not know what the precise terms of reference were.[2] Ouimet promised his cooperation with a stiff upper lip. On May 10th, in the parliamentary committee, he repeated his decision not to reinstate the two hosts.

FAIRWEATHER: Then what is Mr. Keate doing on this? Is he here to look at the tulips?
OUIMET: He is conciliating.
LEWIS: What?
FAIRWEATHER: Yes, what?
OUIMET: I do not know. He was not given any particular terms of reference. I do not know.[3]

On May 1st, the day of Keate's appointment, a CBC spokesman had already made it clear that the decision about the hosts was irreversible. When Leiterman heard this he said that if there was any misunderstanding about the terms of reference, the question of a strike would be reconsidered immediately.[4]

Judy LaMarsh, however, took a positive view of Keate's task.

The phraseology of the instructions was left sufficiently fluid that Mr. Keate would be able to look into all the circumstances of the controversy that obtain at the present time in the narrow sense of the program in question and in the wider sense of the lower part of the iceberg.[5]

Keate was not a mediator in the technical sense. He was not appointed by order-in-council. He had no authority to subpoena witnesses and only his expenses were paid. Once before he had been called in to help make peace in a dispute in the world of culture. A year or so earlier, the Vancouver Opera Association was upset because the Metropolitan Opera National Company was invading its territory. He gave a lunch at the Vancouver Hotel. In consequence, the parties began to talk to each other.

Keate conducted lengthy interviews with twenty-four people involved in the dispute and half a dozen outsiders who could offer advice. He soon came to the conclusion that both sides had behaved badly. The CBC had been ham-handed in its firings and Watson and LaPierre had been insufferably arrogant in their assaults on their bosses.[6]

The report, written with urbanity and wit, contained many perceptive observations. The national hysteria which had attended the debate about *Seven Days*, he wrote, was reflected in a daily newspaper which published a two-column headline "U Thant Warns World of Nuclear Disaster" in a modest position on page one, well below a banner headline, with pictures, "on the Perils of LaPierre". He deplored the Halifax decision by the CBC board not to reopen the case of the two hosts even though the

CBC candidly admitted that the line of authority had been broken.

> This, it seems to me, is at the root of the public protest. The board's intransigent stand was an affront to an instinctive Canadian sense of fair play.

Every person he had interviewed agreed that management had a right to manage. Richard Nielsen of the Producers' Association had even gone a step further. He said management also had a right to mismanage.

Keate quoted a memo from the Producers' Association in which it was suggested that the purpose of management's actions during the dispute was "to cut Mr. Leiterman down to size, to make him and his program more 'manageable'".

> As an Association, we neither approve nor disapprove of this objective. We simply assert that the methods employed involved a kind of program interference which is unacceptable.

LaPierre's forthright speeches seemed to Keate to indicate at times a death-wish.

> On a day on which we proposed to Mr. Ouimet that the case of the hosts be re-opened, newspapers headlined a report of a LaPierre speech in Vancouver: LAPIERRE ASKS CBC LEADERS BE REMOVED.
>
> This suggestion did not appeal to the President.

Keate did not think that LaPierre had been disciplined for a single tear, "dropped at the end of an excruciatingly banal interview".

> There is, after all, a substantial tradition of tears in radio and TV. One remembers Arthur Godfrey's honourable weeping at the funeral of Franklin D. Roosevelt and the near-hysteria of the announcer who witnessed the crash of the Hindenburg at New Jersey. Mr. Jack Paar cried every Thursday on American TV, and amassed a fortune in the process.

He thought there should be a place for LaPierre in Canadian television. He took a similarly broad view on frictions between creative people and management in the media. These had always existed everywhere.

> It will be recalled that the late Fred Allen made a lifetime career of harassing NBC vice-presidents whom he described in his autobiography as "men who come to their offices at 9 a.m., find a molehill on their desks, and have until 5 p.m. to build it into a mountain".

Keate also referred to *Seven Days'* coverage of the Fawcett case.

Much had been made by the CBC of the *Seven Days* penetration of an asylum, their cameras concealed in picnic-baskets, to photograph a story on Fred Fawcett.

Mr. Leiterman's defence is that this was journalistic enterprise, completely justified by the fact that Mr. Fawcett was improperly incarcerated and was subsequently released.

To understand this approach it is necessary to appreciate what Robertson Davies has described as "the raffish, slightly declasse air" of journalism. It is my belief that most metropolitan dailies would have awarded their staff a bonus for such a successful exercise in social justice.

Seven Days, Keate observed, had enjoyed wide latitude in the fifty programs it presented. This was in the best CBC tradition of freedom. The impositions of genuinely stultifying censorship were few. He singled out a few instances where he thought management was right in the position it took. For example, he did not blame it for considering the program's treatment of Pierre Sévigny an invasion of his privacy. He felt that most Canadians, placed in Sévigny's position, would have reacted precisely as he did.

The most valid criticism of *Seven Days*, it seems to me, is in respect of its interviewing technique. The art of the interview, an American authority once observed, is "to ask shrewd questions in a friendly way".

In my opinion, this genuine concept was abused on *Seven Days*. Too often, the interview descended to the level of a brutal, almost savage, inquisition.

Leiterman, "the generalissimo of the current battle", struck him as a gifted journalist and producer, a man prepared to work for ninety hours a week, who was in the forefront of the move to expand the boundaries of television and eager to test management at all levels.

As such he has been stubborn, prickly and relentless in the cause of his show.

Leaving open whether or not he approved—he may well have done—he quoted a passage from an article Leiterman wrote for the Ottawa *Citizen* of May 20th:

Those who do not understand the program, or the nature of television, have said that *Seven Days* can do "an even better job" if you take away the parts of the program they don't approve of, and dismiss the people who host and produce it.

They may succeed. If they do, they will make mockery of a statement of President Ouimet to the Commonwealth Broadcasting Conference in Nigeria. He said: "We must never fear to show our present-day society as it is, even if the picture may sometimes be disturbing or unpleasant. We must never fear to make room for new ideas, artistic innovations, new ways of thinking, notwithstanding the protests of certain elements in the audience."

At one point Keate decided it might be useful if a last-ditch confrontation could be arranged between Messrs Haggan and Leiterman on one side and President Ouimet and Vice-President Coderre on the other. But Ouimet would not agree. He was dealing with the Producers' Association and Haggan was not a member. He thought no useful purpose could be served by such a confrontation. Keate quoted Ouimet:

> However, my door is always open to Mr. Haggan and Mr. Leiterman, through the proper channels.

In a section titled "Present Assessment" Keate wrote that Leiterman expected to reconstitute the show.

> But its future is uncertain and will probably be determined by the board. Mr. Ouimet takes the view that "an entirely new set of circumstances" has developed since the *Seven Days* blowup; Leiterman's testimony before the House Committee, and his role in the ensuing propaganda war in the mass media, will have to be assessed to determine whether the damage done is irrevocable.

In his conclusions Keate quoted a number of authorities who took a gloomy view of the crisis. Fowler had spoken of "smouldering dissatisfaction among producers". Two witnesses had said "The CBC is being torn apart". Walker told him they had been on a collision course for years. Haggan said: "This could finish off the public affairs department for some time. Perhaps there will be a small rump left of quite capable people, though not in television."

Keate did not seem to think that so much gloom was justified. He suggested that better things were in store for the Corporation after the present generation of leadership fades away.

> The CBC is fast approaching a watershed in its colourful and distinguished history. Some of its key executives are at or near retiring age. They have grown up in what may roughly be described as "the age of radio", and have brought great honour to their country by building a system which is acknowledged to be one of the world's best.

He recommended that at the next board meeting, at the end of the month, the question of the hosts be re-examined and an amplifying statement issued. The parliamentary committee should move to other considerations on its agenda and the government should produce a White Paper as quickly as possible. The Producers' Association should suspend its strike threat.

••••

On May 26th, the same day Keate submitted his report, Pearson wrote him a letter.

Dear Stuart,

There are times when I feel severely handicapped by our lack of state honours to recognize outstanding public service. My receipt of your report on the CBC dispute was one such occasion. Your immediate response to my call, your contribution of your services, the dispatch with which you reported and the soundness, balance and readability of that report—for all these I am deeply grateful.

At this time it is impossible to predict the outcome of your labours, but that does not lessen their worth.

I look forward to seeing you again soon.

With sincere thanks and warm regards,

Yours sincerely,
L.B. Pearson

In the House of Commons Diefenbaker rose. His reference to the report was sarcastic:

Mr. Speaker, may I ask the Prime Minister, since delivery to him of what might be described as Stuart Keate's commentaries, whether he has talked with the president of the Canadian Broadcasting Corporation, or any of the senior executives, and have given any indication that they are willing to compromise on their decision...

Pearson answered that indeed the report had at once been referred to Ouimet and the Producers' Association.

When first reading it Leiterman was elated. The recommendation that at the end-of-the-month session of the board the question of the hosts was to be re-examined, followed by an amplifying statement, suggested to him that Keate had come out on his side. The board was to meet in Ottawa the following morning. He sent Keate a wire of congratulations and declared that it was an excellent report. He hoped, he said, that *Seven Days* would return intact next year. But in Vancouver Keate went to great lengths to explain to the press that he had not specifically recommended a reopening of the host question. "Management made it clear to me," he said, "that the CBC would not negotiate on this, and that is that".[7] Leiterman immediately issued another statement. If the board refused to reconsider its decision, he declared, "I fear the whole mess will be back where it started and mass resignations may become inevitable."[8]

In Montreal LaPierre thought the report left room open for a solution to the problem. The issue was not his and Watson's fate, he told reporters, but "the entry of management into production affairs. The primary issue is that the producer must be guardian of his artistic integrity".[9] Watson was in Saskatoon participating in the city's anniversary celebrations. He told the press there was nothing new in the report and he saw no reason why the CBC should pay any attention to it.[10] In Ottawa," David Lewis called it a "fence-sitting job". Reading between the lines, he said, it appeared Keate was saying top management was unfit to deal with programming. "Why couldn't he have said so in polite, clear language?"[11]

The Producers' Association was in a difficult position. The CBC had admitted its procedural mistake and promised to respect producers' rights in future, so no great matter of principle was at stake any longer. Public excitement had died down and the holiday season had started. The executive was in touch with CBC management. Therefore management knew that any renewed strike threat, as envisaged by Leiterman, was not to be taken seriously.

However, the three negotiators were upset by Keate's statement that he had *not* recommended a re-examination of the host question even though he had asked the board to reconsider. If they had not taken exception to this statement, it would have seemed to the *Seven Days* people they had clearly sold them down the river when they agreed to the manner in which Keate was appointed on May 1st. Therefore, they sent off a *cri de coeur* to him in Vancouver, with a copy to the board.

> We submit with respect that the prime minister's good offices have served merely to prolong and make more intractable a dispute which threatens the future of effective public broadcasting in Canada. For in the body of your report you clearly indicate that your inquiry failed to turn up "cogent reasons" for management's decisions. You state unequivocally that that decision failed to observe due process and violated a previous understanding with producers. Yet, you are now reported as saying that you have not suggested that the board re-examine its decision. If not, why not? You suggest in your press statement but not in your report that the reason that you did not ask for re-examination of the case is that CBC management refused to negotiate the issue. This was management's position when you were appointed. That is why Toronto producers demanded a third party review of the case. The prime minister was in no doubt that the Toronto producers accepted

your appointment because of the clear understanding that you were free to make specific recommendations. In your report you state that the prime minister specifically requested that you make suggestions for a resolution of the dispute. Your failure to do so despite a report which confirms in detail the criticism made against senior management by the producers leaves us no alternative but to inform you that we as negotiators for the association will recommend to our membership that they reject your request that we suspend our proposed withdrawal from service.[12]

There is no record of any response to this communication. On May 30th the Association held a general meeting and unanimously accepted the negotiators' recommendations not to withdraw the strike threat. It also resolved to appeal to parliament to restate the aims of public broadcasting in Canada and sent a recapitulation of its position to the parliamentary committee. This long communication was duly tabled and printed in Hansard.[13]

●●●●

According to Roy Shields of the *Toronto Star*, Ouimet, Briggs and Walker were reported to have said that they would resign if the board did not uphold them at the Ottawa meeting on May 27th.[14]

There was no need. The board was still as incensed as it had been a month earlier at the interference by the politicians and was in no mood to make concessions. After a five-hour meeting it supported Ouimet and his two colleagues "out of deep concern for the maintenance of CBC policies and to continue with the program *Seven Days*."[15] But two of the eleven members dissented.[16] While they would not have gone as far as Dalton Camp, they may at least have had some understanding for the bitter irony of his comments:

> We have now clearly established the right of management to mismanage. Every anachronistic incompetent is now snug in his ivory tower. All who disagreed should have known better. Form matters more than content: it is better to be big than to be good, and seniority must never be tried by sensibility.[17]

Comments such as this no doubt had an influence on the third and most dramatic session of the board four weeks later, at the end of June.

CHAPTER 12

DEMISE

It was *Götterdämmerung* time in the *Seven Days* offices in Toronto as spring turned into summer. The atmosphere was filled with confusion, theatrical heroics, intrigue, exhaustion, anger and despair. Sardonic jokes compared the place to the Berlin bunker in 1945.

Only the indomitable Leiterman remained optimistic. The closer he came to the end, the more convinced he was that victory was around the corner. With inexhaustible zeal he, Hoyt and other activists pulled whatever strings they could among the politicians, among members of the CBC board, among their friends in the media and in the universities. Below the level of respectable lobbying, *Seven Days* operatives used all kinds of cloak-and-dagger techniques. Whoever was not with them was against them. The world was full of enemies. One of the researchers, Brian Shaw, used to be a professional detective and now proved invaluable. Soon after arriving in Ottawa, Keate was amazed to discover that somebody he met knew where he had been the day before. Apparently he had been followed by talkative *Seven Days* agents.

In this atmosphere neither side was capable any longer of clear thinking and of understanding the other side's motivations.

Leiterman made every effort to persuade his colleagues in the Producers' Association to renew the strike threat. But there was little response, nor was Haggan prepared to support such an effort. Leiterman did not allow these temporary setbacks to deflect him from his main objective—to work out a compromise with Ouimet.

If the cause of *Seven Days* was not the cause of the Producers' Association, nor was it that of the national public affairs department. Still, without exception, they were appalled by the authoritarian way senior management was dealing with Haggan. Early in June, sixty members, including radio producers, signed a document declaring their support of him.[1]

Reeves Haggan had few illusions. Deeply depressed, living

from day to day in semi-chaotic gloom, he thought that very likely his days as general supervisor, and therefore in the CBC, were numbered. He doubted very much that they would fire him. He had declared to the parliamentary committee on April 28th that "it is a serious matter to fire the general supervisor of public affairs".[2] He knew this to be particularly true now when such an action might be construed as being in contempt of parliament. He expected that they would try to squeeze him into some other box on Ouimet's famous organization charts. But he was far too proud to allow them to do that, although a good case could have been made for waiting for a new regime in which he might play a leading role. After all, if his days were numbered, so were, in the slightly longer run, Ouimet's. But that was not the way his mind worked. He knew he was going to leave. But it was he, not Ouimet, who would choose the right moment.

●●●●

On Tuesday June 21st Leiterman was invited to Ottawa. He had earlier expressed a desire to see the president. This occasion gave Ouimet an opportunity for a calculated show of strength. Later, Leiterman referred to the confrontation as "The Star Chamber". On the bench sat Ouimet, flanked by Briggs and Walker. Facing him, on the hot seat, was Leiterman. They fought him with his own weapon.

For an hour he was subjected to a litany of his misdeeds.

> At the end of an hour I said to Mr. Ouimet that I felt the only hope of progress was for him to see me alone. He agreed and we had a useful chat for an hour, in which I said I was certain there were compromise proposals which could give both management and public affairs a reasonable settlement if we tried to reach it. He said he would think about it.[3]

The compromise to which Leiterman referred included a link between the *Quarterly Report* and *Seven Days*—a prospect Ouimet was not prepared to consider, with the result that the concept of *Quarterly Report*, invented three months earlier with such joyous bicultural enthusiasm at Mont Gabriel, was to be buried under the smoking ruins of *Seven Days*, not to be revived until June 1977, eleven years later, in a different form. A better name had still not come along.

By the beginning of June Ouimet had appeared to have abandoned hope that *Seven Days* could return in the fall under Leiterman's leadership. Ouimet considered his position strong. While many of the columnists, cartoons and front-page stories were hostile to him, he had much support on the editorial pages, as

Blair Fraser had pointed out on CBC radio on April 24th. And he received a great deal of mail encouraging him to remain firm. A businessman in Schumacher, Ont., wrote that in his view *Seven Days* was "a sick program, conceived and presented by sick people".

> Under the guise of pseudo-adultism *Seven Days* has succeeded only in achieving disturbed puerility, a smuttiness, which is more in keeping with adolescent wall scrawling.
>
> As a taxpayer and a father trying to raise a family with a reasonable set of guidelines concerning decency, I urge you to do more than merely dismiss the hosts of *Seven Days*. I urge you to "clean house" with the entire program in order that it might succeed in its necessary function of presenting informed and objective opinions on current events.

During his third appearance before the parliamentary committee on June 2nd Ouimet had made a number of statements about the future of *Seven Days*. When speaking of his confidence in Leiterman he used the past tense.

> It is necessary now to...reassess the feasibility of including the program in the 1966 fall schedule. The reason for this is that not only has Mr. Leiterman, the executive producer on whom we were counting, challenged Corporation authority by acting, as Mr. Keate reported in his recent statement, as "the generalissimo of the battle"...but he has also challenged the Corporation's policies in his recent manifesto which was published in the press. These developments have compelled the Corporation to review the whole thing and this will be done as soon as possible: I hope by the end of the month. You will recall that Mr. Leiterman's views as published recently include the contention that producers should be given the right to editorialize in controversial matters. He also contends that such procedures as the invasion of private property and the use of extra-legal means can properly be used in collecting information for CBC programs such as *Seven Days*. Such views are unacceptable to the Corporation.[4]

Later he was asked directly whether *Seven Days* would be renewed.

> We are not renewing the contracts as usual at this time in a wholesale fashion because we have to decide first whether we have reasonable assurance that we can get *Seven Days* back. One thing you may be sure of is that we will have a magazine type program which will be virile and vigorous and interesting. But I am not sure that it will be exactly the *Seven Days* that you have now. I am not saying it will not be back. That is a decision which has yet to be made.[5]

Leiterman's days as executive producer of *Seven Days* were

clearly numbered, as far as the president of the CBC was concerned.

•••

If it had been up to the parliamentary committee, the program would most certainly have returned in the fall in its existing form. The committee's report, presented to the House on June 28th, clearly showed what sympathetic politicians, public pressure and *Seven Days'* determined lobbying efforts could achieve. The people's elected representatives were overwhelmingly on Leiterman's side.

The Committee had no intention, the report stated, "of intervening in the CBC's internal decisions by passing judgment on the actions of any individual member of the CBC's management or personnel, or on the content of any individual program". It had not embarked on a new journey when it set out to explore the *Seven Days* issue; most of the circumstances were strikingly reminiscent of the findings of previous enquiries, such as the Glassco Commission and the Fowler Committee. The testimony from both English and French networks made it clear that the existing malaise—to avoid a stronger word—was in no way limited to the *Seven Days* issue, but pervaded the whole department of public affairs. The dissension, which seemed deeply rooted in the very structures of the CBC, could not be allowed to go on without jeopardizing both the prestige and the efficiency of the Corporation. Therefore, the Committee strongly recommended a collective agreement with the producers comparable to that existing in Montreal. Moreover, lines of authority were not well defined, which had led to "extreme nervousness or jumpiness on the part of management with regard to public reactions and extreme touchiness or irritability on the part of the creative personnel". This spelled out the very formula for disaster. Furthermore, there should be more opportunities for "younger, more dynamic elements to reach top echelons of management" and the failure to achieve this goal indicated that a certain amount of sclerosis had crept in. Management had not acted wisely in isolating the public affairs department from the normal lines of authority, and therefore in both production centres senior vice-presidents should be appointed who would be responsible for production and programming. (The CBC board was just about to make the same recommendation.) Furthermore, a serious fault in the present structure of the CBC was to be found in the definition of the president's function and authority. He was expected "to be at the same time versed in all aspects of culture, politics and social evolution; aware of all the latest developments in communication techniques as well as an able administrator capable of supervising the management of a budget that exceeded one hundred million dollars".

In the matter of program policies, the committee did not feel that CBC neutrality in controversial issues should be so scrupulous as to detract from liveliness and that a balance could be found between personal editorializing and dullness inspired by fear of public reactions. The CBC needed performers with strong individuality and personal opinions who were aware of their own biases and capable of keeping them in check. Objectivity was as difficult to attain as it was difficult to define. "All journalists have to strive for it, but none, including those employed by the CBC, should be expected to achieve it automatically." The best one could hope for was sincere and constant effort towards high standards of journalistic honesty. Finally, the committee was concerned that steps be taken to ensure adventurous programming during the next season.[6]

On the evening of Monday June 27th the majority of the committee adopted an amendment to the draft report deploring "the manner in which public opinion was injected and drawn into the *Seven Days* crisis by the producers". Twenty-one of the twenty-five members were present. On Tuesday afternoon a meeting took place with only twelve members present, the smallest attendance of any of the thirty-four meetings the committee had held. During that meeting the amendment was voted down. Harold Stafford was unavoidably absent on Tuesday afternoon. On Wednesday he wanted to move the amendment in the full House but he was outmaneouvred. He bitterly complained about this in an article he published two months later in which he told the story of "how an important parliamentary committee went about the job of whitewashing the rebellious producers who got not even a word of reproach for their highly public insubordination".[7]

During the Question Period on Wednesday June 29th Diefenbaker rose.

> Mr. Speaker, the question I should like to ask is directed at the Prime Minister. In view of the substantial criticism of CBC management contained in the report of the committee...is the government going to give consideration to an immediate change in the top management of the CBC? Will the government assure us that the CBC management will be required to review the handling of the case of *This Hour Has Seven Days*?

PEARSON: Mr. Speaker, the report was tabled only an hour ago
and I have not yet had an opportunity to study it.

Fairweather had a supplementary question for Judy LaMarsh.
He asked her whether she would convey to the Corporation that
"a large number of Canadians would welcome the return of the
program *This Hour Has Seven Days*, unrevised and unrepent-
ant?"

LAMARSH: Mr. Speaker, I have a woman's intuition, if you want to
call it that, that they may already know this.[8]

On the following Monday, July 4th, LaMarsh tabled the White
Paper on broadcasting in the House. Some parts of it were critical
of CBC management. It disapproved of the recent build-up of
central authority in Ottawa and made one reference to *Seven
Days*.

> The government considers that the headquarters of the Corpo-
> ration should remain in Ottawa, but that the headquarters
> staff should be of the minimum size compatible with the
> general direction of the Corporation.
>
> The recent difficulties in the relationship of management to
> production staff forcefully underline the necessity for signifi-
> cant improvement in internal communications. The Govern-
> ment therefore expects that action to effect the necessary
> organizational changes will be given high priority by the Cor-
> poration.

In a press conference LaMarsh denied any suggestion that
Ouimet was being removed from power. There was nothing in
the White Paper, she said, which would cause Ouimet to resign
in protest. On the other hand, in response to a specific question,
she declined to confirm that the government would reappoint
him as president once the new legislation was passed.[9]

• • • •

The fate of *Seven Days* was on the agenda at the four-day
annual meeting of the CBC board in Ottawa, beginning on June
27th. If the board upheld Ouimet, *Seven Days* would be permitted to return in the fall, but without Leiterman. If this could not
be arranged, another "virile, interesting and vigorous" program
would take its place. If it failed to uphold Ouimet, Leiterman
would continue in the fall as executive producer of *Seven Days*.

There was no clear answer.

The minutes of the meeting suggest that on the matter of
Leiterman's future Ouimet was outvoted. A majority of the board

was prepared to have Leiterman continue. But the evidence is not unequivocal. The relevant motion, opposed by both Ouimet and Briggs, contained five sections, of which the section on the future of Leiterman was only one. The vote was taken on the whole motion, not on specific sections. It is therefore impossible to know for certain which part of the motion made it impossible for Ouimet and Briggs to support it. But under the circumstances, it seems safe to assume it was the Leiterman section.

The condition the board imposed on Leiterman's return was that he give a written assurance he would in future "accept CBC policies, procedures and direction." (Such an acceptance was already a standard part of the contract which Leiterman and other producers had signed.) Presumably, the question of whether or not he was prepared to sign such a special document would constitute a final test of some sort. No doubt at least some members of the board hoped he would pass it. Others hoped he would not. But at any rate the majority thought it was the fair—and, in the light of the parliamentary committee's report, politically sensible—thing to do.

In the other sections of the resolution, the board expressed agreement with the committee's observation that program policies must be regularly reviewed; it re-affirmed its public statement that it had accepted the principle of an internal grievance procedure; it accepted the idea of establishing positions for two vice-presidents in Toronto and Montreal; and it noted "with concern that there had been deficiencies in the supervision of *Seven Days* and requested management to make necessary changes to improve the supervision."[10]

The criticism of Haggan's supervision could easily have been predicted in view of his testimony before the parliamentary committee. It was the board's decision about Leiterman which was unexpected and extraordinary.

But by now the atmosphere had deteriorated to such an extent that neither Leiterman nor any of his friends grasped the situation. The condition the board had imposed on Leiterman's continuation as executive producer was interpreted as merely another outrageous example of Ouimet's obstructionist chicanery.

The story was not over yet.

● ● ● ●

The meeting of the board concluded on Thursday June 30th. July 1st was Dominion Day. On Tuesday, July 5th there was a bizarre twist in the last scene of the drama. The central figure was Bud Walker.

On the first day of the board meeting, the *Toronto Star* had carried this red-lettered headline: OUIMET ON CBC CARPET FOR NOT FIRING WALKER.[11] On the second day, Osler had moved a resolution that Walker be removed from his job and offered an equivalent responsibility, or be retired on full pension. The motion was defeated. On the fourth day, a motion was carried providing for the appointment of a senior vice-president in Montreal and in Toronto.

Walker decided to break through the dark clouds gathering around him and make a pre-emptive move to the centre of the Toronto stage—the "Kremlin" on Jarvis Street—and establish squatter's rights on the (not yet established) vice-presidential chair. The date was Tuesday, July 5th.

Before making this trip he checked with his assistant Robert McGall in Toronto. McGall assured him that he would be well received.

He was not. No move at this moment could have been more misguided. When David Lewis heard about it, he said the CBC board and Ouimet would be "cutting their own throats" if they permitted such an appointment.[12]

At three thirty in the afternoon Walker held a short meeting in his former office, now occupied by McGall, and announced that he would be moving to Toronto on October 1st so that he could carry out his present duties more effectively.

Hardly had he spoken when someone rushed to the telephone —Walker thought later, rightly or wrongly, that it was Watson— and phoned Judy LaMarsh.

> I received an anguished phone call from Toronto. It was an old friend, long employed by the CBC, who was saying that Bud Walker had just appeared at CBC headquarters in Toronto indicating that he was in line for the new job of vice-president of the English network. He announced that in order to be close to the operation he intended to move his family to Toronto in a few months' time.
>
> Here was the man they hated most, sent down to lord it over them. This time I called Ouimet myself and asked him what in hell he was trying to pull off, whether he was himself deliberately fomenting another palace revolt. He was genuinely surprised and dismayed. Within a few hours he phoned back with a crisp report. He had checked out the truth of my informant's call and had prepared a short statement over Walker's name. In it, Walker took himself forever out of the running for the vice-presidency and indicated that he would not be moving to

Toronto as announced. He was recalled to Ottawa. This time he had gone too far.[13]

On that same Tuesday afternoon, Leiterman was formally asked to comply with the board's request to sign an undertaking to observe CBC policies. In the evening, Norman dePoe interviewed him on *Newsmagazine*. Walker's move came up.

LEITERMAN: I am asked to sign a loyalty oath saying I will accept Corporation policies and procedures and direction. I have done this. The man who failed to do any of these things is General Manager H.G. Walker.

DEPOE: After a public statement like that will you, or in fact can you, work for Mr. Walker?

LEITERMAN: Well, I must tell you that I find it completely astonishing—a most incredible kind of rebuke to my supervisors, to the public affairs department, to the program, that the Corporation should announce today... that Mr. Walker is now to be appointed to be the boss in Toronto. I really find this unbelievable. I don't think it leaves much room for doubt that management has very little confidence, perhaps no confidence, in the *Seven Days* staff, in myself, in my supervisors, or in the public affairs department.

DEPOE: You didn't answer the question. Will you or can you work for Mr. Walker?

LEITERMAN: I don't think I can answer that. I have been working for the officers of the Corporation as long as I've been in it. Mr. Walker is one of them. It seems to me that my loyalty is to the Corporation. It is to the principles that the Corporation has always stood for. As long as the Corporation is operated according to those principles of course I will work for it and of course I will take direction from the men who are appointed to direct it. I do think however that the appointment of this particular person to the Toronto area is just a total repudiation of everything that has been said about the *Seven Days* dispute.

Leiterman said he was "profoundly sad" at the way things were developing. The refusal of the Corporation to reopen the host question, he said, amounted to a blacklisting of Watson and LaPierre. His right to employ anybody as host on the show except those two was not questioned, in spite of the fact that neither the Keate report nor the parliamentary committee had found that they were guilty of the charges made against them. He found the demand to give a special undertaking to abide by Corporation policies "very puzzling and totally mystifying", because he had always done that to the best of his abilities and intended to continue to do so as long the Corporation saw fit to employ him.

LEITERMAN: I feel that if I was to sign another document...it would seem to cast doubt on whether my signature on the present document had any meaning. I think it has meaning. I hope the Corporation thinks it does.

DEPOE: You're saying then that you probably would sign such a document.

LEITERMAN: I suppose so. I suppose I could sign a dozen of them. It just seems to have no meaning.

The next day, on Wednesday, July 6, Leiterman told reporters that the demand for his signing an "obedience oath" was "childish and redundant" and that Walker's appointment was provocative. Senior management was deliberately trying to force the resignation of large segments of the public affairs department.

It's only reasonable to assume that Mr. Walker will become the top man in Toronto. And Mr. Walker is probably the most unacceptable person in the entire Corporation to be sent to Toronto. We have at all times tried to be reasonable and go halfway and all we have met with is rebuffs.[14]

Later on Wednesday, Ouimet authorized two announcements. This was the first one:

I note that rumours are circulating that Mr. H.G. Walker had been appointed to the senior vice-president position at Toronto... These rumours, which began in Toronto yesterday afternoon, have since been currency on radio and TV. They are false.

The idea of establishing positions of senior vice-presidents at Toronto and Montreal was accepted by the board less than a week ago, and there certainly has been no time to consider appointments to them.

The second release was issued under McGall's name.

H.G. Walker...announced today he is not a candidate for the new position of senior vice-president at Toronto, referred to in the CBC Board of Directors issued on July 5.

Mr. Walker said "the possibility of my appointment to the new post has given rise to a great deal of rumour and speculation. Under the circumstances, I feel it would be in the interest of the Corporation if I made my position clear."

Mr. Walker added that, to avoid confusion or ambiguity as to his intentions, he would not carry out his plan, announced yesterday, to move from Ottawa to Toronto, in connection with his present duties.

Early on Wednesday, Leiterman had suspended all work for the fall season of *Seven Days*. To the press, Leiterman gave as his reason Walker's announcement of his projected transfer to Toronto. Jim Carney instructed his people to stop all activities in connection with the summer show *Compass* and a notice went up on the board on Maitland Street to the effect that all work on Watson's *Document* ceased as of three p.m.

To the *Toronto Star* he declared that "the *Seven Days* switchboard will be manned, but filming, planning, taping and production will cease".

Gauntlett issued a memo.

> All the staff and contract employees are reminded that they are bound by the conditions of employment to remain at their posts.

Failure to honour their obligations would result in "immediate cessation of remuneration".

••••

Bill Hogg had suffered a nervous breakdown during the parliamentary committee meetings. Just before the board meeting he asked to be relinquished from his position. On Tuesday, July 5th his successor was appointed. It was Marce Munro who had been head of television since December 1964, a fair-minded practical administrator with a wide range of interests. Munro had suffered serious back injuries as a hardrock miner in his youth and this gave him the air of distinction of a man with an adventurous past. The frailty of his body was in marked contrast to his robust strength of purpose, and his sonorous speech pattern revealed the devotion of an ex-announcer to literate English.

Munro's first act in his new post was to request Haggan to pass on to Leiterman the board's condition. Later, he asked Haggan to tell Leiterman that if he was unable to accept the board's condition the CBC was prepared to negotiate a contract with him for the production of film documentaries. His answer was to be received by Friday afternoon at five.

On Wednesday after lunch, Munro told Haggan that he considered the work stoppage a violation of the unit's contracts and asked him to find out whether the *Seven Days* people were intending to offer their resignations. He also advised Haggan that, instead of utilizing his time to consider his situation, Leiterman was holding unauthorized press conferences and releasing press statements. Therefore, the deadline for giving his reply was now no longer Friday at five but Thursday at four.

In the afternoon Haggan sent a "secret and most urgent" telex to Ouimet.

Statements of the board of directors... severely damage efforts undertaken in good faith by my department in cooperation with French network department and following upon meetings in Ottawa with you and some of your officers to maintain program service of highest quality and to fulfill bicultural responsibilities of the Corporation.

Requiring Leiterman to provide in a special document undertakings clearly contained in his contract is regarded as insulting and degrading. This producer has given to the Corporation and to the country the most vital and significant program in the Corporation's history.

Surely it is something new in corporate practice for a board to make public derogatory remarks about employees in responsible positions as the CBC board did in referring to deficiencies in the supervision of *Seven Days*. Repeated calls from newsmen make it abundantly clear that this is taken as a direct attack upon Hugh Gauntlett, Peter Campbell and me. I cannot agree with the statement. Given the novelty and complexity of this program and the many difficulties naturally attendant, I consider that it has been supervised with skill, patience and determination. I cannot believe that you do not agree with this.

Unrelenting efforts here and in Montreal to find a workable solution resulted in my telex to you of June 24th. Considering the importance of the matters contained in it, I find it hard to understand why, apart from a brief acknowledgment of receipt from Walker, I have heard nothing by way of reaction from that day to this.

This department and the Corporation are now placed in a position of utmost difficulty. It seems to me that the board statement with its implied but clearly visible expressions of lack of confidence in public affairs supervisors and in Leiterman make it impossible to produce *Seven Days* from both the executive producer's and the supervisors' points of view. Failure to produce *Seven Days* is to deprive the audience of a series they value highly...

I feel I should comment on statements which have been made to the effect that "rumours" about H.G. Walker began in Toronto yesterday afternoon. In fact, Walker announced to McGall, Munro, Haggan, Campbell, Gauntlett...that he would be returning to permanent residence in Toronto on October 1st to enable him to carry out his present duties more effectively. This was part of an official statement and if it has been read by some as indication of Walker's eventual appointment to the new vice-president post this is hardly surprising.

I hope you remember the unrelenting efforts I made prior to

the *Seven Days* controversy reaching the press to bring about a sensible internal solution to the problem. In this telex I am appealing to you to try to find a way to undo the destructive effects of the board's last statement. I don't know if it can be done but I hope I need not assure you that I and my colleagues will spare no effort to help in any way I can.

Obviously I do not question the right of the board to make whatever statements it sees fit. This telex refers only to the effects of the last statement and my wish to mitigate these.

•••••

Reports of the work stoppage once again prompted Diefenbaker to rise in the House.

DIEFENBAKER: Mr. Speaker, I direct my question to the Prime Minister. May I ask the Prime Minister whether he has been made aware of the emergency situation created in the CBC which has had the effect of putting the administration of its public affairs department in a shambles?... What does the Prime Minister intend to do regarding this matter? What action is the government going to take?

PEARSON: Mr. Speaker, I am not aware of any emergency situation in the Canadian Broadcasting Corporation, but I should be very glad to bring to their attention the observations of my right honourable friend and ask them to report on the matter.

Diefenbaker turned to the Secretary of State, Judy LaMarsh, and repeated his question.

LAMARSH: ...I do not know that a delay of a day or so will constitute any sort of emergency... The programs are prepared over some length of time in advance. It would seem to me that this is the kind of decision for which parliament selects managing officers and instructs them to manage. I would not suggest to the House that any of us would be in a position to decide whether this could be a matter of emergency. Certainly it will be some months before the fall season starts, some time in September or October. Another day or so surely will not have any effect on the matter.

I have no doubt that the president, vice-president and the board will be making some statement later in the day and taking appropriate action.[15]

••••

On Thursday morning at ten a.m. Leiterman presented two memos to his supervisors. His deadline was at four p.m.

This was the first memo.

My action in suspending the production of *Seven Days* is not an intention to terminate my contract. I have asked the staff to suspend operations because of the uncertainties created by the president's statement which implies lack of confidence in me and my supervisors...

I find it reassuring that Mr. Walker has withdrawn that announcement, though I find it difficult to understand why it should now be referred to as a rumour. However, I must continue to instruct the *Seven Days* staff that work on the program cannot be resumed until the uncertainties referred to above are cleared up and the management begins serious discussions with Mr. Haggan and Marc Thibault of the June 24th proposal. To proceed on *Seven Days* production without these assurances would be a meaningless waste of Corporation funds.

In the second memo Leiterman advised his superiors that he assumed his normal contract, which he was prepared to sign again, covered the board's condition. He did not refuse to sign a supplementary declaration. However, he wrote that he could not accept any contract which qualified the clause in the normal contract which gave the executive producer "responsibility for the selection of scripts and principal artists". At eleven in the morning Munro told Haggan that he interpreted the memo as a rejection of the board's offer. Moreover, Leiterman had not specified that he was prepared to produce the show without Watson and LaPierre. Haggan pointed out that this was not a term in the board's offer and that he had presented the offer in the terms specified by the board.

Munro then alleged that he had instructed me to include the matter of the hosts in the offer. He suggested that I call Leiterman to try to get oral acceptance of a contract offer including agreement to produce the show without Watson and LaPierre. I did so and Leiterman, since the terms of the offer had been changed, then asked for a further twenty-four hours to consider his reply. After a telephone call to Ottawa this was refused.[16]

The next few hours were filled with moves and countermoves as Munro tried to negotiate with Leiterman through Haggan. At one point Munro told Haggan that the offer to sign a contract with Leiterman to produce documentaries if no agreement about *Seven Days* could be reached was also covered by the four o'clock deadline. This was new to Haggan. He said it again changed the terms of the offer. He suggested strongly to Munro that he should make representations to senior management to remove the deadline regarding Leiterman's production of documentaries. Still,

Haggan asked Leiterman whether he was prepared to produce documentaries. Sure, Leiterman said, that was better than total disaster.

After the four o'clock deadline had expired Munro asked Haggan to make absolutely sure that Leiterman understood the situation. This is Leiterman's account:

> At about four thirty p.m. Thursday Haggan phoned me from McGall's office and said he must ask me whether I would sign two statements in addition to my contract. One was a loyalty oath, and the other was a declaration that I understood *Seven Days* would be produced without Watson and LaPierre. I said I would sign another loyalty oath if they insisted but that I required twenty-four hours in which to consider the other declaration. I wanted to consult with my colleagues and, hopefully, the association.[17]

Haggan declared later that, from his experience in dealing with CBC management, "it was clear to me by four p.m. that they were determined to be rid of Leiterman that day regardless of anything he might accept".[18] Still, Haggan put forward another idea. A proposal could be prepared, he said, to provide one-hour documentaries, plus *Quarterly Report*, plus "a judicious scheduling" of other documentaries "which could provide effective strong programming for the Sunday night spot". *Seven Days* could then return in the 1967–68 season. Munro undertook to consult head office and asked Haggan to stand by for further communications.

In the evening Munro and McGall were in McGall's office. At ten o'clock Leiterman spoke on the *National News* on radio. It was a remarkable scene. Two senior CBC officials watched anxiously as events unfolded on the very medium of which they were in charge. Leiterman announced that he had decided to accept the Corporation's offer but said nothing to suggest that he intended to comply with the board's conditions.

This was the breaking point, whatever had been going on in their minds or in the minds of their superiors earlier in the day. McGall and Munro decided it was futile to carry on any further discussions with Leiterman. Here he was saying he accepted the terms when clearly he was not. They knew Leiterman was due to appear on the *National News* on television at eleven. Therefore a statement was drafted and sent over to the television news department, stating specifically that Leiterman's acceptance was not in accordance with the requirements of the board. At five minutes to eleven Munro telephoned Haggan and asked him to advise Leiterman immediately that his reply to the offer of a contract was not deemed acceptable and that on the next day, Friday, the CBC would announce that no useful relationship with Leiterman could be maintained at this time.

"I knew," Haggan explained later, "that I would not survive him for very long. I did not wish to resign but...my stomach turned and I got out."[19]

At ten minutes past eleven Haggan phoned Leiterman. "You're fired," he said, "and I have resigned". Leiterman asked him whether the resignation was irrevocable. Haggan said it was. In response to questions from reporters at two a.m. Leiterman said he understood he was fired but if that was not the case he "resigned as of now in support of Mr. Haggan".

Haggan released a formal statement to the press at one a.m.

> I have tonight, with regret, resigned from the Canadian Broadcasting Corporation.
>
> I have been considering this action for many months. I have remained in my post only from the strongest sense of obligation to the national purpose of the Corporation. I have been aware for as long as I have been general supervisor of public affairs that my determination to make CBC public affairs a lively part of the nation is at variance with that of the Corporation's senior management.
>
> I am resigning tonight because of the sordid manoeuvres the Corporation has been going through to rid itself of Douglas Leiterman who has spared himself no effort in providing a unique service to the country in his excellent program *This Hour Has Seven Days*, and providing lively television journalism.
>
> I do not approve of some of Leiterman's activities in the last few days. At the same time I know that he has been pushed too far by an intransigent and insensitive senior management. I have done all in my power to reach a productive relationship with this senior management. Their attitude has made it impossible.
>
> The CBC as a great instrument of national purpose is more important than any individual. I believe that it will outlive the present difficulties and will again be able to serve the people of Canada with courage and honour. I particularly regret that I cannot follow through upon the start I have been able to make with my colleague Marc Thibault on the French network, toward cooperative programming that could enable the Corporation to fulfill for the first time one of its major responsibilities—to help draw the two founding nations closer together.

The *Seven Days* War was over.

CHAPTER 13

AFTERMATH

Eight years after the death of *Seven Days*, a Canadian camera crew shot a film at the brutal Washington State prison of Walla Walla. After hovering in the background for an hour or so, one of the inmates, a convicted murderer, took his courage in his hand and approached the cameraman.

"Do you know what I think about every night in my cell?" he asked, after confessing that he, too, was a Canadian. "I think about *This Hour Has Seven Days*."

If today, twenty years after its demise, those who remember it think of it with the same nostalgia as that homesick murderer they lament not only their lost youth but also the change of values from the exhilarating radicalism of the sixties to the hardheaded conservatism of the eighties.

The program's overall philosophy would today be called "left-lib"—but no more so than, for example, the *Toronto Star*. There were some who objected strongly to this direction. Of these the most consistently outspoken journalist was Lubor Zink.

> The way I see it, the essence of the issue... is whether or not a group of left-wing radicals who see themselves as the torch-bearers of progressive thought in Canada is to be given a free hand in forcing its one-sided views on the public under the guise of creative freedom.[1]

This point of view was elaborated in an eloquent and careful speech delivered by John R. Matheson, M.P. for Leeds. He had taken a great deal of trouble to support his case that "battle lines are being drawn at last between those who would debase Canada and those who would elevate it." His argument against *Seven Days* was based on his subjective definitions of political categories and on his own statistical analysis.

> Regardless of who was the producer for the evening, the *Seven Days* trumpet never had an uncertain sound. It was always blown in the same key. When one surveys four hundred and ninety-nine items appearing in the fifty programs, one discovers a striking concentration on subject matter and a remarkable consistency of treatment.

Here are some extracts from his tabulation.

National Unity:	A series of programs seemingly calculated to rake the French-English issues, including six interviews on the subject with four separatists and two English-speaking Quebeckers reacting with emotion. In addition, some twelve French-Canadians were hot-seated, pilloried, mocked or their comments distorted.
Religion:	On twenty-eight occasions *Seven Days* dealt with religious subjects. Twenty-two of these were sarcastic and antagonistic in presenting some bizarre and unrepresentative aspect of religion. In the last program the slogan "Kill a Commie for Christ" was repeated several times.
Business:	Of approximately forty-six times, thirty-six ridiculed, condemned or stressed wrongs and errors of companies and business leaders.
Race:	All twenty-nine items on problems of race played up bitterness, injustices and extremism. Nothing was produced to show the notable advances made in legislation, education and other areas. Nothing positive was offered. The emphasis was inflammatory, not constructive.
Drugs:	Two major programs stressed the delights of drug-taking, glue-sniffing and LSD without adequately portraying the serious dangers.
Anti-Americanism:	Some eighty items touched on American subjects or on the U.S.A. itself. Sixty-two were either overtly anti-American or played on U.S. problems and ills. Sixteen items dealt with the Vietnam War. Fifteen of these created impressions opposed to the U.S. role in Vietnam and could have brought nothing but comfort and encouragement to Hanoi.
Communism:	On fourteen programs communism was given sympathetic treatment. Not once in two years was there any substantial criticism of a communist country or of communist philosophy.
Police and Justice:	Fifteen out of some sixteen items dealing with these matters showed police and jus-

	tice in a very bad light. Credit was withheld for work well done in many areas, notwithstanding some spectacular accomplishments during the period.
Canadian Government:	An estimated sixty-nine items dealt with government institutions, parties or personalities—ten only from a favourable viewpoint. Forty-eight were critical, undercutting institutions of government and/or satirically critical of members of the Liberal, Conservative, Social Credit or Créditiste parties.[2]

••••

If many thoughtful Canadians had shared Matheson's or Zink's views, *Seven Days* would not have lasted as long as it did. Eminent conservatives such as Senator Gratton O'Leary and Dalton Camp rushed to its support because they welcomed lively social criticism. In most respects *Seven Days* operated within the mainstream of Canadian journalism. There was nothing sinister or subversive about its idealism and optimism and it is not surprising that those who opposed it seemed to vast sections of the public to be cynical, self-interested and reactionary upholders of the status quo. The good faith of men like John Matheson and Lubor Zink was appreciated only by fringe groups. In today's more conservative climate their views have a substantial following and there is increasing criticism of the continuing "left-lib" orientation of important sections of the media.

••••

The morning after Haggan's resignation on July 7th 1966, Peter Campbell called a meeting of the senior staff of the public affairs department. By the time they gathered, Munro had informally appointed him acting head of public affairs. Campbell read to them Haggan's statement of resignation.

"The department has suffered a serious blow," Campbell said. "I suggest you refrain from doing anything rash. Please go home and, over the weekend, carefully reflect on what your attitude should be."

Nobody did anything rash. Campbell and Gauntlett, with the support of Munro and senior management, then proceeded to demonstrate to the world that it was possible to mount a courageous and enterprising magazine program without Leiterman and Watson.

The man chosen to launch the new show—*Sunday*—was Daryl

Duke, whom Braithwaite had called "the esthete's esthete". He had contributed the Carol Doda item to *Seven Days*, the topless go-go dancer in San Francisco. He recruited, among many others, two leading *Seven Days* survivors—Robert Hoyt and Larry Zolf.

This is how Zolf described his resurrection:

> I was personally fired by CBC President J. Alphonse Ouimet. In typical CBC fashion, I was stabbed in the front. Again, in typical CBC fashion, a necrophiliac collective kiss by contrite Corporation brass restored me to broadcasting. Soon, as CBC's token public affairs Jew on the air, I was to interview so many neo-Nazis that, in gratitude, the CBC awarded me the Iron Cross.[3]

Duke said that in *Sunday* he was intending to present "total journalism" and "run the gamut of human experience" and to achieve the "emotional audience involvement of a medieval bear-pit or of a bullfight arena", adding that it would be "mind expanding *psychedelic* television".[4] He wanted "a rodeo" and "Grand Central Station" and his overall purpose was to merge public affairs, poetry, theatre and rock 'n' roll in such a way that there would be a "multiplicity of impact". The viewers would never be aware when one territory was being crossed for another and there would be constant surprise. In *Sunday*'s bear-pit political interviews were to be a blood sport.

The first four programs of *Sunday* included the following material:

November 6th	Garterbeltmania, paintings by Dennis Burton of women in underwear.
November 13th	Sex education film and what preteens thought of it.
November 20th	Poet Allen Ginsburg with four-letter words in his ode to his mother.
November 27th	Sexual experiences, pleasures and preferences of an unmarried British couple, seen in bed and elsewhere.[5]

The last of these four items (a BBC production) was reviewed in the Senate on November 29th.

> SENATOR LIONEL CHOQUETTE: Compared to this program *Seven Days* was mild. There was lesbianism and homosexuality. People were asked "Do you have as much thrill with a man as you have with a woman? Do you have as much thrill with a lesbian as you have with a man?—and similar questions—all before the eyes and ears of our children.
>
> Honorable senators, let us not look to legislation which is unnecessary and uncalled for at the moment, but let us look at these problems which are urgent.[6]

In the House of Commons, Gordon Fairweather, who had sat on the parliamentary committee and was a supporter of *Seven Days*, asked whether the secretary of state, Judy LaMarsh, belonged to "that fraternity which regrets the loss of that old-fashioned program *This Hour Has Seven Days*".[7] LaMarsh did not reply. It went beyond the means of the parliamentary stenographer to record the expression on her face.

On December 1st Ouimet issued a statement.

> It is the opinion of CBC management that the item in question failed to find its place as an integral and justifiable part of the responsible treatment of a very sensitive subject and, accordingly, that the broadcast of the item was a mistake.

The demoralized and paralysed caretaker management allowed *Sunday* to run its course but it was not renewed for a second season. The program never attracted anything like the passionate allegiance *Seven Days* had, though it reached an audience of nearly two million viewers.

Some of the psychedelic activities portrayed on television ran parallel to similar activities conducted in the production offices on Maitland Street. It was fortunate that the season ended without a major scandal.

●●●●

As the sixties turned into the seventies there was a change in atmosphere. Martin Knelman described it succinctly in an article about *Seven Days* in *Saturday Night* in October 1975:

> The tone of the whole culture (has) changed... The snappy style of *Seven Days* was implicitly justified by being harnessed in support of moral fervour, but without that conviction the style is hollow and dated. It may be possible to get the audience involved in the same way now, because a certain amount of disenchantment has gradually become a built-in part of the mass response. We've been programmed for cynicism by the television serials of the assassinations, Vietnam and Watergate, by commercials that mock everything including their own corruption, and by up-to-date movie-heroes who are wised-up enough to understand that the world is a rotten place and there's no use trying to change it.

In England and the United States, as well as in Canada, the sixties had brought about drastic changes in public attitudes towards the role of broadcasting in the respective societies. In England, Hugh Carleton Greene's "cultural revolution" meant the end of the first era of broadcasting, usually identified with the BBC's first director-general, Lord Reith.

The first era was one of the total institution, during which

Reith sought to construct a BBC which itself recruited, trained and employed all those who provided the material of the broadcasts... This approach collapsed under the impact of the new cultural pluralism of the 1960s. It was simply impossible for the BBC to sustain a totalistic attitude towards every strand of the culture in this no longer homogeneous society.[8]

●●●●

In January 1968 Pearson appointed George Davidson, the secretary of the treasury board and an old friend of his, to succeed Alphonse Ouimet. "Whatever you do, George," Pearson was reported to have said to Davidson, "please make sure that I never hear about the CBC again." Laurent Picard, a management expert and the director of the École des Hautes Etudes Commerciales in Montreal, was named executive vice-president to succeed Briggs.

These appointments dashed Judy LaMarsh's hopes, and those of many others, that men with proven affinity with the creative community would henceforth occupy the two top positions in the CBC. She referred to the appointments in her memoirs:

I have known George Davidson almost since I arrived in Ottawa, and I consider him to be highly intelligent and a skilled member of the public service. I do not, however, know of a single talent which he possesses which fitted my concept of what the Corporation urgently needed, other than the fact that he was bilingual... I had met Picard and interviewed him once or twice. He had impressed me considerably, but he knew absolutely nothing about broadcasting or about the CBC's organization. Their appointments brought polite burps and a sort of so-what-else-is-new attitude.[9]

Davidson and Picard managed "to keep a lid on" the CBC. There were no more scandals. The public affairs department ceased to have an autonomous existence and was joined with the news service (which was rapidly growing in influence and sophistication) in a new box on the organizational charts called "Information Programming". Martin Knelman used a vivid phrase to describe the effect of these changes. He wrote that they had led to a "scorched earth period in public affairs broadcasting".

Seven Days, however, was the direct ancestor of straightforward CBC programs like Ombudsman and Marketplace and many programs specializing in investigative journalism. Moreover, it influenced a whole generation of Canadians for whom the Beatles and Seven Days were decisive events in their formative years. Above all, few would dispute the lasting effects of Seven Days' courageous and enterprising taboo-smashing. The whole country benefited from it, not just television programs like CTV's *W5*.

The pristine classicism of Ouimet's ethical code, in the form he presented to the parliamentary committee on May 6th 1966, raised a fundamental issue. He said no CBC program must consistently advocate social change. The Corporation's job was to reflect public opinion, not to change it, a position *not* shared, at least by implication, by the report of the parliamentary committee. While Ouimet's position seemed to be unexceptional in theory, it failed to take into account the nature of journalism everywhere and at any time, not only in the sixties. Good news is not considered interesting, bad news is.

Moreover, most serious journalism, then and now, tends to have a strong reformist component. Journalists consider it part of their job to criticize society, not merely to serve as a mirror. For many it is the most important part of their job. Muckraking and rocking the boat are honourable, necessary activities.

Even before *Seven Days*, the CBC public affairs department had assumed that the purpose of informing the public and giving it well-balanced presentations of conflicting opinions was to improve society. In that sense, its policies had never been neutral and merely reflective. While *Seven Days* was more populist and engaged in crusading in a way that had not been permissible before, it still came within the traditional framework of the department. So did one of its most important innovations, the ombudsman component, which had the specific purpose of exposing abuses by governments and large institutions. This was one of the reasons why it became "the people's show".

••••

Ouimet's fear that a terrible precedent was being created by politicians playing CBC program directors proved unjustified, and so did Nathan Cohen's Cassandra-like prophecy that the producers "would rue the day" when they mobilized them. There has been no recurrence of collusion between aggrieved producers and politicians, nor, on any major scale, any conflict between producers and head office. *Seven Days* had increased the respect with which senior management regarded them.

Haggan's prediction that the defeat of *Seven Days* would lead to a mass exodus of television talent, leaving CBC public affairs depleted of talent, proved equally unwarranted. Once the smoke had lifted, all the *Seven Days* people who wanted to stay in Canadian television or film in fact did. But the unprecedented resignation of a whole production unit left the scene devastated and in the summer of 1966 it looked as though Haggan might well be right.

To him, the possible loss to Canada of Leiterman's contributions seemed particularly sad. For him, Leiterman was not a congenial character. He had good reason to be fed up with him. But this is what he said about him a few days after both had resigned:

> He's the only authentic genius I've known in my time. He's an authentic genius in the field of communications. He is extremely difficult to work with, but at the same time I must say stimulating to work with. He is a man who, when he has made up his mind, finds it difficult to change it. He sees an objective and he goes straight to it and it is difficult to deflect him. But the cost of putting up with a chap like Leiterman is nickels and dimes compared to the cost of losing him.[10]

Immediately after the collapse of *Seven Days* Leiterman offered his services to all three networks in the United States. Bill Leonard of CBS News had heard of the program's success from a relative in Winnipeg, even before he read Jack Gould's piece in the *New York Times* about *Seven Days* and, more specifically, about Beryl Fox's *The Mills of the Gods*.

> Mr. Leiterman and his producing colleague, Pat Watson, appeared to have achieved not only an element of excitement in covering the news but ability to make news themselves. Their show is very much an in-thing with college students and top Canadian leaders have been aware of its influence. The show enjoys finding weak links in the accepted order of things and its "hot seat" for guests is now a minor Canadian institution. American TV news coverage might be stimulated if it was similarly inclined to get out the needle; it certainly makes for different viewing.[11]

Leiterman showed Leonard and other CBS people some of his kinescopes. They realized at once that it was too revolutionary to fit into their framework. "This is not CBS News", they said. But the network had launched a long-term project to look into the possibility of presenting a one-hour magazine show. Eventually, *Sixty Minutes* was the result. Leiterman joined the unit and participated in the deliberations. He also wrote a twenty-page memo for them about the problems involved in producing a television magazine show, full of cautionary advice.

After two years in New York, Leiterman returned to Canada to work in private television and film.

••••

So who—or what—killed *Seven Days*?

Canadians older than, say, thirty-five who think of *Seven Days* as the greatest CBC program they have ever seen commonly assume that it was top management, characteristically insensitive and supercautious, which had killed the program. They have never forgiven it for this brutal crime.

But eight years after the demise of *Seven Days* Watson took a very different line. Michael Enright interviewed him on the CBC radio program *This Country in the Morning*.

ENRIGHT: What was at stake? What was at issue there?

WATSON: What was at issue was whether or not the people who ran the program were going to allow themselves to be run by the management of the Corporation. It was a very straightforward management crisis. We were a bunch of unmanageable cocky little...you know...who wouldn't do what we were told... We had our own accounting system which was not the CBC accounting system and really were creating an empire in a kind of counter-power centre within the CBC, and that was intolerable to any management.

ENRIGHT: Do you think it would be today?

WATSON: Yeah... I think so...if it were as abrasive as that one was.[12]

However, Watson would be the first to insist that it was management's chronic insensitivity and supercaution which had provoked the producers to build an empire within an empire in the first place. He has often spoken with eloquence about the suicidal clumsiness of corporate tactics.

Who provoked whom? One can look at the matter in quite a different way. Wasn't it the producers who had provoked management? Their egos vastly swollen by their unprecedented success, the tactics they had chosen, especially the mobilization of the politicians, doomed the program just as much as management's stubborn intransigence. Moreover, middle management also bore its share of responsibility. It failed to build the necessary bridges between the intellectual department of public affairs and the non-intellectual head office.

Everybody was guilty.

Under normal circumstances the conflict could have been resolved through normal institutional procedures. Until 1959 disputes within the Corporation had normally been conducted with reasonable civility and restraint. But in that year the Montreal producers' strike had clearly demonstrated that times were no longer normal and that in an atmosphere of acute social tension confrontations within the CBC could easily get out of hand.

The Corporation has always been a microcosm of Canada. Its role in the society, and the battles fought within it, reflect the tensions in the country as a whole, and the ever-changing values. The attitudes of both sides during the *Seven Days* war were shaped by the attitudes of various interest groups in conflict with one another—the young, the old; the established, the less established; the left, the right; the intellectuals, the non-intellectuals; the pro-Americans, the anti-Americans; the urban, the rural— and, above all, those impatient for social change and those terrified of it.

Ouimet was a father-figure and during the sixties fathers were unpopular. The exercise of traditional authority was soon perceived as tyranny. Similarly, idealistic reformers in their early middle age like Leiterman and Watson appeared to their superiors as wildly radical revolutionaries. And suddenly it was no longer a matter of perceptions. Each actually began to play out his role in strict accordance with an invisible script. At what time except in the sixties would a minister of the crown, Judy LaMarsh, surreptitiously arrange a cloak-and-dagger meeting with an employee of a crown corporation, Douglas Leiterman, in a car going down the Queen Elizabeth Way, to discuss with him the timing of the removal of the employee's boss, the president of the CBC? Not in the forties or fifties, nor in the seventies or eighties. Only in the sixties could such an encounter have been thinkable.

The conclusion is inescapable. It was the sixties which killed *Seven Days*.

●●●●

On the day before he resigned, Leiterman phoned Michael Hind-Smith, CTV Vice-President of Programming and a former CBC colleague. If things went wrong, Leiterman told him, you can have the *Seven Days* unit lock, stock and barrel.

"No thanks," said Hind-Smith. "I don't want it."

The suggestion, Leiterman told the press later, was made in jest.[13]

●●●●

Two decades have passed. Discussions about the role of the CBC are being conducted in a different climate. There are new attitudes towards regulation and deregulation and new technological developments. Many aspects of the problem are different. The position of the CBC in Canadian life has declined. Until *Seven Days* and its aftermath it had many features of a secular church with the president as pope and the Broadcasting Act as gospel. Today few would describe it in those terms.

The climate is changing and new allocations of functions between the public and private sector are being worked out. There is good reason to assume that the CBC will remain the paramount broadcaster and that it will continue to have the capacity to influence Canadian life. What it also requires is the courage, vitality and idealism with which it launched *This Hour Has Seven Days*.

Patrick Watson and Dinah Christie: Scrubbed clean

WHAT ARE THEY DOING NOW?
THE MAIN PLAYERS

Reeves Haggan

"Too rich for CBC's blood"—his words—Haggan was hired by the Department of External Affairs where within a year he became senior adviser to the secretary of state. He left in 1972 to become an assistant secretary to the cabinet in the Prime Minister's Office. After a number of years in the ministry of the solicitor-general engaged chiefly in developing federal-provincial coordination in the field of criminal justice, he returned to the privy council office to work on patriation of the constitution. In 1980 he was posted to London where he negotiated passage of the patriation legislation with senior British cabinet ministers, public servants, and the Lords and Commons at Westminster. After his return to Ottawa he became senior adviser to the government of Canada on constitutional matters, specializing in native rights. He retired in January 1986.

Laurier LaPierre

After *Seven Days*, LaPierre returned to full-time academic work at McGill, which made extensive use of him as a fundraiser for the alumni association. He also became active in the NDP. He ran unsuccessfully in Lachine in the federal election of 1968 and for a year or two tried to keep himself in the public eye "by being atrocious and outrageous". But once the sixties were over this activity ceased to be appealing to him and to his public. He wrote extensively and continued his work in television. From 1975 to 1978 he was host of *LaPierre* on CBMT in Montreal and from 1977 to 1979 president of the Commission of Inquiry in the Education of the Young Child. In recent years LaPierre has lived in Vancouver, where he is host-interviewer on CKVU TV's daily *Vancouver Show*. He has taught Canadian studies at Simon Fraser University, hosted a French series for TVOntario, broadcast on the western region French network and written a newspaper column. He is much in demand as a broadcaster and lecturer and in 1985 was writer and host of the series *Disasters: Acts of God or Acts of Man?* on CBC Stereo. He owns Nibbles Restaurant in Vancouver.

In 1966 the Association of Canadian Television and Radio Artists (ACTRA) filed a grievance on LaPierre's behalf against the CBC's decision not to renew his contract, on the grounds that top management had interfered with the normal processes of engaging performers. This, they contended, constituted a breach of their collective agreement with the CBC. The case went to arbitration. Hearings were held in the Four Seasons Motel in Toronto during the climactic days of July 7th and 8th 1966. On September 2nd Mr. Justice Rhodes Smith announced his decision in favour of the Corporation. He held that neither by the terms of the collective agreement nor by understood accepted practice had executive producers any exclusive or uncontrolled power to engage performers.

Douglas Leiterman

After Leiterman left New York in 1970 he formed a film production company in Toronto with his partner Philip S. Hobel. He soon discovered that as a private producer the only films he could sell commercially were films on history, nature and the future. Under the wing of Murray Chercover, President of CTV, the company produced more than two hundred films. Leiterman also received a cable licence for Wired City Communications Ltd. which provided him with a formidable education in the realities of big business. Instead of producing innovative local programs, as he had hoped, his time was spent demanding that his program people produce on ever-lower budgets so that the cash-flow would be sufficient to fight off attempts by brokers to wrest control. One memorable winter night, flanked by his lawyer, he adjourned a shareholders' meeting and walked coatless into the snow with an armful of proxies to prevent a takeover. In the end he sold the company and went back to making nature and business films, guaranteeing their completion on budget. In 1976 he set up a third-party completion guarantor company and a brokerage firm which grew into Motion Pictures Guarantors Inc. to become the third-largest film bonding company in the world, with branch offices in the U.S., Australia and France. In the winter of 1984 this company took over *Joshua Then and Now* and a French film. Both were expensive mistakes which cost him nearly two million dollars. He survived by selling real estate from his children's trust fund which he had bought in lusher days. By 1986 his companies had fully recovered and now occupy a pivotal position in the feature film industry.

Leiterman is prepared to produce *Seven Days* again. "All it would take would be a CBC president with a cast-iron stomach, a prime minister who would insist his cabinet keep 'hands off', a budget around the cost of a cruise missile, and a crew as talented and courageous as we had way back then".

Alphonse Ouimet

After his retirement, Ouimet became chairman of the board and of the executive committee of Telesat Canada. In 1980 he resigned as chairman, but remained as director until the end of 1984. From 1969 to 1974 he was also a member of the executive board of UNESCO Canada, as well as a founding member, and later honorary chairman, of the Canadian Communications Research Information Centre. Ouimet was also among those who started *L'Institut International de la Communication*. Between 1973 and 1976 he was chairman of the CBC's corporate Olympic committee. In 1978–79 he served as member of the consultative committee on the implications of telecommunications for Canadian sovereignty.

As writer, lecturer and consultant, Ouimet has been actively concerned both with the past and the future of communications. He has written extensively on the history of broadcasting for the Public Archives and has been consultant to the Department of Communications and to the CBC. He has conducted a major study for the *Delta* project and for the international periodical *Intermedia* and contributed an important article on "The Communications Revolution and Canadian Sovereignty" to *Gutenberg Two*, edited by Dave Godfrey and Douglas Parkhill, and published by Porcepic Press in 1979.

Two years ago "I decided it was time to devote all my energies to the management of my old age ... I think I'm rather successful at it but I still can't help but worry about the growing erosion of Canadian sovereignty".

H.G. Walker

In 1966, having declined the offer of early retirement, the Canadian government asked Walker to undertake a feasibility study of broadcasting services and structures in the Caribbean. The purpose of this study was to explore the contributions television and radio networks might make to strengthening a sense of regional identity. Once completed, this study received much praise, but, as he had predicted, the people of the Caribbean were not as yet ready to implement his recommendations.

On his return to the CBC, Walker spent four rewarding years as director-general of the External Services Division until his retirement in 1972. He now lives in Ottawa, devoting much of his time and energy to volunteer work. For five-and-a-half years he was chairman of the education program of the Cancer Society. He is also a member of the Education Committee of the Council on Aging, of the Psychogeriatric Committee of the Ottawa General Hospital and of a subcommittee of the Lung Association's board of directors on matters concerning general health.

He jogs every morning at six, winter and summer.

Patrick Watson

In 1968 Watson formed his own company, Patrick Watson Enterprises Ltd. He has continued to win high praise for his work in film and television, both in Canada and in the United States, as producer, writer and host-interviewer. The *Toronto Star* called him "the best television interviewer in the business" and *The New York Times* described him as "polished, articulate". CBC viewers are familiar with *The Watson Report*, his hosting of Peter Newman's *The Canadian Establishment*, *Lawvers*, *Venture* and many other programs.

He is now at work with his own film company on the most ambitious documentary project of his career, the ten-part series *The Struggle for Democracy*. It will be ready for presentation in various countries early in 1988.

Watson is interested in all kinds of communication. Among his many enterprises was the adaptation in 1983 of *The Book of Job* into a one-man stage performance, accompanied by percussionist John Wyre and produced and directed by John McGreevy. Among the five books he published are *Alexander Dolgun's Story*, Knopf 1976, and *Alter Ego*, Lester and Orpen Dennys, and Viking 1978. But his activities are not confined to communications: he acquired a commercial pilot's licence, which enabled him to work as a charter pilot and instructor. In middle years he became an enthusiastic pianist and practises Bach fugues every day.

W.E.S. Briggs spent the last years of his life in a seaside home near Hubbards, the village forty-eight kilometres from Halifax, near a CBC "camp". He died in 1975.

Peter Campbell, who succeeded Haggan as General Supervisor of Public Affairs, became Director of Policy in 1968. He retired in 1985 but continues to act as consultant for the CBC. Campbell conducts a weekly seminar on broadcasting at York University and is a Fellow of Winters College.

After occupying a number of administrative positions, *Hugh Gauntlett* is now in charge of CBC network programs on art, music and science.

Bill Hogg died in 1979, after ten years of retirement.

Robert McGall lives in retirement in Victoria, B.C. From 1969 to 1976 he was regional director of the CBC in British Columbia.

Keith Morrow retired in 1982 and now lives in Charlottetown, P.E.I. From 1967 to 1973 he was regional director of the CBC in Newfoundland.

After a fundamental policy disagreement, *Doug Nixon* resigned from his position as director of entertainment programming in 1969. He formed his own company and made several documentaries in Spain. He died in 1977.

Marce Munro has been living in retirement in Victoria, B.C. since 1974, after having served as assistant general manager for the English Services Division in Toronto for six years.

Bernard Ostry served as secretary-general, National Museums Corporation, from 1974 to 1978, as deputy minister of communications in the federal government from 1978 to 1980, and as special adviser to the secretary of state on cultural and communications technology for western Europe, based in Paris, in 1980 and 1981. After moving to Toronto and serving as deputy minister in various departments of the Ontario government, he was appointed chairman and chief executive officer of TVOntario in 1985.

THE TEAM

Heinz Kornagel Story editor, film director	Freelancer.
Ken Lefolii Producer	Engaged in diverse business enterprises in the area of communications.
Sam Levine Story editor	Executive producer, CBC drama.
Carol McIntyre Film coordinator	Freelance researcher.
Ross McLean Producer of satire and celebrity material and *Document*	Freelance producer, columnist, member of School of Journalism, Ryerson Institute.
Kim Malcolmson Script assistant	Health Care researcher, planning and program development.
Jim Mercer Cameraman	Cameraman, CTV's *W5*.
Mavor Moore Writer of lyrics	Eloquent fighter for all the arts, writer for the *Globe and Mail*, actor. Until 1984, chairman of the Canada Council.
Brian Nolan Story editor	Producer of documentaries, professor at Carleton University, teaching in the journalism and film studies departments.
Peter Paterson Production manager	Recently settled in Halifax, N.S., to write mystery stories, after relinquishing the editorship of the award-winning *North Island Gazette* on Vancouver Island.
Stephen Patrick Story editor and chief organizer of *Save Seven Days* committees	Producer, writer.
Peter Pearson Story editor	Executive director, Telefilm Canada.
Beverley Roberts Researcher	Director, Information and Publications Branch, TVOntario.
Nancy Ryley Researcher	Freelance producer.
David Ruskin Director	Practises law in the entertainment and communications field.
Alexander Ross Story editor	Editorial director of *CB Media Ltd* which publishes *Canadian Business* and *Your Money*, author of *The Traders*, Collins, Toronto 1984, a study of Canadian stock markets.
Paul Saltzman Researcher	President of *Sunrise Films*, the company producing *Danger Bay* and other films for television.
Merle Shain Researcher, story editor, interviewer	Author of *Some Men Are (More Perfect Than Others)*, *When Lovers Are* *Friends* and *Hearts That We Broke Long Ago*, published by McClelland and Stewart and in paperback by Bantam Books in 1973, 1978 and 1983.
Peter Tiedeman Budget manager	Unit Manager, CBC Children's Programs.
Warner Troyer Interviewer	Freelance broadcaster and writer, living in Aylmer, Que. Recently returned from CIDA assignment to Sri Lanka.
Maggie Watchman Script assistant	Production assistant, TVOntario.
Vincent Vaitiekunas Film editor and director	Film editor/director and associate professor of film, Department of Film and Video, York University.
Larry Zolf Producer and interviewer	CBC television producer, political commentator, critic, journalist, personality. Author of two books about Trudeau, *Dance of the Dialec-* *tic*, published by James Lewis and Samuel 1973, and *Just Watch Me*, published by James Lorimer 1984, and of a book about the Senate, *Survival of the Fattest*, published in 1984 by Key Porter.

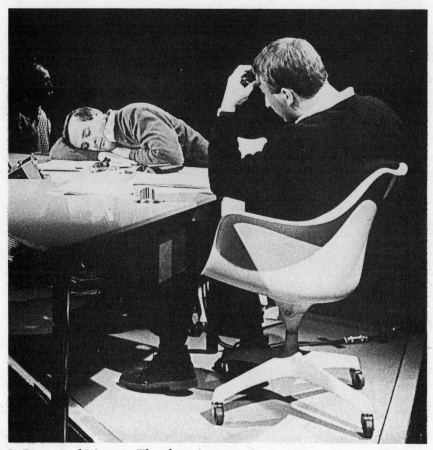

LaPierre and Watson: The show is over

ENDNOTES

PART ONE

CHAPTER 1

1. Frank Peers, *The Politics of Canadian Broadcasting*, University of Toronto Press 1969, p. 29.
2. Erik Barnouw, *The Image Empire*, Oxford University Press 1970, p.43.
3. Fred Friendly, *Due to Circumstances Beyond Our Control*. New York, Random House 1967, pp. 29–41, and CBS-TV, October 4th, 1954.
4. CBS-TV, April 6th, 1954.
5. News Power, the fourth program in the series *Television* produced by Granada in the U.K.
6. Debates, House of Commons, 1962, Vol. 1, February 14th, p. 856, quoted by *Time* magazine, March 16th 1962.
7. Debates, House of Commons, 1964, Vol 2, p. 1350.
8. Anthony Smith, *The Shadow in the Cave*, University of Illinois Press 1973, p.115.
9. Debates, House of Commons, 1964, Vol 5, p. 4493.
10. Interview, September 2nd 1981.

CHAPTER 2

1. By permission of The Second City, Chicago, Illinois.

CHAPTER 3

1. *Canada Since 1945*, Robert Bothwell, Ian Drummond and John English, University of Toronto Press, 1981, p. 269.
2. Ibid.
3. Notes, October 1981.
4. *Globe and Mail*, June 24th 1964.
5. Notes, October 1981.
6. Martin Hunter in *Toronto Life*, November 8th 1985, p. 91.

CHAPTER 4

1. Roy Faibish, Papers of the Committee on Broadcasting, cited by Frank Peers, *The Public Eye*, University of Toronto Press 1979, p. 302.
2. Report of the Fowler Committee on Broadcasting 1965, p. 72.
3. Frank Peers, p. 283.

4. *Years of Impatience*, by Gérard Pelletier, Methuen of Canada 1984, p. 222.
5. *Toronto Star Weekly*, June 13 1959, and *En greve* by Jean-Louis Roux, Editions du Jour, Montreal 1963, p.265.
6. Report of the Parliamentary Committee 1959, p. 557.
7. Ibid, p. 604.
8. Ouimet Papers.
9. E.A. Weir, *The Struggle for National Broadcasting in Canada*, McClelland and Stewart 1965, p. 312.

CHAPTER 5

1. Notes, October 1981.

PART TWO

FAVREAU

1. Memo, September 21th 1965.
2. Memo, October 22nd 1964.

THE QUEEN

1. *Globe and Mail*, October 12th 1964.
2. Ibid.

ROCKWELL

1. Debates, House of Commons, 1964, Vol. 1X, p. 9413.
2. *Globe and Mail*, October 28th 1964.
3. *Toronto Star*, October 28th 1964.
4. *Montreal Star*, October 26th 1964.
5. *Morningside*, CBC radio, January 15th 1976.
6. Ibid., January 16th 1976.
7. *Globe and Mail*, November 19th 1964.

HORSBURGH

1. Minutes of President's Meeting, November 16th 1964.
2. *The Horsburgh Affair* by Ronald Smeaton, Toronto, Baxter 1966.
3. *Winnipeg Free Press*, April 15th 1966.

DIEFENBAKER AND LÉVESQUE

1. Undated Memo signed by R.L. Warner.
2. Interview with Helen Carscallen, early 1966.
3. *Toronto Star*, December 12th 1964.

FAWCETT

1. Canadian Criminal Cases 1963 (Vol 3) p. 134.
2. Letter of Robert McGall, March 24th 1965.
3. *Toronto Star*, May 29th 1965.
4. Memo to Robert McGall, March 23rd 1965.

VIETNAM

1. Committee, p. 1082.
2. Bernard B. Fall, *The Two Vietnams*, New York Praeger 1963.
3. Memo from H.G. Walker to Bill Hogg, March 14th 1966.
4. Memo from Peter Campbell to Bill Hogg, March 18th 1966.
5. *Edmonton Journal*, May 4th 1965.
6. Memo from Knowlton Nash to Bill Hogg, January 19th 1966.
7. Memo from Walker, January 17th 1966.
8. *The New York Times*, January 18th 1966.
9. Letter to Leiterman, December 7th 1965.

THE ELECTION OF 1965

1. Committee p. 247.
2. Committee p. 735.

THE POPE SKIT

1. CBC Audience Research Report TV/ 65/106.
2. Speech to the Women's Canadian Press Club, April 18th 1966.
3. Committee p.685.
4. Quoted in *Ottawa Journal*, November 8th 1965.
5. Letter to Ouimet, November 9th 1965.
6. *Maclean's* magazine, November 1st 1965.

"SLEAZY"

1. Betty Friedan, *The Feminine Mystique*, New York, Dell 1963.
2. Committee, p. 243.
3. *Seven Days* Complaints, CBC head office document, November 24th 1965.
4. *Globe and Mail*, December 14th 1965.
5. Pat Pearce, *Montreal Star*, December 13th.
6. *Globe and Mail*, December 14th 1965.
7. Committee, p. 415.

KU KLUX KLAN

1. CBC Audience Research Report TV/ 65/114.

2. *Seven Days* Complaints, CBC head office document, November 24th 1965.

VICTOR SPENCER

1. *Globe and Mail*, September 23rd 1966.
2. *Toronto Star*, April 20th 1966.

GERDA MUNSINGER

1. Debates, House of Commons, 1966, Vol II, pp 2209–11.
2. *Toronto Star*, March 11th 1966.
3. Douglas Leiterman, *You can't tell TV: don't peek, Maclean's*, July 23rd 1966.
4. Memo from Hogg to Gauntlett, March 16th 1966.

STEVEN TRUSCOTT

1. Published by McClelland and Stewart.

THE ORGY

1. Debates, House of Commons 1966, Vol. 11, p. 4570.
2. Confidential report to the C.B.C., May 12th 1966, R.C.M.P. file reference 66-O-431–69.

PART THREE

CHAPTER 6

1. Committee, p. 428.
2. Max Ferguson, Unforgettable Captain Briggs, *Readers Digest*, November 1982.
3. Ibid.
4. Letter from G.F. Brickenden, March 9th, 1982.
5. Memo from E.S. Hallman, vice-president of programs, to H.G. Walker, October 27th, 1964.
6. Debates, House of Commons 1964, Vol. IX, p. 9413.
7. Committee, p. 461.
8. *Globe and Mail*, December 21st 1965.
9. Ibid., December 10th 1964.
10. October 15th, 1964.
11. Minutes of President's meeting, January 11th 1965.
12. Memo to Ouimet and Briggs, May 13th 1965.
13. Memo to Briggs, June 9th, 1965.
14. Ibid.
15. Interview with Helen Carscallen, early 1966.
16. August 5th 1965.

CHAPTER 7

1. Peter Newman, *Toronto Star*, April 20th 1966.
2. January 16th, 1966.
3. Heather Robertson, *Maclean's*, March 1975, p. 76.
4. *Memoirs of a Gilded Bird*, McClelland and Stewart, Toronto, 1969, p. 241.
5. Committee, p. 16.
6. Peers, *The Public Eye*, p. 360.
7. Committee, p. 255.
8. Baton Broadcasting Ltd. v. CBC (1966) 2 O.R., p. 169.
9. November 13th 1965.
10. Interview with Helen Carscallen, early 1966.
11. November 16th 1965.
12. Memo to Hogg, copy to Walker, December 13th 1965.
13. December 15th 1965.
14. Memo to Briggs, November 15th 1965.
15. *The Sunday Times*, March 16th 1969.
16. Letter to the author, November 25th 1981.
17. Letter to the author, November 25th 1981.
18. Hugh Greene, *The Third Floor Front*, The Bodley Head, London 1969, p. 135.
19. Committee, p. 250.
20. *Globe and Mail*, December 17th 1965.
21. Committee, Marc Thibault's testimony, pp 812–838.
22. November 15th 1965.
23. Committee, p. 470
24. Committee, p. 740
25. Committee, p. 472
26. Committee, p. 437
27. *Maclean's*, March 5th 1966, p. 26.
28. Interview with Helen Carscallen, early 1966.

CHAPTER 8

1. Telegram from Thibault and Haggan to Marcel Ouimet and H.G. Walker, February 3rd 1966.
2. March 28th 1966.
3. Committee p. 35.
4. April 14th 1966
5. May 16th 1966.
6. April 15th 1966.

CHAPTER 9

1. Peter Newman, *Toronto Star*, April 21 1966.
2. January 14th 1976.

3. Committee, p. 113.
4. November 19th 1974.
5. *Globe and Mail*, April 18th 1966.
6. *Globe and Mail*, April 25th 1966.
7. Heather Robertson, *Maclean's*, March 1975.
8. *Memoirs of a Bird in the Gilded Cage*, McClelland and Stewart, 1969, p. 254.
9. Watson in *Maclean's*, November 26th 1966.
10. Telephone interview with E.B. Osler, March 23rd 1982.
11. Debates, House of Commons 1966, vol. IV, pp. 3977 and 3983.
12. Harold Stafford in *Canada Month*, August 1966, p. 8.
13. Ibid.
14. Dennis Braithwaite, *The Globe and Mail*, April 28th, 1966.
15. Committee, p. 333.
16. *Toronto Star*, April 18th 1966.

CHAPTER 10

1. *Montreal Star*, April 19th 1966.
2. *Toronto Star*, April 21st 1966.
3. Association Notes.
4. Committee, p. 17.
5. Telegram from E.B. Osler to Ouimet, April 30th 1966.
6. Jeremy Brown, *Toronto Telegram*, April 23rd 1966.
7. Committee, p. 88.
8. Committee, p. 86.
9. Debates, House of Commons 1966, Vol 1V, p. 1128.
10. Committee, p. 136.
11. *Globe and Mail*, April 27th 1966.
12. Debates, House of Commons 1966, Vol 1V, p. 4310.
13. *Montreal Star*, April 28th 1966.
14. Committee, p. 323.
15. *Globe and Mail*, April 28th 1966.
16. *Toronto Star*, April 28th 1966.
17. Committee, p. 139.
18. C.P. Story, April 27th 1966.
19. Debates, House of Commons 1966, Vol V, p. 4417.
20. Committee, p. 447.
21. Committee, p. 434.
22. Committee, p. 482.
23. *Globe and Mail*, April 29th 1966.
24. *Globe and Mail*, April 30th 1966.
25. Debates, House of Commons 1966, Vol V, p. 4499.
26. Martin Goodman, *Toronto Star*, May 2nd, 1966.
27. Roy Shields, *Toronto Star*, April 30th 1966.
28. Martin Goodman, *Toronto Star*, May 2nd, 1966.

29. Minutes of the Board.
30. Letter to author, March 2nd 1982.
31. Minutes of the Board.
32. Committee, p. 499.
33. Committee, p. 503.
34. Committee, p. 536.
35. Committee, p. 529.
36. Committee, p. 605.
37. Ottawa *Citizen*, May 20th 1966.
38. Committee, p. 605.
39. Committee, p. 611.
40. Committee, p. 615.
41. Committee, p. 692.

CHAPTER 11

1. *Toronto Star*, May 3rd 1966.
2. *Globe and Mail*, May 2nd 1966.
3. Committee, p. 697.
4. *Globe and Mail*, May 2nd 1966.
5. Debates, House of Commons, 1966, Vol V, p. 4571.
6. Letter to the author, March 2nd 1982.
7. *Globe and Mail*, May 27th 1966.
8. *Montreal Star*, May 27th 1966.
9. *Globe and Mail*, May 27th 1966.
10. *Toronto Telegram*, May 27th 1966.
11. *Montreal Star*, May 17th 1966.
12. May 27th 1966.
13. Committee pp. 1090–1095.
14. *Toronto Star*, May 25th 1966.
15. CBC Press Release, May 30th 1966.
16. *Toronto Star*, May 27th 1966.
17. *Toronto Telegram*, May 30th 1966.

CHAPTER 12

1. *Toronto Telegram*, June 3rd 1966.
2. Committee, p. 446.
3. Leiterman, Summary of Events, summer 1966.
4. Committee, p. 1049.
5. Committee, p. 1069.
6. Committee, pp. 1233–1241.

7. *Canada Month*, August 1966.
8. Debates, House of Commons 1966, Vol. V11, p. 7024.
9. *Globe and Mail*, July 5th 1966.
10. Minutes of the Board.
11. *Toronto Star*, June 28th 1966.
12. *Toronto Telegram*, July 6th 1966.
13. *Memoirs of a Bird in a Gilded Cage*, McClelland and Stewart, 1969, p. 257–8.
14. *Toronto Telegram*, July 6th 1966.
15. House of Commons, Debates 1966, Vol V11, p. 7267.
16. Haggan's Notes re Dismissal of Leiterman, July 12th, 1966.
17. Statement by Leiterman, July 12th 1966.
18. Haggan's Notes re Dismissal of Leiterman, July 12th 1966.
19. Interview with Doug Fisher on CJOH-TV, July 10th 1966.

CHAPTER 13

1. *Toronto Telegram*, April 28th 1966.
2. Speech to Canadian Club, Winnipeg, December 8th 1966.
3. *Globe and Mail*, January 17th 1981.
4. Braithwaite, *Globe and Mail*, October 19th 1966.
5. Listed under the heading *Always on Sundays*, *Globe and Mail*, December 1st 1966.
6. *Toronto Star*, December 3rd 1966.
7. Debates, House of Commons 1966, Vol X, p. 10579.
8. Anthony Smith, *The Guardian*, June 17th 1985.
9. *Bird in a Gilded Cage*, p. 274.
10. Interview with Doug Fisher on CJOH-TV, July 10th 1966.
11. *The New York Times*, January 30th 1966.
12. November 19th, 1974.
13. *Globe and Mail*, July 8th 1966.

INDEX

270